GW01168072

Kristu Bhakti
and
Krishna Bhakti

Interfaith Treasures Uncovered

Under this Series, the Publishers endeavor to focus on Comparative Studies pertaining to Christian Faith & Living in the central matrix and Hinduism, Buddhism, Sikhism, Islam, Judaism, etc., on the peripheral. The Studies shall cover topics like Literature & Poetry, Indigenous Philosophizing, Ethical response towards Agriculture, Health & Healing, Science & Technology, Ecofeminist Theology, Sociological approach towards Human Rights, Law & Politics, Arts, History of Ideas, Ancient Civilizations, Cultural Contiguity, Religious Cosmologies & Mysticism, Footsteps of famous Theologians, World Peace & Harmony, Global Capitalism, Network Marketing, Cybertheology, Population & Demographics, Epigraphic Studies, Contextualized Education, and many others. We welcome a Mss. on any topic/s mentioned, whether they are original works, scholarly monographs, collections of conference papers, revised dissertations, or translations of historical documents. Through the Series, we are striving to put forward published works that may help Institutions, Academic Bodies, Researchers, Scholars and the World at large in furthering their respective knowledge and understanding on the concerned subject. We welcome your comments on our efforts and further suggestions on how we can foster the upcoming books on parallel interfaces between and among Christianity and other religions.

Interfaith Treasures Uncovered - 8

Kristu Bhakti and Krishna Bhakti

A Christian-Hindu Dialogue
Contributing to Comparative Theology

Israel Selvanayagam

CWI

Christian World Imprints™

© Israel Selvanayagam

Israel Selvanayagam asserts the moral right to be identified as the author of this book.

First Published in 2017 by

Christian World Imprints™
Christian Publishing & Books from India
H-12 Bali Nagar, **New Delhi-110015**
info@christianworldimprints.com
www.ChristianWorldImprints.com
Phone: +91 11 25465925

ISBN 13: 978-93-5148-198-0 ISBN 10: 93-5148-198-0

Cataloging in Publication Data--DK
Courtesy: D.K. Agencies (P) Ltd. <docinfo@dkagencies.com>

Celvanāyakam, Israyēl, author.
Kristu bhakti and Krishna bhakti : a Christian-Hindu dialogue contributing to comparative theology / Israel Selvanayagam.

pages cm. -- (Interfaith treasures uncovered ; 8)
ISBN 9351481980
ISBN 9789351481980

1. Jesus Christ. 2. Krishna (Hindu deity) 3. Bhakti. 4. Hinduism--Relations--Christianity. 5. Christianity and other religions--Hinduism. I. Title. II. Series: Interfaith treasures uncovered ; 8.

BQ7276.C5C45 2017 DDC 261.245 23

All rights are reserved. No part of this publication can be reproduced, distributed, performed, publicly displayed, stored in a retrieval system, made into a derivative work, transmitted or utilized in any form or by any means; electronic, mechanical, photocopying, recording or any information storage system, without the prior written permission of the copyright holder(s), as indicated, and the publishers.

Jurisdiction: Any conflict or dispute in relation to this publication shall be adjudged in accordance with the laws of India and the matter shall be subject to the jurisdiction of the Courts, Tribunals or any other Forums of New Delhi, India, only.

Disclaimer: The views and contents of this publication are solely of the Author(s); the Publisher may not subscribe to them.

Printed in India.

To
Julius Lipner

Contents

Foreword ix

Introduction xv

Chapter 1: What is Bhakti? A Summary of Definitions and Discussions 1

Chapter 2: Jesus and Kṛṣṇa: Multi-faceted Figures 27

Chapter 3: Jesus and Kṛṣṇa: Process of Ascendency to Supreme Divinity 49

Chapter 4: Selections from St John's Gospel Pertinent to Kristu Bhakti 81

Chapter 5: Highlights of the Rāsalīlā 109

Chapter 6: Kristu Bhakti and Kṛṣṇa Bhakti: A Comparative Analysis 129

Conclusions 159

Select Bibliography 181

Index 187

Foreword

A source of substantial satisfaction for any mentor is the significant success of his or her mentee. Indeed, Dr. Selvanayagam does me honour by asking me to write a foreword for this critical and innovative piece of interreligious dialogue, a comparative examination of devotional theism in the Christian and Hindu religious traditions by examining two texts, one Christian and the other Hindu.

There have, of course, been numerous explorations of Christian *bhakti*, the religious tradition that Rudolph Otto defined as "faith in salvation through an eternal God and through saving fellowship with Him (sic)."[1] For the beginnings of Christian bhakti one has to go back to the early 19th century when Ram Mohan Roy was attempting to interpret Christianity through his own brand of unitarian non-dualism. At the same time, convert Tamil Christian poets such as H.A. Krishna Pillai,[2] deeply steeped in the Hindu *bhakti* tradition from which they had come, were already writing Christian lyrics which laid the offering of *bhakti* at the feet of the Christ. Here there is love and personal devotion; here there is experience of God's grace; here there is self-abandonment to the love and power of God which has distinguished so many *bhaktas*, devotees Hindu and Christian. Small wonder, then, that to so many,

---

[1] R. Otto, Christianity and the Indian Religion of Grace (1929). p.13.

[2] See A.J. Appasamy, *Tamil Christian Poet* (1966), Kingsbury and Phillips, *Hymns of the Tamil Saivite Saints* (1921).

as to the Christian poet from Maharashtra, Narayan Vaman Tilak,[1] there has seemed to be a direct bridge linking the world of Hindu bhakti with that of Christian faith, a bridge over which the *bhakta* may cross, and still feel that s/he has not strayed from home.

And yet in the midst of all this surfeit of complex richness, I know of no discussion quite like the present one. In and through it Dr. Selvanayagam, fully cognizant of all that has gone before, has launched out into previously unchartered waters, i.e., "a dialogical study of Kristu *bhakti* and Krishna *bhakti* in comparison with the limited scope of taking two texts with a probing approach to find new aspects to be added to the already existing views and definitions of bhakti and suggesting if hybridization is possible or not, or an alternative may be possible." Further, one does not often find a comparative study such as this which takes seriously the methodological issues attendant on a recognition that the Christian materials are typically reckoned to deal with a historical person, Jesus, while the Hindu materials relating to Krishna are commonly considered to be mythic, narratives of gods and superhuman beings.

Although, I have no intention of attempting to add to the book itself, I am pleased to have the privilege of joining conversation with the author regarding the significance of his research for one among many of the more lively current discussions and debates. Clearly the issue of hybridity or hybridization is of major concern to the author. There can be no gainsaying that fundamental to any understanding of hybridity is the critical issue of identity, i.e., who a person is, where he or she belongs and the qualities that make them different from others. Nowhere is this more true than in examining the role of religions.[2]

Self-identity, that sets a person apart from others, is rooted in that with which one associates and with a sense of belonging

---

[1] J.C. Winslow, *Narayan Vaman Tilak: The Christian Poet of Maharashtra* (1930), N. Macnicol, *Psalms of the Maratha Saints* (1919).

[2] See "Rethinking Religious Identity, Commitment and Hybridity" in Meredith B. McGuire, *Lived Religion: Faith and Practice in Everyday Life* (2008).

within given boundaries that provide a sense continuity and integrity, and a story-enlivened sense of a significant past and a significant future destiny. Identities not only empower but more importantly provide a sense distinctive status in relation to others, first the kinship of a shared status, but also the potential enmity of otherness.

While earlier societies with a social order based firmly in tradition would provide individuals with more or less clearly defined roles, increasingly in late modernity the search for self-identity is seen as the individual working out a personal identity, constructing a unique individual narrative. Critical here is the tension between personal and communal identity, a tension that is equally present within religious experience between the closely knit inner faith group and wider communities outside that faith group. There are, however, also powerful compulsions within different religious traditions that make for modes of human inclusiveness. Faith not only intensifies feelings of being distinctive, it can also lead to a greater awareness of the wider human community.

Analysis of the role of religion in shaping human identity makes it necessary to give far greater importance to the peculiar inner dynamic of religious life and to the interactive dimensions of religion. Hence, there is need to recognize the distinctively religious dimensions of key modes of self-identity. At the same time, the interaction of religious life with other historical realities, including other religious traditions, needs to be given serious attention. The problem is that it is unusual (except among religious studies specialists) to find significant recognition of the diversities of religious identities, even diversities of identities within what are commonly viewed as single traditions, e.g., Hindu, Christian, Muslim, etc. Further, even inner groupings, e.g., *saiva*, Protestant, *sunni*, etc, can and often do refer to widely contrasting worldviews. Nor is it only from outside that family uniformities are too facilely assumed.

The sense of belonging which is intrinsic to one's self-identity is increasingly complicated by exposure to the reality of religious diversity and knowledge of the teachings and practices of different religious traditions, bringing about shifts in the sense of religious identity and belonging.[1] Amply obvious is the fact that rather than simply and totally identifying one particular religious tradition, an ever growing number of individuals have come to affirm belonging to various religious traditions. In many cases, this involves Christians who have grown up in a household in which Christianity was practiced who also are attracted to certain schools of Hinduism or Buddhism. While some identify predominantly with one tradition and partly with another, others find themselves between traditions, moving back and forth between the normativeness of one or the other in various aspects of faith and practice. This, John Dunne[2] speaks of as 'passing over,' a shifting of standpoint from one's own to that of another religious tradition. This is followed by an equal and opposite process that might be called 'coming back', coming back with new insight to one's own religious tradition. A notable example of this is Raimon Panikkar who famously declared about his journey into another religion 'I "left" for India a Christian, "discovered" myself a Hindu, "returned" a Buddhist, all the while remaining a Christian.' Panikkar offers important caveats in terms of several indispensable prerequisites including a deep human honesty, significant intellectual openness and a willingness to forego prejudice in the search for truth, while maintaining a profound loyalty towards one's own tradition. The practical application of this principle is explained by Panikkar with reference to Hindu and Christian understandings of each other. "A Christian will never fully understand Hinduism if he (sic) is not, in one way or another, converted to Hinduism. Nor will a Hindu ever fully understand Christianity unless he (sic), in one way or another, becomes a Christian."

---

[1] Catherine Cornille, *Many Mansions?: Multiple Religious Belongings and Christian Identity* (2002).

[2] John Dunne, *The Way of all the Earth: Experiments in Truth and Religion* (1972).

[3] Raimon Panikkar, *The Unknown Christ of Hinduism* (1981), pp. 35, 43.

Indeed the religious self, like the culture or social self, is at core and in its conduct essentially and dynamically hybrid. This means that religious identity is not purebred. It is not singular, it is plural. It takes shape through an ongoing process of standing in one place and stepping into other places, of forming a sense of self and then expanding or adjusting that self in engagement with other selves. There is, in fact, no such thing as a neatly defined, once-and-for-all identity. Buddhists certainly have it right: there is no isolated permanent self. The religious self, along with other selves, is constantly changing through a hybridization process of interacting with others who are often very different from us. But being religious hybrids does not mean that one does not have an identity. Each individual has an identity, but that identity in its origins and its continuing life comes to be and continues to flourish in interaction with other selves. It does not, however, exclude some of the relationships that form the individual's identity from having a primacy over or greater influence than others.

For those who are interested, academically as well as existentially, in a different kind of interreligious dialogue characterized by perceptive discernment, a corrective criticism, and a dynamic mutual enrichment among two religious traditions, this is to be found in Dr. Selvanayagam's study, for which we owe him a debt of gratitude.

Rev'd. Dr. David C. Scott
Emeritus Professor of Religion and Culture
United Theological College, Bangalore

Introduction

Brooke Foss Westcott (1825-1901), a famous Professor of Divinity in Cambridge, New Testament scholar, writer on the fourth Gospel, guide to the formation of Cambridge-Delhi Mission-Brotherhood and bishop, 'believed that the most profound commentary on the Fourth Gospel was still to be written, and that it could not be written until an Indian theologian would undertake the task.' It is agreed that Bishop A.J. Appasamy (1891-1975) partially fulfilled the task. His successful Oxford doctorate was titled 'The Mysticism of the Fourth Gospel in Relation to Hindu Bhakti Literature.' The best fruits of this research were his books *Christianity as Bhakti Marga* (1928) and *What is Moksha?* (1931). Later, he wrote a book on the theology of Hindu Bhakti. In this book he quotes the missionary scholar J.N. Farquar's excellent summery of bhakti in Bhāgavata Purāṇa, the finest of the six major Vaiṣṇava Purāṇas:

> Bhakti in this work is a surging emotion which chokes the speech, makes the tears flow and the hair with thrill with pleasurable excitement, and often leads to hysterical laughing and weeping by turns, to sudden fainting fits and to long trances of unconsciousness. We are told that it is produced by gazing at the images of Krishna, singing his praises, remembering him in meditation, keeping company with his devotees, touching their bodies, serving them lovingly, hearing them tell the mighty deeds of

> Krishna, and talking with them about his glory and his love. All this rouses the passionate bhakti which will lead to self-consecration to Krishna and life-long devotion to his service.[1]

However, there is no attempt to work out the possibility of a hybridization that would have helped Christians have greater appreciation for not only Hindu bhakti in general but also Kṛṣṇa bhakti in particular. In turn, such possibility would help Hindu partners in dialogue to understand the unique Jewish tradition on which Kristu bhakti is built, thus moving away from the superficial slogan that the (undefined) essence of both (and even all) the religions are the same. Today, with the revival of studies of Hindu bhakti and of Kṛṣṇa bhakti and its globalization, and that of fundamentalist-conservative obsession of the churches in India, there is a need to critically analyse the hitherto studies and to make concrete suggestion for mutual enrichment as well as being together in the experiential dimension of religious life however limited it might be.

St John's Gospel, apart from the stories and teachings of Jesus, presents moments of his talk about the intimate union with God the Father on the one hand and his disciples on the other. The Holy Spirit as the 'Go between God' joins the union of the Father and the Son, thus completing the Trinitarian bond. Earlier, Jesus' 'I am sayings' which are similar to the 'I am sayings' of Kṛṣṇa in the Gītā, portray his supremacy and accessibility. His sayings 'I and my Father are one' and 'My Father is greater than me' seem to suggest the centrifugal and centripetal rhythm in his relationship with God and humanity.

In John chapter 15 we read Jesus telling his disciples, after mentioning the analogy of vine and branch, 'Dwell in me, as I in you. No branch can bear fruit by itself, but only if it remains united with the vine; no more can you bear fruit, unless you

---

[1] Appasamy, *Theology of Hindu Bhakti*, Madras: CLS for the Senate of Serampore College, 1970, 103f (quoted from Farquhar, *Outlines of the Religious Literature of India*, 230f).

remain united with me.' Little later he tells, 'you are to bear fruit in plenty and so be my disciples. As the Father has loved me, so I have loved you. Dwell in my love. If you heed my commands, you will dwell in my love, as I have heeded my Father's commands and dwell in his love.' Consequent of this union, Jesus calls his disciples friends as there is no secret in between them. Further, according to Jesus the oneness between him and the Father is the same as the desired oneness between them and his disciples. Such expressions are explained in terms of mystical union as well as dynamic intimacy.

Bhakti is the most important dimension in the development of Hindu religious traditions. Although there were traces in Vedic literature, and later the two classical texts – *Śāndilya Bhakti-Sūtra* and the *Bhakti- Sūtra* of Nārada (dates unknown) to define bhakti in relation to the question if the Brahman is with qualities or attributes (*guṇa*) or without, the earliest instance of a full-fledged experience and narrative of devotion is found in the Bhagavad Gītā (c 2nd century BCE). God in the form of Kṛṣṇa and his dear most devotee in the form of Arjuna set a background for describing the nature of bhakti. There were moments of physical thrill and emotional excitement on the part of Arjuna while experiencing the *viśvarūpadarṣana* and then listening to Kṛṣṇa acclaiming Arjuna to be his most beloved devotee. He also elaborates that with any means (leaf, flower, water) and any condition (low-born: Vaiśya, Śūdra and women) he accepts people who approach him in love. Even the act of exhalation and inhalation can become offering to him in loving devotion.

More than ten centuries later (c 9th century CE) came the famous Bhāgavata Purāṇa. Again Kṛṣṇa is the divine hero, supreme God and enjoyer of his devotees' love. In two important counts, bhakti in the Bhāgavata is distinctive. First, the mythical presentation of Kṛṣṇa satisfies the devotional longing of his different types of devotees. Second, there is corporate devotion present in the Purāṇa. The gopīs (milkmaids or cowherd women) epitomize closest devotees of Kṛṣṇa in all the ages and all the places. Aspects of bhakti such as divine attraction, separation and reunion with the greatest outpouring of devotion have found place in the tenth book or canto of Bhāgavata Purāṇa. It is in this section the famous Rāsalīlā, Kṛṣṇa's sportive dance or love game with the gopīs happened on a river bank as well as in the waters in moon light. Here he multiplies his form in order to meet the need of every gopī to have him in either side. It is the belief of the writer that an interactive reading of St. John's Gospel and the Rāsalīlā will bring out insights from their depth for guiding a creative dialogue today, even if a straightforward hybridization may not be possible.

The Background of Interest

For the first time, I encountered the Bhāgavata Purāṇa's section of the Rāsalīlā in 1982 at the United Theological College, Bangalore as it was one of the prescribed texts for the Masters in Hinduism. I was particularly struck by Kṛṣṇa's explanation to his beloved gopīs about his absence for a while and re-presence with greater glamour, grace and gaiety. He says that it was to enhance and intensify their devotional state of mind: 'The case is like that of the poor man who is not conscious of anything else when the wealth that he had gained is lost, but continues to contemplate that wealth obsessively' (BhP. X.32.20). Christians and devotees of other religious traditions are no strangers to such ideas as they are mentioned in their own scriptures and devotion, or mystical traditions. In fact since then I have mentioned the story in talks and sermons with necessary camouflaging.

However, it so happened that my dissertation was on a piece of Tamil Śaiva devotional literature, i.e. the famous poet-saint Māṇikkavācakar's *Tiruvācakam* (Sacred Utterance). It was a great moment of learning of bhakti in the Tamil Śaiva tradition but I had very little space to make a comparison with a Vaiṣṇava piece of literature or the distinctive nature of Christian bhakti. Further, my doctoral research was on the post-Vedic development in the understanding of sacrifice (*yajña*) and the response of the Bhagavad Gītā. This research took me into the fascinating world of Kṛṣṇa, particularly his elevation from a hero of a cowherd clan to an avatāra of Viṣṇu and further the one identical with Viṣṇu, the supreme. But I could not return to the Bhāgavata in any detail. A side-benefit of this research is to be able to question and articulate the relationship between the grace-filled bhakti and the performance of elaborate Vedic ritual with a belief in its inherent power, which continues to dominate in the major Hindu worship traditions.[1]

The course on Hindu Bhakti I have taught since 2010 for the Masters at Gurukul Theological College and Research Institute Chennai has given me some impetus to take up a study of Vaiṣṇava bhakti with reference to the famous Bhāgavata, again with special and limited reference to its crown, the Rāsalīlā section. Soon, I realized that a plethora of studies had been done on Vaiṣṇava bhakti in general and Bhāgavata in particular. I consulted a few scholars in the field and received overwhelming encouragement.

A Note on Method

I am aware that in the ever increasingly sophisticated research industry of the field of religion and religions, one would expect a discussion on what is known as methodology. I wish I had sufficient space to demonstrate the different senses, even contradictory at times, in which the term 'methodology' is used. The word therefore is very intimidating for students, particularly in India. Consequently, from the simple way of doing the research (using printed materials and empirical research) to the complex and complicated procedures are noted by them. Especially, with regard to these procedures and approaches like historical, hermeneutical, sociological, psychological, anthropological, phenomenological, philosophical, and so on are noted without explaining the relevance and analytical tools they provide. Since these approaches have been developed in the western academic contexts, researchers have developed novel theories on the basis of data collected from different parts of the third world and communities (i.e., Islanders, Hindu cults and African

[1] For an initial and preliminary discussion, see I. Selvanayagam, *The Dynamics of Hindu Religious Traditions*, Bangalore: Asian Trading Corporation, 1996, 64-83.

clans). Though it is not always acknowledged, one can notice that the tools used in such studies are aspectual, polyvalent, and specific and unless some twists are made the theories cannot be made universal. Thankfully, religio-theological scholars such as Wilfred Cantwell Smith (1916-2000) of Canada have criticized and chided scholars who go into remote parts of the world, collect data and interpret in such a way that it will suit their preconceived theories. Though such activity might help them to find places in universities, it hardly helps to understand the human experience of transcendence in whichever way it may be perceived. Also, more recently, 'dialogue' in general and interfaith dialogue in particular is interpreted as an indispensable tool for understanding religious experience and action. In the light of this preliminary observation, let me point out some presuppositions that govern the research in hand.

First, it is a scholarly fallacy that serious religious commitment necessarily hampers objective observation and unbiased interpretation. As a matter of fact a bhakta who uses his/her reasoning is in an advantageous position to listen to and understand another bhakta. As far as Christians who take the core insights of the Bible seriously are concerned, they are commanded not to bear false witness against their neighbours and to distort their visions and experiences. The definition of the attitudinal principle of dialogue as 'a mood, spirit and attitude of love in relationship' (Stanley Samartha, 1920-2001) need not be bracketed when a serious research of this kind is done.

Second, early missionaries who dared to study religious literatures they encountered in their 'mission field' and introduced to people of their home country, advocated approaching them with respect and courtesy. For example, George U Pope (1820-1908), an Anglican missionary from England who worked in Tamilnadu, southern India, as a groundbreaking attempt, translated *Tiruvāakam* into English, as we mentioned earlier. In his introduction he advocates an open approach to people of other faiths with a search for common truths and deeper layers of Truth without any unreasonable, unsympathetic and antagonistic attitude. He also points out that we have to get into the shoes of the poet we study and develop an empathetic feeling.

Third, as will be clear in this study, bhakti has both common and special features. One may argue that the basis of bhakti lies in human life itself and it has been already identified as soul, life-force, sacred awareness, feeling of transcendence and religiosity. Then, specifically, its manifestation is different depending on the grounding of it in a particular tradition. In this study, aspects of bhakti in John's Gospel have inalienable connection with the Hebrew/Jewish tradition. Its sacred values of liberation, justice and equality, and God's preferential option for the victims of various kinds, mix with what Jesus and his disciples did. Bhakti there is not focused on one moment and place but permeated throughout the events, dialogues and discourses. In the Rāsalīlā section of the Bhāgavata, on the other, it is focused and is grounded in the Vaiṣṇava tradition within a remarkable phase of Kṛṣṇa becoming the supreme God though there is mention of Viṣṇu and Vāsudeva towards the end. Whether the Kṛṣṇa-gopīs' experience of romantic behaviour or erotic mood in the play is actual or allegorical, we try to understand within the parameters of the bhakti tradition.

Fourth, related to the above, the historical quest of Jesus and Kṛṣṇa is acknowledged with reference mainly to the texts, but not explored in this study with debatable claims of historiography. Studies on the historical quest of Jesus abound. And though many have argued that narratives of Jesus are not as historical as in the modern sense of the term, though they are faith narratives and interpreted narratives, no one has claimed that they were myths and legends without any historical base. In the case of Kṛṣṇa there are informal claims about his historicity, but serious and detailed studies are yet to emerge. It is intriguing that at the end of the Rāsalīlā section it is noted that the sportive experience happened in an ahistorical realm as, apart from the presence of the celestial world, the husbands of the gopīs did not miss them as they had them with them intact. But what makes the narrative most significant is that it continues to inspire millions of Kṛṣṇa bhaktas. The same is true of the narratives of Jesus and his disciples for Christians.

However, the way bhakti manifests in the two narratives, is the limited focus of our study.

Fifth, Raymundo Panikkar (1918-2010) in his seminal book *The Unknown Christ of Hinduism* (1964) points out the need of mutual fecundation in Hindu-Christian dialogue. He has somewhat identified a meeting point in his study of the Advaita-Vedāntic category of Īśvara with Christ. We need not evaluate his work here, but note in passing that Panikkar's interpretation was that of a tiny tradition and its interpretation by a tiny number of exponents and proponents, which was refuted by other traditions of interpretation within Vedānta. It was taken out of the master narrative of the brāhmaṇic tradition or *The Vedic* Experience. This is not to deny the possibility of lively meeting points and mutual fecundation of one tradition by interaction with another, but Panikkar has not demonstrated how this can happen in relation to the interaction of two traditions. We do propose in this study the possibility of mutual enrichment between true Kṛṣṇa devotees and Christ devotees. Particularly, the self-forgetting dynamism of Kṛṣṇa bhakti might incorporate aspects of the deep intimacy of Christ with an emphasis on bearing fruit in the world. Christians could incorporate the whirlpool movements of the Bhagavan and his devotees to re-conceive the communitarian dimension of the Trinity. Hybridization cannot be preempted to happen unless when representative devotees of two or more communities come together with absolute openness to work out something that could be uplifting them individually and corporately. In the conclusion we will come back to this fashionable yet ambiguous issue and clarify the possibilities as well as difficulties.

Sixth, a long experience of Hindu-Christian dialogue is in the background of this study. The oputcome has not been as it was expected. Mutual defence of both sides, and the repeated slogan of 'one truth-many religions' on the Hindu side and 'one truth-one religion' on the Christian side, have not helped to move on with openness and new experiences. 'Dia-logue' is not simply speaking and chatting, nor remaining in silence in the name of mystery. Dialogue requires a commitment to listen more and speak less and a dedication for sustained sharing and if possible collective action. It is hoped that this study will motivate more studies from both sides.

Seventh and finally, the last point above needs some elaboration. One of the unique images of Kṛṣṇa, as presented in the Bhāgavata, is a player and dancer. His frolicks, pranks and lovegames with the gopīs are normally interpreted as signifying his independence, spontaneity and effortlessness. More importantly, it is explained as his divine action without any specific purpose unlike the other avatāras. It is not a means to an end but the end itself. He is self-content and self-fulfilled without any external support. But in the case of Jesus as presented in the John's Gospel, most of the time he provides solidarity with the least, last and lost among his community, confronts the conservative wing, and gives a new vision of reality. A comparison of both may sometimes look inconsistent and incoherent. Every care will be taken to avoid confusion. Moreover, it should be noted that scholars of Hindu-Christian themes, inside and outside India, repeat most of the ideas already studied and documented, discovers some new areas and offers helpful analysis and interpretation. But when presentations are made in the Indian context they appear to share the 'playful' posture of Kṛṣṇa, stressing the benefit for scholarship itself with stretching the intellect and fail to draw insights for addressing the Indian socio-economic realities. Precisely for this reason, reformers and social activists dealing with India's agelong problems of poverty, corruption, untouchability etc., judge the scholarly exercise as useless. This study is aware of this tension but with no claim to solve it.

The Structure and Sequence

This study acknowledges the difficulty of setting forth the most convincing definition of bhakti. The first chapter gives a summary of the ongoing discussion on what is bhakti. One may be surprised at the variety of definitions and interpretations. In the light of this study, some observations are made with a view to establish the variety and complexity of religious life, particularly religious experience.

The second chapter presents Jesus and Kṛṣṇa as two figures of divinity who have attracted the devotion of millions. They represent two new traditions while they are already rooted in two major religious traditions. It is an unjust act to remove Jesus from his Hebrew/Jewish tradition within which he found his mission that included both confrontation and comfort. His life and titles have hardly any significance outside his tradition during his life time. Kṛṣṇa also comes from a particular tradition which had in the background an amalgamation between the Brāhmaṇic tradition and Bhāgavata tradition. Here, Vedic dharma is both affirmed and transcended. He appears to return to his community without breaking the Viṣṇu connection. His visit to Vraj (Bṛndāvana) and calling the gopīs for a play represents his return and reconnection with the cowherd community to which Kṛṣṇa originally belonged.

The third chapter deals with questions about the ascendency of Jesus and Kṛṣṇa from multifaceted human figures to supreme divinities or visions of the supreme God. Scholarly discussions are more consulted on this section. This is an important point in the development of bhakti to them. Jesus and Kṛṣṇa did not instantly discend from heaven. They had their human stories and through various stages they attained the status of a supreme being. Admittedly, the process was not straightforward and unilineal as debates and discussions show. Particularly, the image of Bāla Kṛṣṇa poses a difficulty. He was a fascinating divine child frolicking and pranking, thus signifying his sportive power, independence and transcendence. But the stage and location of this image and perception may not be aaccertiained. In the case of Jesus, however, the progression from human identity to divine status somewhat is easier to read.

The fourth chapter, after some notes on historical background and literary genre of the fourth Gospel, presents the most important selections which come around or close to bhakti. Jesus' confrontation with the conservative leaders who refused to accept a new thing that God was doing, his struggle with the slow-thinking disciples to make them understand the new dispensation, and his claims and the problems therewith are brought out with sufficient detail.

The fifth chapter brings out a summary of the Rāsalīlā section of the Bhāgavata. Classical commentaries and scholarly studies of this section are referred to. As it is shorter than John's Gospel in many places texts are just reproduced. Its sequence in progression is maintained.

A comparative analysis fills in the sixth chapter. The word 'comparison' may be misleading unless it is explained. We deal with two distinctive traditions with different stories, terms, experiences and expressions. We seek to explain the common features of experience in the two texts and their unique aspects and in the process one helps the other to elucidate the meaning of its bhakti narrative. The distinctive backgrounds include both the long traditions behind the particular expressions of bhakti and the locations of the basic encounters. Each has a stated purpose and literary style. More importantly, Jesus and Kṛṣṇa, the fascinating figures and rallying centres of the two bhakti traditions, have their different contexts of having different titles, shifts and final ascendency towards becoming supremely divine. As we have already noted, the process is not simple and straightforward. The author of the fourth Gospel seems to struggle to maintain a hair-line between Jesus' humanity and divinity. At the same time, the title Son of Man suggests the most radical view that just as some Hebrew prophets experienced themselves and perceived God's very nature as providing solidarity with victims of all forms of injustice and oppression, Jesus does the same and asks his disciples too to do so. Kṛṣṇa, on the other hand, is connected with the long development of the Vedic deity Viṣṇu whose identification with the Bhāgavata divine hero Kṛṣṇa was most decisive in the complex history of intertwining traditions and tensions. In the fluid stages of the concept of avatāra which provided an all embracing and inclusive framework, Kṛṣṇa was one of the cardinal avatāras as declared in the Gītā (4: 7ff). But the same Gītā at a crucial point (e.g. the viśvarūpa darśana in ch. 11) presents him the pan-entheistic figure and even identical with the Vedāntic Brahman. Though the Vaiṣṇava purāṇas have different lists of the avatāras with or without Kṛṣṇa, the Bhāgavata is so distinctive in projecting him as the Lord supreme, replacing Viṣṇu or at least his name. What is intriguing is the mention of his consort as Lakṣmī or Śrī who is normally Viṣṇu's consort as Kṛṣṇa's most beloved gopī Rādha is conspicuously absent. Also, towards the end the names Viṣṇu and Vāsudeva occur and there seems to be no convincing explanation about these anomalies. Separate research is needed to solve them, particularly the relationship between Vedic Viṣṇu and Bhāgavata Kṛṣṇa. For our purpose here, we will continue to maintain that Kṛṣṇa was experienced both as the supreme God and the kinsman and friend of the cowherd community of Vraj. This reaffirms the observations that for an authentic bhakti experience, God must be both far and near, supreme and intimate, unapproachable and accessible, transcendent and immanent and so on.

Conclusion is the final section. After suggesting some additions of dimensions to the ongoing discussion on bhakti in the light of the highlights of each chapter, there will be detailed discussion on the compatibility between two narratives of bhakti. Some of the important questions that motivated me to embark on this study will be raised. For example, what new insights emerge from this study that can contribute and correct the ongoing attempts to define bhakti in general and Hindu-Christian bhakti in particular? In what way, mutual enrichment and fecundation can happen in a conscious interaction between Kristu bhaktas and Kṛṣṇa bhaktas? Is a true hybridization possible between the vision and experience of John's Gospel and that of the Rāsalīlā section of the Bhāgavata Purāṇa, while each already represents a process of hybridization in their own way and form? If at all hybridization is possible, what form will it take and who will own it and practice it? Even if some dismiss it as a wishful thinking, is there a possibility for the Kristu bhaktas and Kṛṣṇa bhaktas to maintain a sort of devotional fellowship and work together for the regeneration of the Indian society where the need of a thorough cleaning is recognized by the governments? Is a critical approach to religion and society possible within a devotional commitment? And, what are the issues for further dialogue between these two communities and how initiatives may be taken and dialogue sustained in a spirit of love and openness?

Acknowledgements

Originally I consulted Eric Lott of Leicester, a former Wesleyan mission scholar in India who was my teacher and research guide in the United Theological College Bangalore and Julius Lipner of Cambridge who supervised my doctoral research for ten months. After reading my 'proposal' they gave me the enthusiastic support. Later, David Scott of Washington, DC, another Methodist mission scholar in India who happened to be the final guide of my doctoral dissertation, showed much interest in my work and agreed to read chapters of the initial draft and make corrections and comments. He has done extensive studies on bhakti. I am immensely grateful to this trio of my 'doctoral brothers'.

From the beginning, I wanted to keep this study dialogical, within, with the texts and with as many devotees as possible. On 20 August 2013 fifteen scholars from the Gurukul seminary spent the day at the ISKCON centre/temple of Sholinganallur on the outskirts of Chennai. We not only enjoyed the fellowahip and hospitality but also a fruitful dialogue with the Japanese Äcārya and fourteen of his associates. There was so much of openness. It was clear that the centre is not engaged in any social involvement but fully concentrated in spiritual development. And the Äcārya was not hesitant to proclaim that Kṛṣṇa is the supreme and all other deities including Śiva are inferior. Further, we were guided to attend their worship which was enthralling.

While continuing to read the Vaiṣṇava bhakti literature, unexpectedly, recommended by my friend Kenneth Cracknell, I received an invitation to participate in a Christian-Vaiṣṇava consultation on 'Love of God and the Theological Bases for Vaiṣṇava-Christian Dialogue' held at the Śrī Kṛṣṇa Temple and ISKCON Centre at the foot of the seven hills on which situated is the famous Śrī Venkaṭeśvara Temple, Tirupati, 4-6 January 2015, under the leadership of an American Ācārya. It was good to see again friends of the ISKCON Chennai including the Ācārya, scholars such as Ravi Gupta and Francis Clooney and theologians such as Michael Amaladoss. I was assigned to make a presentation on Christian theological basis for dialogue. It was a memorable and enriching experience to be in the company of 20 Vaiṣṇava and Christian scholars staying in a comfortable guest house in the close precincts of the magnificent Kṛṣṇa temple. It was both inspiring and intriguing to bump into more than hundred brahmacāris with their unceasing utterance of the root mantra (*'Hare Kṛṣṇa, Hare Kṛṣṇa, Kṛṣṇa Kṛṣṇa, Hare Hare...*). I did not miss any opportunity to converse with both bhaktas and scholars to pick up and clarify matters pertaining to my research.

I place on record with gratitude the grants I received from the Teape Foundation and Spalding Trust which helped me to read in the Divinity School Library and main university libraries in Cambridge and Oxford in May 2013. I thank the librarians and staff of those libraries. I do hope that this research will throw some significant light on the understanding of Kristu bhakti and Kṛṣṇa bhakti and contribute to a comparative theology as well as to a sustained dialogue.

In my long experience of publication I have found the Christian World Imprints to be the most prompt in correspondence and most courteous and straightforward in dealing.

A Note on Translation: (unless stated otherwise).

New International Version of the Bible (1984)

Rāsalīlā section of the Bhāgavata Purāṇa by Edwin F. Bryant (2003); *Bhagavad Gītā*, translation of Swami Cidbhavananda (undated). Sanskrit words transliterated into English have the diacritical marks according to the standard practice except where they are in common English parlance, such as bhakti, yoga and dharma. However, quotations are reproduced just as they are in the original without any attempt to synchronize.

Chapter 1

What is Bhakti? A Summary of Definitions and Discussions

Setting the Background

The Sanskrit word *bhakti* does not refer to a self-evident concept and consistent practice. Translated usually in English as 'devotion' the contexts and contents of its usage suggest an amazing variety of meanings and experiences. Its rendering or similar expressions in the vernacular and non-Indian languages may well add to this variety. However, it is a useful exercise to trace the complex development of the word and meaning of *bhakti.* One may surmise that it is not as simple as has been thought so far.

As recognized in the 'scientific study of religion' experience is one of the dimensions of religious life. There is a variety of religious experiences identified and studied ranging from mystic absorption to ecstatic outburst. Phenomenologically, the idea of holy, mysterious fascination, prayer etc are suggested.

In orer to understand the meaning(s) of bhakti in the Bhāgavata tradition we need to map out major strands of the complex and polyparadigmatic religious tradition called Hinduism. Basically, there are four major strands in religious Hinduism:

1. *Ritual tradition*: It is traced back to the Vedic religion. It is centred on sacrifice (yajña) which developed from simple food offerings to gods and ancestors to an elaborate ritual mechanism which is believed to generate sacred power that sustains the life of the universe and human life and maintains the social order according to different varṇas. Though in the beginning some gods were invoked for granting boons and blessings, personal devotion to a deity was not prominent and in fact they too needed nourishment by rites such as *soma* cult.[1]

2. *Yogic tradition*: It is believed to have been developed outside the Vedic circle by a group of yogis, wandering ascetics or *śramaṇas* and later incorporated into the evolving Vedic system. It is still debated whether devotion to God was constituent of the eight-step classical yoga which was codified by the sage Patañjali. Today the term yoga is used very commonly referring to exercises to foster well being with proper postures, and to control of senses and breathing. Since the Bhagavad Gītā has ably demonstrated that yogic practices can be helpful to have undivided and unswerving concentration on God, devotees may practice yoga not simply to have well being but to gain full concentration on God, whatever their vision or image of God may be.

3. *Theistic tradition*: It is a long and complicated history to survey the development of theism or belief in a personal God. It is observed that polytheism, henotheism, monotheism, monism, pantheism, panentheism and polycentrism today roll together in different combinations. The most popular gods are Śiva and Viṣṇu, along with their consorts, avatāras or appearances or family members. The Goddess is also on a par with the Gods. At one level, these represent sectarian traditions and at another level

---

[1] The core of the *soma* cult is the soma plant, which grows in the mountains, but its true origin is believed to be heaven, whence it was brought to earth by an eagle. The pressing of *soma* was associated with the fertilizing rain, which makes possible all life and growth. In the post-Vedic classical period, *soma* is identified with the *moon*, which wanes when soma is drunk by the gods but which is periodically reborn. See *The Oxford Dictionary of World Religions*, ed. by J. Bowker, Oxford University Press, 2004, 913.

supreme beings. *Bhakti* plays a vital role in their cult and personal relationship.

4. Popular Diverse cults. They are communal, celebratory and ecstatic. Though there are voices for recognizing their unique distinction, studies suggest that at some point they have been influenced by the above traditions. On the whole, elements of bhakti may be found in all these strands in varying measure and magnitude.[1]

In parallel, the biblical tradition has many shades of 'devotion' to God. The root story of the Bible is the liberation of Hebrew slaves from bondage in Egypt by God in the enigmatic name of Yahweh. Their social cry was regarded as a powerful prayer by God Yahweh. God made a covenant with them which established the fact that they were called God's people who were supposed to cooperate with God to establish justice, peace and love in the world by following God's commandments. Whenever they deviated from this call they were chided, reprimanded and even condemned by the prophets, the spokespersons of God. The Hebrew scripture, apart from stories and discourses, is full of 'devotional expressions' in the forms of prayers, psalms and lamentations. But they are of great variety of intentions, meanings and moods. It was in this tradition came Jesus who had his own prayer life and he taught his disciples how to pray meaningfully in few words and to avoid long public prayers of display. There was an evolving perception of Jesus, from a devout Jew to the one coexistent with the Father God from eternity. It is believed that he inaugurated a new dispensation of the reign of God, now reigns spiritually in inseparable union with the Father and the Holy Spirit. His second coming is awaited in hope when he completes the process of establishing a new heaven and new earth. There are visions but no blueprints. But as far as the popular devotional exercises among Christians are concerned there is confusion about the above story, there are denominations and sects, and they account for a variety

[1] For details see I. Selvanayagam, *The Dynamics of the Hindu Religious Traditions,* ch. 2.

of devotional expressions ranging from contemplation, fixed liturgies and ecstatic outbursts.

It is within the aforesaid two settings we discuss bhakti as a prelude to the main task of proposing a comparative theology of Kristu bhakti and Kṛṣṇa bhakti.

The Word Meaning and History

A.J. Appasamy, a pioneering Christian exponent of Hindu and Christian *bhakti* observes: bhakti 'has had a long history in India and the varieties of meaning through which it has passed are numerous.' He quotes L.J. Sedgwick, an English civilian well-read in Indian literature, who defines bhakti as 'Personal faith in a personal God, love for Him as for a human being, the dedication of everything to His service, and the attainment of "Moksha" (final bliss) by this means, rather than by knowledge, or sacrifice or works.'[1] He also quotes an Indian scholar who writes of Gujarati religion the soul and spirit of which is bhakti – 'a word which, with its numerous associations has no English word for it. Worship, prayer and even devotion are words which fall short of the full annotation of bhakti. It means standing in the presence of God, serving Him, loving Him, hearing Him, and in fact enjoying the deity.'[2] He negates certain spurious definitions. For him the word bhakti occurs for the first time in the *Śvetāsvatara Upaniṣad*. This book was the last of the classical Upaniṣads and was probably written about 250-200 B.C. by an unknown author. But though the word 'bhakti' does not occur earlier than in this Upaniṣad the idea of the love of God is already present in early Hindu texts.[3]

To compound the problem of defining *bhakti*, it is often identified with mysticism. A.J. Appasamy, in his introduction to *Christianity as Bhakti Marga*[4] says that the book grew in six years in 1930: 'The first draft of it was submitted to Oxford

---

[1] A.J. Appasamy, *The Theology of Hindu Bhakti*, 1.

[2] Ibid.

[3] Ibid., 17.

[4] A.J. Appasamy, *Christianity as Bhakti Mārga: A Study of the Johannine Doctrine of Love*, Madras: CLS, 1991, vii.

University in 1922 for the degree of Doctor of Philosophy under the title *The Mysticism of Hindu Bhakti Literature especially in its relation to the Mysticism of the Fourth Gospel.*' He seems to have a pre-conceived idea that mysticism and bhakti are the same! He mentions the counsel and help of B.H. Streeter, J.N. Farquhar, Rudolf Otto, Baron Fredrich von Hūgel (and his friend Sādhu Sunder Singh). Later, the common term 'spirituality' too was identified with bhakti. Referring to many definitions, Appasamy sums up:

> By mysticism, however, I mean the type of religious life which emphasizes the communion of the human soul with a personal God. So, stated, the word Mysticism might seem to indicate the heart of all religious experience, but as a matter of fact, the word is used to indicate not so much the heart of *all* religious experience, as one particular type of that experience. To distinguish between that type of religious experience and other types is most difficult.[1]

One other type is ethical. We will soon point out Appasamy's own distinction between Hindu *bhakti* and Christian ethics.

A key biblical term to be recognized at this juncture is 'presence', i.e., an acute awareness of the presence of God. Even in the story of creation Adam and Eve lived in the presence of God and after their deviation went out of it (Gen. 3: 8; 4: 16). The Israelites during their exodus felt the presence of God through the symbols of pillar of fire, pillar of cloud, smoke (Ex. 13: 21-22; 19: 18) and tabernacle (25: 30; 35: 13; 39: 36). The promise of God for the leaders of liberation such as Moses was, 'my presence will go with you' (33: 14). When the community was settled in Canaan, when they were tempted to build a temple for God, the reminding reply from God through a prophet was, 'I have not dwelt in a house from the day I brought the Israelites up out of Egypt to this day. I have been moving from place to place with a tent as my dwelling' (1 Sam. 7: 6). However, certain kings yielded

[1] Ibid., 6.

to the temptation of building a temple as a symbol of the glory of their kingdom (yet usurping the LORD's name), but it proved to be disasterous. There were individuals who restored the idea of acute awareness of God's preseence in their life. For example, a psalmist prays:

> O LORD, you have searched me and you know me. You know when I sit and when I rise: you perceive my thoughts from afar. You discern my going out and my lying down; you are familiar with all my ways. Before a word is on my tongue you know it completely, O LORD. You hem me in-behind and before; you have laid your hand upon me. Such knowledge is too wonderful for me, too lofty for me to attain. Where can I go from your Spirit? Where can I flee from your presence (Ps. 139: 1-7).

The Hebrew prophets transposed such awareness to see God's struggle in the midst of unjustice and oppression in town gates, temple, royal courts and market places and spoke agains them in God's name. In this process, they faced suffering and disappointment. Some of them questioned God's presence in their life. Thus, Jeremiah laments: 'Why is my pain unending and wound grievous and inclurable? Will you be to me like deceptive brook, like spring that fails?' (Jer. 15: 18). There is an instance of a distinctive *viraha* bhakti here!

Coming in this tradition, Jesus gave an unque expression of living in the presence of God by identifying with the lost sheep and assuring them of God's active presence. We will elaborate this in our study of the John's Gospel. After the death and resurrection of Jesus the experience of living in the presence of God gave a new dimension to his apostles such as Paul, i.e. 'to live in Christ' (Phil. 1: 19-26). The new dimension had a new story, new memory and a new field of force. With this they could sing in jails, praise God in beaches, worship in catacombs and celebrate communion in houses. The first chapter of the last book of the Bible gives a strange but meaningful picture of someone like a son of man among the seven lampstands, signifying the seven struggling and persecuted churches of the Asia Minor. He holds in his right hand seven stars symbolizing the leaders of these churches (Rev. 1: 12-16). Unfortunately, Christian mystics and bhakti theologians like Appasamy have not mentioned the biblical idea of presence but it is very important to understand 'Kristu Bhakti'.

In discussing scholarly opinions with special reference to G.A. Grierson's article[1] in the *Encyclopedia of Religion and Ethics* Karen Pechilis Prentiss notes the following: 'Grierson defined the term *bhakti* as having the primary meaning of "adoration" while the related term *Bhāgavata* (which the author always capitalizes) means "the Adorable One" (in the sense of "One who is adored"). In discussing how Indian monotheism originated and became centred on this figure – the embodiment of bhakti – Grierson grudgingly identified a first stage in nature worship, representing his nod to a discourse that was marginal in academic scholarship on bhakti but dominant in the scholarship on the Vedas. Grierson suggested that early bhakti may or may not have been related to worship of the sun. The idea was that the sun is unitary; some of the earlier Orientalists had, in fact, likened Viṣṇu's *avatāras* (forms in which a deity descends to earth) to rays of the sun.'[2]

Based on a more recent and detailed and thorough study of bhakti, Krishna Sharma, suggests:

> The word bhakti is derived from *Bhaj* by adding the suffix *ktin*(ti). *Bhaj* can be used in any of the following meanings: to partake of, to engage in, to turn and restore to, to pursue, to declare for, to practice or cultivate, to prefer or choose, to serve and honour, to love and adore. The suffix *ktin* is usually added to a verb to form an action or agent noun. Thus, bhakti (*bhaj+ti*) can mean participation as well as recourse, experience as well as practice, reverence as well as love and adoration. Semantic studies bear out the

---

[1] G.A. Grierson, "Bhakti-Marga" in *Encyclopedia of Religion and Ethics*, ed. by James Hatings, New York: Charles Scribner's Sons, 1955, II, 539-551.

[2] Karen Pechilis Prentiss, *The Embodiment of Bhakti*, New York: Oxford University Press, 1999, 14.

occurrence of the term in all these meanings in the Indian classical texts. According to the rules of Panini, bhakti indicates a *bhava* or condition. In the relevant *sutra* in the *Ashtadhyayi*, he uses the word in the sense of excessive fondness and devotion, and illustrates its meaning by relating it with different objects and personalities.... Hence, the use of phrases like guru-bhakti, desa-bhakti, swami-bhakti etc...it can mean devotion to God only in a general sense, with no implication of any particular image or conceptualization of God. That is indicated only when a prefix is added to the term bhakti as in the case of Vishnu bhakti, Krishna bhakti etc. By itself it does not suggest any theology, nor any mode of worship. Thus, bhakti as a feeling of religious devotion, constitutes a part of every religion. The nature of its manifestation in a particular religious tradition, however, is conditioned by the nature of the cognition of God found therein, and by the beliefs and practices connected therewith. To the extent the different denominations of the Hindus conceive God in different forms, personal as well as impersonal, bhakti in the sense of religious devotion remains common to them all. However, variations can be caused in its character and overt expressions on account of the pluralistic character of the Hindu religious tradition.'[1]

Of course this is not a conclusive definition in the ongoing and popular attempts to define bhakti.

The Upaniṣads do not talk only and mainly about *brahman-atman* oneness as repeatedly noted by most Hindu scholars. The rituals of the earlier parts of the Vedas continue and they contain legends and introduction of the idea of *karma saṃsāra* which later became the fundamental problem of the pan-mythic Hindu faith, and bhakti was one way of getting liberated from it. At the same time, there had been deeply pantheistic trends inherited from the

[1] Krishna Sharma, *Bhakti and the Bhakti Movement: A New Perspective*, New Delhi: Munshiram Manoharlal, 1987, 40f.

Upaniṣads as well. Nevertheless, it is equally true that from the sixth to eighth centuries onwards there was the most vital religious energy manifested itself in the form of *bhakti*.

This renaissance of *bhakti* is known to have received its main impulse from South India. And it was presumably this fact which initiated the tradition preserved in the *Padmapurāṇa*, namely, that *bhakti* was born in the Dravida country. In South Indian Saiva tradition there were 63 Nāyanārs (leaders), who flourished between sixth and eighth centuries CE. They opposed the Buddhists and Jains, reconverted many of them and even supported their persecution with royal patronage. Their remarkable life-experiences of Śiva's grace and miracles and intense *bhakti* they developed in their life carried a melting appeal and meaning to the public. Some of them became 'madly in love with the mad Śiva' as in the case of the most popular poet-saint Māṇikkavācakar. The hagiography of these poet-saints has been translated.[1] The twelve canonical texts of the cardinal poet-saints became the basis of the Tamil Saiva tradition and Saiva Siddhāntha. Referring to the theistic traditions such as Saiva Siddhānta, the Indian Christian theologian Chakkarai observes:

> In all these instances of divine revelation God stands, as it were, outside man's consciousness and inspires him with some divine message or renders him some needed help. God stands like a light behind the crystal dome of man's mind, and reflects the divine light as far as he can do it. This is the imagery that the Saiva Siddhānta often employs as an illustration of divine contact with men.... but the Incarnation posits a different and more intimate union between God and man, like that between body and the mind or the body and the soul. Against such a union no mere *a priori* theories of God have any validity. Equally intelligible theories of God can be propounded with which to support the possibility of a real Incarnation. God's

[1] See Alastair McGlashan, *The History of the Holy Servants of the Lord Siva*, Canada: Trafford Publishing, 2006.

> being, as well as man's, is a mystery, and the Incarnation of Jesus only emphasizes it.[1]

God's universality and appeal to humans are amazing. 'He is the eternal diamond in the crown of life, presenting a thousand facets to men's vision...It is unique, universal, and mysterious.'[2]

Around the same time a group of 12 Āḻvārs (those who immerse, i.e. in the love of God) in Tamilnadu flourished and propagated the Viṣṇu bhakti. Their 'compendium of four thousand verses' reflects their bhakti experience. For them Viṣṇu or in the form of Kṛṣṇa was both far and near, supreme and accessible, transcendent and immanent. The Sanskrit stories of Viṣṇu's transcendent and playful acts were given imaginative interpretations with personalizing intimacy.[3] Deep intimacy and devotional delight run through their songs and sometimes the distinction is blurred. Therefore it is not surprising that the great Vaiṣṇava theologian Rāmānuja found in the Āḻvārs ingredients for the construction of his philosophy which was both theological as well as devotional.

Important Historical Locations and Distinctive Definitions of Bhakti

Vaiṣṇava *bhakti* underwent a truly exuberant ramification in northern and central India in the medieval period. Rāma bhakti came to centre in Ayodhya. Kṛṣṇa bhakti spread widely, particularly in Bengal and Maharashtra. Before we move forward, a note on the rough historical locations of the development of bhakti is in order. As we have noted, it is held by scholars with evidence that bhakti originated in the South. Then the logical outcome should be that the experience and writings of the Nāyanmārs and Āḻvārs should have found mention in North Indian bhakti literature. But what is striking is the opposite. This calls for more thorough

[1] V. Chakkarai, *Jesus the Avatār*, Madras: CLS, 1926, 6.

[2] Ibid., 13.

[3] See S. Robertson, *Bhakti Tradition of Vaiṣṇava Alvars and Theology of Religions*, Kolkata: Punthi Pustak, 2006.

research though it may not be wrong to take the view that oral stories were floating around to be grabbed by bhaktas before they were written.

When stories of divine encounter and bhakti in response spread, devotees experienced and expressed it in new ways depending on their geo-political atmosphere and distinctive personality. For example, following the line of Rāmānuja (11/12 cent.) and Madhva (13th cent.) Vallabha (c1479-1531) claimed that

> One who worships Kṛṣṇa with devotion is relieved of all misery. His motive in all things is sport (*līlā*), the motive of Bhagavān. Knowledge without devotion is useless since devotion supplies what is lacking in the path of knowledge, namely, a keen sense of Kṛṣṇa's personality. The fruit or reward of knowledge is inadequate. Since the individual self is a part (*aṁśa*) of Bhagavān, his grace alone is a sufficient instrument for bringing about the highest attainment of Bhagavān. Knowledge leads to the impersonal (*akṣara*) *brahman*, but devotion leads to the bliss of Bhagavān Kṛṣṇa.[1]

He further clarified that although Kṛṣṇa pervades the individual selves, his bliss is obscured and is only potential in them. Kṛṣṇa's sport alone evokes and brings it to fruition. 'When the bliss of union, as in the ecstatic play of Kṛṣṇa with the cowherd girls (*gopīs*), occurs, it is only a transitory feeling of emotion (*vyabhicāri*), which deepens and enhances the true end of devotion, hat is devotion itself. There is no room here for any earthly passion (*kāma*). The ecstatic play (*rāsalīlā*) is an allegory of the love of God for his devotees in terms of the human passions of union and separation. Separation (*viraha*) is the highest form of devotion since in it the heart hungers and craves for the absent Kṛṣṇa, whom it perceives in everything. The ecstatic play of the gopīs symbolizes the ideal of unselfish devotion and total dedication to Kṛṣṇa. Their love

---

[1] Daniel P. Sheridon, *The Advaitic Theism of the Bhāgavata Purāṇa*, Delhi: Motilal Banarsidas, 1981, 125.

is a spiritual love for Kṛṣṇa, untainted by physical desire. It is the ideal towards which the devotee should strive.'[1] When that is achieved there will be moments of thrill, excitement and tears of joy. Indeed, *bhakti* is rightly described as an end as well as a means. In one sense it indicates the mental attitude of the aspirant; in the other, it stands for an accomplished state of mind.

The Caitanya (c1485-1533) tradition teaches a radical metaphysical anthropomorphism.

> The phenomenal world and the individual self are just shadows of the transcendent world and the Supreme Self. In this system the paths of action, knowledge, and yoga have value only if they prepare the way for devotion. Devotion is an all-absorbing passion (*anurāga*) for God, but it also has its stages. First is devotion which resorts to means (*sādhana bhakti*) and is twofold. Prescribed devotion (*vaidhī bhakti*) follows the instructions of the *Bhāgavata* for the practice of the nine-fold devotion, hearing, singing, remembering about Bhagavān, etc. A second form of the devotion which resorts to means is the devotion of emotional attachment (*rāgānuga bhakti*) to Kṛṣṇa, which bypasses the steps of prescribed devotion. It takes the form of vicarious identification of the devotee with the servants, friends, parents, and lovers of Kṛṣṇa. The goal of the devotion which resorts to means is affective devotion (*bhāva bhakti*) which is the emotional dawn of love (*preman*) for Kṛṣṇa. Love is spontaneous and exclusive attachment to Kṛṣṇa.'[2]

This tradition, also known as Bengal or Gaudia Vaiṣṇavism, takes the concept of *rasa* or sentiment of the Sanskritic and local aesthetic and applies it to Kṛṣṇa bhakti and pushes it to the maximum pitch. 'The highest, most perfect sentiment is the erotic thrill (*sṛṅgāra*), the highest accomplishment of devotion. For

---

[1] Ibid., 126.

[2] Ibid., 131.

example, the gopīs surrendered unconditionally to Kṛṣṇa, whom they loved for his own sake. They seek nothing but to foster his pleasure. They forget their parents, husbands, and good reputation and blindly follow Kṛṣṇa. Yet there is no touch of scandal, for as Jīva Gosvāmi postulates, there are two aspects to the ecstatic play of Kṛṣṇa. As unmanifest (*aprakṛta*) in the inner essence of Kṛṣṇa, the ecstatic play takes place in a transcendental, ideally pure realm. The gopīs are Kṛṣṇa's intrinsic power (*svarūpaśakti*), and thus are his wives untouched by immorality. As manifest (*prakṛta*) in outer essence of Kṛṣṇa, the ecstatic play is a projection of the unmanifest ecstatic play. As such it is not subject to criticism. The manifest play leads the devotee by means of ecstatic devotion to the unmanifest play. The Vṛndāvana līlā is not a mere allegory or symbol but literally history in both its phases.'[1] Later in our study we will raise questions such as, why the gopīs are described as the wives of other men? Does it reflect the pattern of Sanskrit drama in which the unmarried strike love more passionately than the married ones? Is ecstatic devotion (*rāsa bhakti*) possible for all devotees? Is devotion of separation (*viraha bhakti*) applicable only to those caught up in romantic frenzy? Is it available for old persons, for example?

Does Christian bhakti bring into the discussion anything new? For Appasamy 'To abide in Christ means to live so continually in contact with Him and to be so filled with His spirit that it overflows into abounding deeds of love for our fellow men.'[2] He clarifies that 'complete metaphysical equality with God is a mystery which only choice and gifted souls can understand; only men of real penetration can grasp the ultimate fact of the equality between God and man.'[3] To explain further:

> Fellowship with God does not consist in such a realization of our ultimate kinship with God, a kinship which always exists though hidden by mists of illusion and which has

[1] Ibid., 132.

[2] Appasamy, *What is Moksha?*, 27.

[3] Ibid., 58.

> only to be made clear to the soul by some rapturous glimpse of Reality. But it is the harmony of the individual soul with the Divine soul in thought and imagination, in purpose and will, in humble deed and adoring devotion. Oneness with God consists in the continuous orientation of the human personality towards the Divine so that floods of God's love and power keep running into man's soul. The vast energies of God inundate the soul of man (sic) from time to time, and every moment he lives in the consciousness of receiving them. From him proceed prayers, aspirations, longings and decisions which continually keep flowing into God. Thus, there is a perpetual flux of life from God into man and then again from man into God.[1]

The future is hopeful but its nature is unpredictable. 'So through Christ we sweep the heavens and realize the inaccessible depths and distances with all their mystery, stretching to we know not where. Beyond Christ is the great and mysterious God, great and mysterious in His love and goodness as well as in His power and might. We may not measure or fathom or comprehend Him fully. We may only catch the most distant glimpses of Him and have our whole being stirred by the illimitable vistas which spread before our awe-struck gaze and stretch into farther and ever farther distances.'[2] At the same time he consistently maintains that the vertical dimension of bhakti should reflect in our horizontal outreach which elevates us to have a fuller knowledge of God. 'The relations which connect us with our fellow-beings provide us with opportunities for getting a fuller knowledge of God. They point out ways and means by which our union with God may become enriched.'[3]

Our survey of definitions and discussions of bhakti with reference to the Hindu bhakti traditions as well as Christianity gives glimpses into a great, mysterious, God-oriented, loving,

[1] Ibid., 68.

[2] Ibid., 116.

[3] Ibid., 142.

ecstatic and emotional experience called *bhakti*. We have confined to consult the main traditions. Sometimes the nature and experience of *bhakti* is integrally related to theological foundations and beliefs. We do not have space to study them in any detail. Also in both the religious traditions there are numerous sectarian groups and fundamentalists who express bhakti in a particular way but claiming that it alone is the correct way! When we study the relevant sections of the John's Gospel and the Rāsa Līla section of the Bhāgavata Purāṇa and make a comparative analysis we may well expect that more light will be shed on understanding the nature and meaning of bhakti.

Interpretation of Bhakti

Bhakti does not happen in a vacuum. Adherence to a tradition, belonging to a community, performing ritual, attachment to scripture, pilgrimage and emotional talk particularly at times of personal crisis are integral to bhakti. It is obvious, therefore, that as *bhakti* has the dimension of emotion the psychology of religion is germane to *bhakti* studies. Mythology and the fact of imagination too have gained significance in the study of *bhakti*.

There are a number of attempts to identify and establish the components and stages of the bhakti experience. We consult the two classical texts on bhakti whose dates are unknown but as both mention the Gītā and the Rāsalīlā, they should be later than them.

1. Following the pattern of the *Btahma Sūtra*, Śāndilya opens his Bhakti Sūtra with the words, 'Now, then, enquiry into the Doctrine of Devotion.' The next line is 'The primary Devotion is the attachment to the Lord.' Further it asserts that decaying knowledge is of no use and bhakti alone is the way and the fruits of devotion are eternal.[1] Even attaintment of *samādhi* is secondary. Contrasting Bādarāyṇa who held that absorption in the Ātman leads to amancipation, Śāndilya asserts, 'when the understanding is absorbed in both viz. the majesty of the Deity, and the fullness of the Ātman it causes the release, as is evident from the authority

[1] R.N. Vyas, *Melody of Bhakti and Enlightenment*, New Delhi: Cosmo Publications, 1983, 175.

of the Vedas and valid reasoning.'[1] Believing God's power and invulnerability to pain and suffering, the sage points out the following devotional actions: devotion to the manifestions of the powers of the supreme God, singing of the names of the Lord and narrating God's attributes, concentration of mind in the process of meditation,[2] offering etc are secondary. Finally, 'rebirths and deaths originate from want of devotion, and not from want of knowledge, that being inconsistent with the cause.'[3]

2. Narada's *Bhaktisutras* first instructs the devotee to conform to Vedic injunctions without explaining the connection between the central Vedic feature of ritual sacrifice and devotion to a personal loving God. Bhakti is explained as 'attraction for stories of God's play as incarnations', 'surrender of all activities to God and extreme anguish if He is forgotten', 'devotion is superior to the paths of action, knowledge and yoga' (because) 'even God hates pride and loves humility'; and the means for attaintment of devotion are: the renunciation of objects of enjoyment and attraction towards them, grace of God, holy company of God's devotees, giving up all effects and fruits, renouncing action even enjoined by the Vedas, giving up lust for women, pride, vanity and other vices, devoting all actions to God and direct lust, anger, pride etc. towards God only, reading and reflecting devotional texts and performing bhakti-arousing activities, constant worship and maintanence of equinimous mind.[4] Further, Nārada notes that bhakti manifests itself in eleven forms, which overlap some of the above:

> Love of the glorification of the Lord's blessed qualities, love of His enchanting beauty, love of worship, love of constant remembrance, love of service, love of God as a friend, love of God as a son, love of God as the husband,

---

[1] Ibid., 176f.

[2] Ibid., 177ff.

[3] Ibid., 181.

[4] Swami Bhuteshananda, *Nārada Bhakti Sūtras*, Kolkata: Advaita Ashrama, 2009, verses 17ff.

love of self-surrender to Him, love of complete absorption in Him, and love of the pain of separation from Him.[1]

Finally, apart from his own name Nārada recommends the following teachers of devotion: Vyasa, Shuka, Shandilya, Garga, Vishnu, Kaundinya, Shesha, Uddhava, Aruni, Bali, Hanuman, Vibhishana, and so on.[2] And he concludes his Sūtra with a signatory line: 'Whoever believes and follows with faith this auspicious teaching of Narada becomes a lover of God and realizes the Dearest who is the sole aim of life.'[3]

The Bhāgavada Purāṇa lists nine stages or aspects of devotional life: 1. *Śravaṇa* (listenng to scriptural stories of Krsna); 2. *Kīrtan* (singing, usually ecstatic group-singing); 3. *Smaraṇa* (recollecting or fixing the mind on Viṣṇu); 4. *Pādasevana* (serving the deity); 5. *Archana*, worshiping an image); 6. *Vandana* (praising); 7. *Dāsya* (servitude); 8. *Sākhya* (friendship); 9. *Ātmanivedana* (self-surrender).[4] In more general terms, with special reference to a piece of Tamil Śaiva devotional literature (Māṇikkavācakar's *Tiruvācakam*) I have identified three basic components of a bhakti experience: image, imagination and emotion.[5] One can unpack these components with illustrations from across religious traditions.

In terms of an actual encounter between the Lord (Kṛṣṇa) and his dearest devotee (Arjuna) the Gītā represents the earliest expression of an almost full flown bhakti. In an explosive situation of different schools of thought or yogas (ways) the Gītā tries to work out a synthesis between karma yoga, jñāna yoga and bhakti yoga. But does it really synthesize? The Vedāntic interpretations

---

[1] Ibid., v 82.

[2] Ibid., v 83.

[3] Ibid., v 84.

[4] Bhāgavata Purāṇa 7.5.23-24. See Daniel Sheridon, *The Advaitic Theism,* 82; cf.

[5] I. Selvanayagam, "Components of a Tamil Saiva Bhakti experience as evident in Manikkavacakar's Tiruvacakam" in *Spiritual Traditions: Essential Visions for Living,* edited by David Emmanuel Singh, Bangalore: UTC (ISPCK, Delhi), 1998, pp. 418-439.

of the Gītā alone indicate the difficulty of working out such a synthesis unless one has a distinctive meaning of 'synthesis.' The Vedāntins differ in prioritizing the three yogas mentioned in the Gītā. Particularly the contradistinction between the Nirguṇa Brahman and Saguṇa Brahman is still debated. Can one in some way include the other? This question has been answered in different ways. Krishna Sharma points out the following:

> In the *Bhakti-Vardhanī*, bhakti is defined as an overwhelming affection for God, accompanied by a full sense of his greatness. He mentions seven stages of bhakti – of bhāva, prema, praṇya, sneha, rāga, anurāga and vyasana – all indicating purely emotional states of love. The devotee attains the highest state of bhakti only when his love for God assumes the nature of a passion (vyasana). Vallabha regards prema as the seed of bhakti and his followers generally interpret bhakti as a combination of prema, and sevā, (service). Bhakti as sevā can exist for the name (nāma-sevā), as well as for the form (rūpa-sevā). Sevā or service may be of the body (tanujā), of material wealth (vittayā), or of the mind (manasā). Bhakti as sevā in these forms is obviously conceived in relation to the personal deity Kṛṣṇa, his idols, and temples.[1]

She also draws special attention to the view of R.G. Bhandarkar, a contemporary of the Orientalists Weber, Monier-Williams and Grierson: Bhandarkar 'was the first Indian academician to write on Bhakti theme. He tried to demolish the theories advanced by Weber and others who had argued to prove the influence of Christianity on bhakti. Accepting their identification of bhakti with the Kṛṣṇa-cult and Vaiṣṇavism, Bhandarkar sought every possible evidence of the worship of Kṛṣṇa-Vāsudeva and Viṣṇu in the pre-Christian era. Adopting the modern historical methods, he established its native character and antiquity with the support of epigraphic and literary

[1] K. Sharma, Op. cit., 159.

evidence.'[1] From the Christian side it only requires regretting for some Christians today who make unfounded superficial claims about Christian influence on Hindu bhakti.

There are five things identified in devotion: (1) residence in the Vaikuṇṭha heaven with Bhagavān (*sālokya*), (2) the possession of divine powers (*sārṣṭi*), (3) living in Bhagavān's presence (*sāmipya*), (4) the possession of the divine form (*sārūya*), and (5) absorption into his being (*ekāyva*). The latter in this context must mean absorption compatible with remaining with the sphere of the qualities.[2] None of these states of beatitude can compare with the simple state of devotion, which is a state of union (left finally unexplained, though beyond the qualities) with Bhagavān: "That only is called the final discipline of devotion by which one overcomes the three qualities and attains my state." In canto nine each of these types of beatitude is contained within devotion: "Fully satisfied with service to me they do not desire the four types (of beatitude), such as residence, etc. which are attained by service to me. How could they desire these other things which are ravaged by time?"...The states always involve, even in their highest degree, some form of death and rebirth. To the extent that they are not final these states of beatitude are actually states of bondage.[3]

For R.N. Vyas 'Bhakti implies an intimate and intense love for God. A devotee fixes his attention on the feet of God alone and spurns anything that comes by way of an obstruction in the path of this love. God is thought to be beloved, father, mother, brother everything. Bhakti consists in dedicating all the actions

---

[1] Ibid., 88; (cf. Bhandarkar, *Vaishṇavism, Śaivism and the Minor Religious Systems*, New Delhi: Asian Educational Services, 1983, 3, 4, 9, 14, 29, 38.

[2] See Sheth Noel, *The Divinity of Krishna*, Delhi: Munshiram Manoharlal, 1984, 144.

[3] Sheridon, Op.cit. 93; In the Śaiva traditions the stages are four: *sālokya* (living in Śiva's world), *sāmīpya* (living close to Ś iva), *sārüpya* (acquiring Śiva's image) and *sāyujya* (perfect intimacy with Śiva).

performed through body, language, mind, intelligence etc. to God with sincerity and honesty.'[1]

According to Appasamy, Christian mysticism imparts a unique, moral character: 'Communion with our Lord is made possible not by emotional fervor, nor by flights of speculation, or even of intuition, but by the difficult yet joyous discipline of walking along His path of suffering. The attainment of salvation by suffering is not an especially Christian idea; the moral quality of suffering is.'[2]

Moreover, R.G. Bhandarkar and others argued for a kṣatriya development of bhakti monotheism; Grierson in his aforesaid article went a step forward assigning caste groups and geographical locations. 'The map of bhakti in this article was not gratuitous. It was a spatial depiction of the Orientalist sense of the orthodox (center) and the unorthodox (periphery), with bhakti consistently located on the unorthodox side in opposition to Śaṅkara. The origin and tenacity of the Bhāgavata religion depended upon non-brahman kṣatriyas, following Bhandarkar's analysis, who were not traditionally invested with religious power. Grierson's map "explained" the genesis of monotheism, and the development of the Bhāgavata religion, in terms of polarities. But whence came the reformers who created the modern bhakti-mārga? By the time Grierson wrote this article, scholars had linked bhakti to the Vedānta of Rāmānuja and others as even he acknowledged this. His answer was to suggest a gap between the early Bhāgavata religion and modern bhakti-mārga, the latter a reform that 'almost seems as if a new doctrine, coming from some unknown land, had suddenly been revealed, and had swept with irresistible force in one mighty wave across the peninsula.' The image of the wave is in keeping with his, and earlier orientalists' idea of a reform movement and with their persistent image of bhakti as an overwhelming emotional response to God.'[3]

---

[1] Vyas, R.N., *Melody of Bhakti and Enlightenment*, New Delhi: Cosmo Publications, 1983, 56.

[2] A.J. Appasamy, *Christianity as Bhakti Mārga*, 111.

[3] Prentiss, Op. cit., 15.

Bhakti has its own tension as it is acknowledged: 'The tension in bhakti is between emotion and intellection: emotion to reaffirm the social context and temporal freedom, intellection to ground the bhakti religious experience in a thoughtful, conscious approach. This tension was missed by Orientalist scholars, who even in the earliest definitions stressed what they viewed as the uncontrolled emotion of bhakti: 'The whole religious and moral code of the sect is comprised in one word, *Bhakti*, a term that signifies a union of implicit faith and incessant devotion, and which …is the momentary repetition of the name of KRISHNA under a firm belief, that such a practice is sufficient for salvation.' For Monier-Williams, 'the full realization of bhakti's potential for uncontrolled emotion occurred in the "abuses" of the followers of the sixteenth-century bhakta Vallabhācārya. But the Orientalists were mistaken in their analysis; in bhakti texts, emotion is freed from social and temporal constraint, not moral principles.'[1]

There are studies which establish connection between ideology and *bhakti*. For instance, D.D. Kosambi, a Marxist historian, has demonstrated how bhakti suited the feudal ideology. But can it be generalized? We have cases of *bhaktas* who have revolted against oppressive structures. E.g. Māṇikkavācakar, the foremost of the Śaiva Ācāryas, declared that we are not subject to anyone! Māṇikkavācakar was a Brahmin. But bhaktas such as Kabir and Namdev who revolted against caste came from lower castes. Long ago, the Gītā, however, affirmed the four castes were created by God, but in a bhakti framework, people of lower births (Vaiśyas, Śūdras and women) were accepted in loving devotion to Kṛṣṇa (9:32). Perhaps Kosambi was not aware of the fact that praise and glorification could be mutual between God and devotees as Jesus and some devotees have shown. A recent popular Tamil Christian devotional starts with two lines meanng 'while you are seeking God, God is seeking you; while you are singing God's praise, God is singing your praise.'

[1] Ibid., 20.

Focusing on Specific Traditions

Let us move close to the Bhāgavata tradition of the Vaiṣṇava bhakti. The *Bhāgavata Purāṇa* is regarded to be the fountainhead of a great deal of bhakti thought. It is claimed that 'We find here a tendency to consider that a Bhakta may indeed merge in God if he desires such merging. This possibility is always before the Bhakta. He thinks it quite natural that as the goal of all spiritual striving there should be possible this absorption in God. But he prefers the other way of service and devotion. It is quite significant that this possibility of absorption in God is not wholly rejected but is still allowed a place in the religious thought of the Hindu Bhakta.'[1]

Distinction between liberation and devotion is made in Bhāgavata Purāṇa. One interpretation is that 'devotion is a natural inclination of the senses, whose objects are the qualities and whose actions are in accord with Scripture, toward the quality of pure being (*sattva*) which is the quality nearest to Bhagavān. This motiveless devotion is superior to final beatitude itself. It quickly dissolves the body just as the stomach consumes what is eaten. The effort to reach beatitude is imperfect since it is concerned with the self.' The other is found in a testimony that 'the mind incessantly flows to me, who reside in the hearts of all, by means of listening to my qualities just as the water of the Ganges continuously moves to the ocean.' This is devotion without ulterior motive, without cause, an uninterrupted devotion to the Supreme Person.[2] As it will be clear later in this study, stress on one such aspect is limiting on the part of God.

It is significant to note that inner purification and service to the poor are associated with devotion but along with performing the prescribed sacrifices without shedding blood. 'The devotee sees, touches, and worships Bhagavān's image. He sees Bhagavān in all things. Truthful and dispassionate, he is respectful towards great souls and compassionate towards the poor. He is friendly and practices the injunction of Yoga. He listens to spiritual matters,

---

[1] Appasamy, *Theology of Hindu Bhakti*, 120.

[2] Sheridon, Op. cit., 74.

and chants Bhagavān's name, and associates with holy men. Thus, he gives up egoism. These moral virtues and spiritual practices are the religious duties (*dharma*) of the *Bhāgavata*.'[1]

It is also observed that the pre-Rāmānuja and pre-Bhāgavata bhaktas did not claim that their efforts connected them to God. But they will say: 'We have a longing to draw near Him. That longing is planted in our souls by God Himself. With His help we think of Him, steadily and constantly and with deep love, in order to realize that longing. As we do so He enters our souls. We keep meditating on Him if He is to remain in us. His dwelling in our hearts brings with it joy and light and freedom from impurity and release from ever-recurring cycle of births and deaths. And we sing and dance filled with rapture because of this experience.'[2] This is different from self-induced emotionalism as further clarified.

We have already noted, there are different relational stages in the progression of a bhakta's closeness toward God, as servant, friend, bride and so on. The overarching bond is love. Love includes qualification of the recipient, the type of feeling, idea or attitude that motivates the experience, the emotional, aesthetic and moral quality of the experience itself, and the emotional, moral and spiritual effects that it exerts upon those engaged in a love relationship. Making this general observation, Bruce Long refers to the Vaiṣṇava Sahajiyā cult of Bengal (16th century) which holds that the Bhāgavata Purāṇa defines the route taken by the spiritual pilgrim. Accordingly, the route to salvation progresses along five stages of spiritual development, in which the bhakta enjoys an increasingly intimate relationship to God: '(1) *śānta*, the feeling of awe, humility, and insignificance experienced by the devotee who views God as the supreme deity; (2) *dāsya* love in the form of respect or reverence and obedient service, experienced by man (sic) as servant or slave toward God as supreme master; (3) *sākhya*, fondness and affection through a personal relationship between man (sic) and God as friends; (4) *vāsalya*, a parental or fraternal affection; and (5) *māthurya*, the stage of lover and

---

[1] Ibid., 80.

[2] Appasamy, *Christianity as Bhakti Mārga*, 73.

beloved, the ultimate and purest form of love, epitomized in the love of the cowherd girls for Kṛṣṇa.'[1] Is this pilgrimage unilinear without struggle and overlapping? We will point out later how in the experience of the gopīs romance is mixed with friendship, pain and service.

Vyas observes yet another dimension. For him *bhakti* in Bhāgavata implies a willing selfless surrender to God. It means a firm, stable, and unflinching attachment to God, which is unaffected by any personal desire, or worldly ambition. 'Bhakti is thus a transforming experience. It is a transforming experience because a God-oriented attitude is produced in a devotee that brings about a complete change in the attitude of the latter towards the world. His tendencies, which were formerly directed towards worldly desires and aspiration, mundane ambitions, or attainment of super human powers, or even liberation from the world, are suddenly turned completely towards God. A devotee, no doubt, lives a worldly life. But he does not live for himself. He lives only for his God, his beloved. He (sic) becomes a shadow of his master. His heart is full of love for his beloved, his mind is full of admiration for his beloved, his body moves for his beloved. A life of devotion is a life that is no longer personal. It belongs to God alone. The reason is obvious. The mental tendencies of a devotee are surrendered at the feet of God, his speech invariably engaged in reciting His names, and his body is always in the state of paying an obeisance to Him.'[2] Already we find here as elsewhere theological articulation without reference to actual stories and distinctive experiences. As it will become clear, the story of the Rāsa Līla contains the story of the Lord's pastime in an autumn moonlight that included fascination to a sacred music of flute, rushing in absolute priority to meet him, despondence of separation and gaining a new life on the Lord's return. The symbolic acts with sexual imageries suggest what has been known as 'bridal mysticism' or the devotion of deep intimacy of love.

---

[1] J. Bruce Long, "LOVE" in *Encyclopedia of Religion*, New York: Macmillan Publishing Company, 1987, Vol. 9, 34f.

[2] Vyas, Op. cit., 57.

All the aspects of bhakti we have discussed above may be applicable to the experience of devotees or God's people mentioned in the Bible. However, it is not studied in the Indian terms. But there are most distinctive aspects of bhakti in the Christian tradition. As we have already noted, Appasamy felt 'the difficult yet joyous discipline of walking along His path of suffering. The attainment of salvation by suffering is not a specifically Christian idea; the moral quality of suffering is.' This is very true of St John's Gospel. This is in line with the Hebrew experience of a suffering God and his devotees sharing in this suffering in the context of trying to change the society and the attitudes of people. But at the same time, as we will point out, Jesus and his disciples experienced surprise, thrill, sorrow, joy and hope. More importantly, there is a gradual understanding and changing perception of what Jesus was. All this happened within the framework of a corporate unity of three 'persons' within the Godhead in which the disciples and believers could participate and of a functional oneness in a continuing mission.

Summary

Bhakti is not a single term with straightforward meaning. Nor is it a self-evident concept. There are efforts to give a convincing definition and interpretation. The extensive details of the definition, interpretation and personal testimony of bhakti we have discussed thus far, have not helped to construct a doctrine of bhakti. What is evident is that just like religious life in general there are different dimensions and perceptions of bhakti. In the Hindu tradition, particularly the Vaiṣṇava-Bhāgavata tradition, there are clues for shifts of meaning and emphasis. The climax is either absorption into the Supreme or dancing in ecstatic joy with the Lord just as the *gopīs* did with their Lord Kṛṣṇa. Though the moral quality of loving one's fellow beings and of working to change the society to ensure human rights and equality is not immediately evident in the original Hindu texts, new interpretations touch the point. But in the case of the Judeo-Christian tradition, loving God with one's all mind, soul and strength, and loving others as oneself, is noted as cardinal. Any devotion to God without commitment to change positively the life of others and the society is condemned as hypocritical. As Appasamy has pointed out, working for change in solidarity with the suffering God is vital in the Christian tradition. This is not to claim that all the Christians follow this path of integrated spirituality. This recognition is helpful for approaching the texts of our study without any prejudice but with openness.

Chpter 2

Jesus and Kṛṣṇa
Multi-faceted Figures

Introductory Remarks

One repeated problem in comparative theology and interfaith dialogue is a confusing starting point. For example, a Christian, a victim of the propagation of 'Jesus cult', may start with an uncompromising belief in Jesus as God, the only God, the supreme God, superior than Hindu gods and goddesses, more powerful and most reliable. S/he may add that Jesus is the eternal Word who incarnated, and his incarnation was the only one in full human form, only one who was historical, and, if s/he has been trained in some form of devotional/missionary theology, s/he may add that Jesus' is the sweet, precious, wonderful name which alone can save. S/he may also mention that Jesus is the central partner of the mysterious Trinity. This way of presenting Jesus lacks clarity and it confuses the partner in dialogue. The actual fact is that the New Testament portrays a long process of changing perceptions of Jesus which need to be acknowledged in a discussion, particularly with devotional Hindus.

Similarly, the Kṛṣṇa bhaktas always project Kṛṣṇa as the most important avatāra of Viṣṇu or God himself. We have most fascinating accounts of such bhaktas such as Mīrābai and Chaitanya who found in Kṛṣṇa the most compelling form of God who not only satisfied their longing but also presented a new way of life. The International Society of Kṛṣṇa Consciousness (ISKCON) presents Kṛṣṇa all over the world as the God Supreme, the only way for a healthy spiritual life in today's world. Some gurus have presented Kṛṣṇa as a divine figure parallel to Jesus. Again there is hardly any attempt to acknowledge the long process through which Kṛṣṇa has been elevated from an ordinary hero to the divine Lord, ignoring other figures in both Śaiva and Vaiṣṇava traditions as well as in the most diverse and popular traditions.

In this chapter, we will attempt to present different facets and perceptions of Jesus and Kṛṣṇa. Though a thorough historical discussion would be useful, present space limitations compel us to confine our discussion to portrayals in selected texts.

Tradition and Identity of Jesus

Jesus is perceived as having a multiple identity, human and divine. In a unique spectrum of evolving perceptions, on the one hand, he was an ordinary human, son of Joseph and Mary, who lived in Nazareth, a backward village in Galilee. On the other extreme, he was divine, even God the Supreme. In between there are perceptions such as Teacher, Prophet, Son of God, Son of Man, Christ, King, Saviour and Holy One. Some of the perceptions are highly contested. The reason is that it is claimed, 'we have found the one Moses wrote about in the Law, and about whom the prophets also wrote' (Jn. 1: 45). But if we look at the perceptions and the related titles carefully, we will realize it is not as easy as one would think to make such connections. With this note of caution, we will examine the titles accorded to Jesus in the Fourth Gospel.

***Jesus of Nazareth*:** Philip, an early disciple, told a potential disciple Nathanael that he had found the one about whom Moses and prophets had written. Nathanael quipped, 'can any good come from Nazareth?' (1:45, 46). This shows the backwardness of Nazareth in Jesus' time, more insignificant than the 'little town of Bethlehem.' Jesus carried the identification that he was from Nazareth. Those who arrested him said that they wanted Jesus of Nazareth (18:5, 7). At last Governor Pilate's notice on the cross read, 'Jesus of Nazareth, the king of the Jews' (19:19). This shows the evolving perception about Jesus as an ordinary man from the remote village Nazareth, to be the king of Jews. It was not without controversy.

Rabbi: This title defined a Jewish religious teacher. Jesus' disciples, friends and people addressed him by this word (1:38, 49; 6:25; 11:8, 28; 20:16). Unlike many of the religious teachers of his day, Jesus walked what he talked and talked what he walked. This was pointed out sharply following his dramatic act of washing the disciples' feet. He said, 'You call me "Teacher and Lord" and rightly so, for that is what I am. Now that I, your Lord and Teacher, have washed your feet you should also wash one another's feet' (13: 13ff). A Rabbi commanded great respect in the Jewish society and here the word 'Lord' simply meant 'Master.'

Prophet: In the Hebrew tradition 'prophets' played an important role in reminding of the past, checking excesses, pointing out deviations and condemning all kinds of injustice and oppression. They also set before people visions of hope for the future. In fact, performing miracles, foretelling events and expressing what was held in secrecy in hearts and lives were characteristic of very few prophets. After Jesus hinting her past life, the Samaritan woman declared him to be a prophet (4:19). People after seeing him feeding the five thousand said he was so (6:14). On hearing his words, some of the people said, 'Surely this man is the prophet' (7:40). Significantly it was remarked in a controversy about Jesus' identity that a prophet would not come from Galilee (7: 52). Clearly, through his person, life, ministry and teaching Jesus resembled many characteristics of the Hebrew prophets.

Son of God: In 1: 34 Nathaniel declared: 'You are the Son of God and king of Israel' (1:49). This was also repeated by more people: Father's Son, Son of God (4:19ff), Son of God and king of Israel (5:25; 1:49; 5:27; 11:27); just the Son (6:40). Jesus himself said, 'I am God's Son' (10: 36) who was to be glorified (12:23). According to some Jews, as per their law the one who claims to be the Son of God must die (19:7). Part of John's concluding words of his Gospel was that it was written that the readers may believe that Jesus is the Christ, the Son of God, and that by believing him they may have life in his name (20:30ff). Clearly, someone claiming to be the 'Son of God' was a great offence to the tradition and sensibilities of the Jews. And yet this title was closely connected with the other titles such as Christ and Son of Man.

Messiah/Christ: Messiah was the divinely ordained ruler expected in hope by the Hebrews/Jews. It was not clear in Hebrew scripture if he would be a military ruler or suffering servant or both. Also there was confusion about the time of his appearance, his stature and place of origin. Was he only one or more? It was almost a declaration for disciples to say, 'We have found Messiah the Christ' (1:41). Outsiders such as the Samaritan woman perceived the Messiah in Jesus on the basis of their personal experience (4:25-26, 29). Confused authorities concluded that Jesus was not the Christ, and added, 'But we know where this man is from; when the Christ comes, no one will know where he is from' (7:26-27). In the context of a controversy about 'Christ', some people putting faith in him, they said, 'when the Christ comes, will he do more miraculous signs than this man' (7:31)? Others said, he was the Christ (7:41). Still others asked, 'How can the Christ come from Galilee? Does not the Scripture say that the Christ will come from David's family and from Bethlehem, the town where David lived?' Thus, the people were divided because of Jesus' (7:42-44). In connection with healing a blind man on the Sabbath, 'the Jews had decided that anyone who acknowledged that Jesus was the Christ would be put out of the synagogue' (9:22). Jews, experiencing suspense pressed Jesus saying, 'If you are the Christ tell us plainly' (10:24). Jesus' friend Martha, at a moment of bereavement and emotion, declared, 'I believe you are the Christ, the Son of God, who was to come into the world' (11:27). Following talk about his death and glorification, the crowd declared, 'we have heard from the Law that the Christ will remain forever' (12:34). To repeat the signature verse, 'these are written that you may believe that Jesus is the Christ, the Son of God, and that by believing you may have life in his name' (20:31). Thus, Jesus was confessed as the Christ (the Greek word for the Hebrew Messiah, meaning 'anointed') by those who were in trouble physically, psychologically and socially, who lived with intense anticipation of his appearance. For others, who applied particular criteria held by tradition, Jesus was an enigma. At least in one place the titles Son of God and Christ occur together (11:27). Some commentaries suggest that when Peter declared, 'You are the Holy One of God' it indicated a combination of Son of God and Christ (6:69).

***Son of Man*:** While the titles King, Son of God and Christ were almost interchangeable in substance, the title 'Son of Man' conveyed a distinctive meaning. To understand the significance of this title it is necessary to refer to its corresponding verses in the Hebrew scripture, Daniel 7:13ff. These verses speak of 'one like a son of man' coming from the clouds of heaven. He was led into the presence of the Ancient of Days, i.e. God, where he was given authority, glory and sovereign power. All people everywhere worshipped him. His dominion will be everlasting and his rule has no end. The context of this night vision was foreign political oppression being suffered by the Jewish community. The 'one like a son of man' appeared to offer hope, power and stability. For the first time, very early in his ministry, Jesus told Nathanael, 'I tell you the truth, you shall see heaven open, and the angels of God ascending and descending on the Son of Man' (1:51). This narrative would have reminded the Jews of the dream of their ancestor Jacob in which he saw a stairway resting on the earth, with its top reaching to heaven, and the angels of God were ascending and descending on it (Gen. 28:12). Further, God gives assurance of a new life and great future. To the Jewish leader Nicodemus, Jesus said, 'No one has ever gone into heaven except the one who came from heaven - the Son of Man' (3:13). He was to be lifted up like the snake (bronze) was lifted up by Moses in the desert.

Those who believed him would have eternal life (3:14). Again, Jesus told the crowd that followed him for miraculous feeding that they should work, not for perishable food but for eternal life which the Son of Man can give them (6:27). More intriguingly, he told the Jews in debate that unless they ate the flesh of the Son of Man and drank his blood, they would have no life in them (6:53). He also clarified that when they lifted up the Son of Man, then they would know that all he did and spoke was what the Father taught him (8:28). Jesus asked the man who had been healed of his blindness, 'Do you believe in the Son of Man' (9:35)? But the man said that he did not understand the person with this title and Jesus introduced himself as the Son of Man. This man was not the only one to ask, 'who is the Son of Man?' (vide. 12:34). Jesus foretold that the Son of Man would be glorified, which meant buried seeds producing many more seeds (12:23-24). This was connected with his intimacy with the heavenly Father. 'Now is the Son of Man glorified and God is glorified in him. God will glorify the Son in himself, and will glorify him at once' (13:31). On the whole, the title Son of Man itself has many facets. As we will discuss later, one strong meaning in St John seems to be that as Son of Man Jesus was in solidarity with the victims and this qualified him to be their representative.

The Lord: Jesus was given this title by his disciples, his women friends Martha, Mary and Magdalene Mary, Martha-Mary's neighbours etc (4:3; 6:23;11:11, 12, 27, 32, 34; 13:13-14, 25, 36, 37; 20:18, 20, 25). There is confusion about the title 'Lord' both in the Bible as well in the Church. In the most ordinary sense it meant Sir, husband, Master, King and any respectable person. In the extraordinary sense it meant God. In the Hebrew scripture (Ex. 6:2) God reveals himself to the Israelites with the enigmatic name of Yahweh (YHWH). As it was regarded too sacred to be uttered the Hebrew name 'Adonai' was used in its place. When the Hebrew scripture was translated into Greek the word 'Kurios' was used for 'Adonai'. Unfortunately the translators could not find two words to distinguish between the ordinary sense and the extraordinary sense. Realising the terrible confusion the

NIV (following RNEB) uses the form LORD to indicate the extraordinary sense. Vernacular translations are totally helpless to make such distinction.

In most cases Jesus was addressed 'Lord' in the ordinary sense. However, few cases seem to suggest the extraordinary sense or nearing it. The man who was healed of his blindness, in response to Jesus' self-introduction as Son of Man, said, 'Lord I believe' and worshipped him (9:38). Commentators observe that "worship" (*proskyneo*) is used in John to speak of the worship of God. When the man worships Jesus he is acknowledging the presence of God in Jesus. Another instance: 'This Mary… was the same one who poured perfume on the Lord and wiped his feet with her hair' (11:2; 12:3). Again it is not clear what she meant, but the time referent locates the anointing in the same week as Passover and thus serves as a reminder of the proximity of Jesus's hour. The identification of Bethany as the site of Jesus' raising Lazarus also directs attention to the miracle that precipitated the death sentence under which Jesus now stands (11:47, 53, 57). In the same sense during Jesus' processional entry into Jerusalem the crowd shouted, 'Hosanna! Blessed is he who comes in the name of the Lord! Blessed is the King of Israel' (12:12ff). Most intriguingly, when the risen Jesus showed his wounds and asked his disciple Thomas to go forward and touch, the 'doubter' confessed/declared 'My Lord and my God' (20:28). Many questions arise. For instance, was it an exclamatory statement or a doctrine that Jesus was the supreme God Almighty? If the former was more reasonable, one can imagine the excitement, exclamation with beating his chest that caused this emotional outburst. If the latter was true, i.e. Jesus was God, what the Jews suspected earlier about Jesus' claim, came to be true. And Jesus' saying with greater clarity, 'I am going to my Father and your Father, my God and your God' is challenged. In any case we will return to this question in due course.

Only once in the Fourth Gospel the title 'Saviour of the world' is mentioned and it was the perception and affirmation of Samaritans, the enemies of Jews, who had aspiration of their own salvation in the sense of religio-political liberation (4:42). In the

Jewish world and its surroundings 'saviour' primarily meant a successful king who ensured prosperity, protection and liberation of his people.

Controversial King: Monarchy having been established among the Israelites, while God was regarded as the overall king, human kings were expected to be the servants and saviours of the world. In the wake of many kings transgressing their limits and exploiting the people, there was the expectation of an ideal king to transform the world. As we have already noted, the crowd at Jesus' processional entry into Jerusalem declared: 'Blessed is the King of Israel' (12:12-13, 15; cf. Zech. 9:9). 'Are you the king of the Jews?' asked Pilate while Jesus was on trial. 'Is that your own idea, or did others talk to you about me?' said Jesus. 'What is it you have done?' Jesus replied: 'My kingdom is not of this world. If it were, my servants would fight to prevent my arrest by the Jews. But now my kingdom is from another place.' Pilate quipped, 'You are a king, then.' Jesus replied: 'You are right in saying I am a king. In fact, for this reason I was born, and for this I came into the world, to testify to the truth. Everyone on the side of truth listens to me' (18:33-37). Pilate asked those Jews who had brought Jesus to him: 'Do you want me to release 'the king of the Jews?' He used to release a prisoner at the festival of Passover (18:39). People shouted 'No.' Subsequently the soldiers mockingly proclaimed 'Hail, king of the Jews!' And they struck him in the face (19:3). Though Pilate tried to save Jesus, the Jewish leaders and the people instigated by them, roared their disagreement. To call Jesus king was tantamount to opposing Caesar. So, Pilate told the Jews, 'Here is your king' and in return they bellowed 'Crucify.' 'Shall I crucify your king?' Pilate continued. 'We have no king but Caesar' was the crowd's resounding reply (19.14f). At last, belying all expectations, the strange king Jesus was crucified as a criminal. Pilate's notice fastened to the cross read, 'JESUS OF NAZARETH, THE KING OF THE JEWS.' Jewish leaders protested and suggested a correction to Pilate saying,'Do not write King of Jews' but 'this man said 'I am King of the Jews' (19:9-21). The authoritative and autocratic Pilate refused and said, 'What I have written I have written' (19:21). Thus, religious language and political language were confused in the case of Jesus and there was no patient listening and clear speaking to discover the truth about him, the truth he stood for and the truth he was witnessing to, i.e., a servant-king-saviour. In this sense, Jesus was the good shepherd who came to seek the lost sheep, to know and to be known by the sheep, and who was ready to lay down his life for the sheep (10:11-18).

***Lamb of God*:** John the Baptist declared this title for Jesus (1: 29, 35). It is not clear if it meant to be a sacrificial lamb ready for slaughter or a vulnerable lamb in the midst of devouring beasts. In the book of Revelation both the meanings can be found. If we stretch the sacrificial sense we have to visit the sacrificial cult of the Hebrew tradition and find out whether the idea of atonement is meant here. On the other hand, it might very well mean the innocent and vulnerable lamb that challenges powers and authorities in family and society. It is entirely likely, however, that John's title for Jesus in 1:29 draws on a rich heritage of symbols to identify Jesus as the redeemer for the world's sin.

One more fact has to be noted here in passing. At the level of using and identifying with the Jewish categories and titles, Jesus was the leader of a sectarian or heterodox movement within Judaism.[1] Thus, he was the Messiah when many claimed to be so. Jesus, while claiming he was the good shepherd, he referred to other shepherds some of who were thieves and robbers who had no real interest in their life but in their own life at their cost. The heterodox nature of the Jesus' movement is openly acknowledged in few later texts. Jesus foretold his disciples that 'they will put you out of the synagogue' (16: 2). When the early Jesus' movement faced persecution, at the time of a trial in the Sanhedrin, the well respected member and teacher of law, Gamaliel, recalled the rise and disappearance of two such movements following the death of their founders (Acts 5: 33-39). It stands to reason that when Jesus claimed he was the way, truth and life (Jn. 14: 6) he was well aware of similar claim by others. But this does not undermine

[1] See Ashton, Op. cit., 151f.

the validity of his universal claim about connecting his heavenly Father and humanity in general. However, his offer was not an easy one but a call to share in the suffering of God in solidarity with victims and vulnerable. Engaging readers with an acute awareness of the context of John will not miss the meaning of the three words contained in 14: 6. **Way** does not mean shortcut, nor a broad way, but it is the way of suffering. There is no sense of a physical distance between the heavenly Father and people and needed was a spiritual insight into the heart of God which is wounded and bleeding for the victims of injustice and the suffering. The biblical witness is not to the one time suffering of God but everlasting. **Truth** here does not mean an abstract concept, nor a doctrinal capsule. Jesus told Pilate that he had come to witness to the truth. For Jesus truth was the reign of God breaking into the world and those called by God were to be open to its unfolding and manifestation. The truth sets us free. Jesus embodied this concrete truth. **Life** for many may mean the combination of prosperity, protection, progeny, popularity, promotion and peace of mind. Jesus said that he had come to seek and find the lost sheep and was ready to give his life for them. He came to give life in its fullness. Meaningful life is life-giving, life-saving and life-affirming for all.

So far we have identified Jesus with the titles known in his Jewish tradition. One may be tempted to stop with it. The way Jesus spoke of himself in relation to the heavenly Father perplexed his Jewish opponents who criticized him for equating himself to God. Jesus' attempt to explain with reference to a verse from a psalm was not convincing. But greater perceptions were dawning in due course which projected him divine, not in an instant instance but in a gradual realization. There were some conceptual tools available such as the Word which was conceived as eternal, cosmic and all pervasive. Further his 'I am sayings', claim should be connected to 'I and the Father are one' and the disciples' experience of him risen from dead and ever living in communion with God and with themselves. This led the believers to take him more than his simple human and religious identity. In the next chapter we will elaborate the process.

The Tradition and Identity of Kṛṣṇa

A Complex Development

The name 'Kṛṣṇa' means 'black' and it seems to indicate the non-Ārayan origin of Kṛṣṇa who came to be known as a warrior, friendly leader of a shepherd community, a divine hero, an avatāra of Lord Viṣṇu and finally the supreme Bhagavān or Viṣṇu himself. It is no wonder that those who wade through the flood of materials ask the question, is Kṛṣṇa one or many? Approaches and conclusions are varied. There are a few Kṛṣṇas in the Vedas and Upaniṣads. Attention has been drawn to eight Kṛṣṇas in the Mahābhārata: (1) Kṛṣṇa DvaipāyanaVyāsa, the author of the Mahābhārata, known as Kārṣaṇaveda, (2) Arjuna himself, (3) a serpent called Kṛṣṇa, (4) a soldier of Skanda, (5) Lord Śiva, (6) a mountain with plenty of jewels, (7) a ṛṣi connected with the origin of *āyūrveda* called Kṛṣṇaatreya, (8) Lord Kṛṣṇa himself.[1] Further, it is observed: 'The Kṛṣṇas of the Ṛgveda and of the *Chāndogya Upaniṣad* do not seem to be presented as divine beings. On the other hand, the Vāsudeva-Kṛṣṇa of the Sātvatas was considered *devadeva* centuries before Christ. Are these two the same? Is the theory that Kṛṣṇa, who was an ancient sage, was deified later on by the process of apotheosis, a sufficient answer? The identification in the Mahābhārata of Kṛṣṇa with the Gopālakṛṣṇa of Vraja is 'seriously controverted.'[2] A further observation makes the complexity still clear:

> There appear to have been two cycles of Kṛṣṇa stories, in which the hero's life is displayed in two different lights: (1) as a cowherd living in the forests around mount Govardana; (2) as a Kṣatriya after Yādava clan, a friend of the Pāṇdavas and founder of the city of Dwāraka. Probably these were once independent figures, Kṛṣṇa Gopāla, and Kṛṣṇa Vāsudeva, but texts which tell the whole story of Kṛṣṇa's life linked them together by having him born into a Kṣatriya family and smuggled out secretly to grow up in a cowherd village, in order to escape the murderous designs of his kinsman Kaṃsa. The fact that in this story Kṛṣṇa's mother's

---

[1] Quoted, Vempeny, Op. cit., 242.

[2] Ibid., 243.

name is Devaki may also link him with K. Devakiputra who is said in Ch.U.3.17.6 to have been instructed by Ghora Angirasa.[1]

It is further noted that 'Although the stories of Kṛṣṇa Gopala became part of the main Vaiṣṇava tradition later than those of KṛṣṇaVāsudeva, they probably circulated for some centuries earlier among the cattle rearing tribes of northwest and western India. The tribe with which they are most often associated is that of the Abhiras, a nomadic pastoral tribe inhabiting the lower Indus Valley. There is some debate as to whether these tribes were immigrants or natives of the subcontinent, but it is generally accepted that they were settled there by the third century BCE. As far the Kṣatriya Kṛṣṇa, through the connection between the Yādava clan and the Vṛṣṇis, he became fused with the latter's hero-divinity Vāsudeva. Once this fusion had happened, the earliest way of accounting for the fact that the hero had two names, Kṛṣṇa and Vāsudeva, was to say that his father was called Vāsudeva, so that the second name was a patronymic.'[2] For some time Kṛṣṇa was subservient to the Viṣṇu tradition as a mere avatāra and further development was through new myths which carried new doctrines.

Kṛṣṇa's ascendency to supremacy was not without struggle. The Bhāgavata cult is not recognized in the Aśokan edicts, therefore it is proper to maintain that it became popular only after it was amalgamated with Brāhmaṇism during its revival at the turn of the second century BCE through a complex amalgamation with the śramaṇa movement and tribal clans. What is more obvious is that the Bhāgavata cult existed among the Sātvatas, a warrior tribe, a branch of the pastoral clan of the Yādavas who settled in the Mathura region. Apparently they had a good relationship with the *śramaṇas* and the *sāṁkhya-yoga* thinkers. At that time the Brāhmaṇas needed the help of heroic divinities of the Bhāgavata cult to arrest the influence of the *śramaṇas*, particularly the Buddhists (though they took a middle path) and Jains. In lieu they gave them a higher status in society. Apart from the Gītā, the earliest literary sources of Bhāgavatism is the *Nārāyaṇīya*

---

[1] Freda Machett, *Kṛṣṇa: Lord or Avatāra*?, Surrey: Curzon, 2001, 7.

[2] Ibid.

section of the *Mahābhārata*. The pattern of discourse in this section includes curious metaphysical and practical questions and answers. The questions appear "like fleecy clouds before the wind" that confused many. This shows that the situation was full of divergent, even contradictory, view-points. The authorities quoted in support of the answers are mostly the traditional *ṛṣis* as well as some visiting guests who appeared to be wandering teachers.[1]

There was tension in assimilation, particularly Kṛṣṇa's introduction. Majumdar writes:

> Whatever might be the reason, it must have cost the brāhmaṇas a bitter pang. The memorable scene in the *Mahābhārata* in which Śiśupāla poured forth the venom of his heart, against Bhīṣma for honouring Kṛṣṇa as the most "worshipful" seems reminiscent of the spirit of the die-hards, who refused to acknowledge the divine character of one who was not a brāhmaṇa by birth.[2]

In the subsequent fight Kṛṣṇa kills Śiśupāla. 'The identification of Kṛṣṇa, the leader of the Yādus and the kinsman of Sātvatas, with the manifestation of the supreme Lord, is the most significant development in the transition from Vedic brāhmaṇism to Vaiṣṇavism, though a chronology of this development is hardly possible. We have a few references to the name Kṛṣṇa in the *Vedas* and the Upaniṣads, such as an *asura* in conflict with Indra, a demi-god of the Yādus, and a son of Devaki, the disciple of a *ṛṣi* and later a herdsman, a playboy and the supreme Lord – thus a many-faceted God displaying great variety, supported with a number of myths.'[3] Radhakrishnan observes: 'The *Mahābhārata* contains several layers of thought superimposed one upon another in the course of ages representing Kṛṣṇa in all the grades, from

---

[1] See I. Selvanayagam, *Vedic Sacrifice: Challenge and Response*, Delhi: Manohar, 1996, 187.

[2] R.C. Majumdar, *Ancient India*, Delhi: Motilal Banarsidas, 1982, 174.

[3] See Selvanayagam, *Vedic Sacrifice*, 188.

a historical character to an *avatār* of Viṣṇu.'[1] Unusually, he also makes a historical point:

> It is clear that the editors of the *Mahābhārata* felt that some popular hero must be made the rallying centre to counteract the mighty influence of the heretical sects. The figure of Kṛṣṇa was ready to hand.[2]

Kṛṣṇa's conflict with Indra for redeeming the cows was most remarkable. His clan originally had some affinity with the Vaiśya caste before elevated to the Kṣatriya. Identification with Viṣṇu, the Lord of sacrifice, was most significant. He was the centre of heroic divinities and legendary heroes.

One of the outcomes of the Brāhmaṇa and Bhāgavata amalgamation was the refocusing on the prominence of bhakti. Bhakti was a better way than *yajña* and *jñāna* although the latter was explained as a tool to develop full concentration on the Supreme Lord in loving devotion. Further, new figures deserving worship came to the fore. Particularly, Nārāyaṇa and Vāsudeva from the Bhāgavata tradition came to be popular as evident in the Mahābhārata.[3] Moreover, 'At the end of the chap. 12 of the third book of the *Viṣṇu-Purāṇa* it is stated in the account of the genealogy of the Yādavas and the Vṛṣṇis that Sātvata was the son of Aṁsa, the father of Bhima, and all his descendents were called Sātvatas. The Bhāgavata represents the Sātvatas as calling the highest Brahman Bhagavat and Vāsudeva (Bh.P. IX.9.49), and having a peculiar mode of worshipping him. It mentions the Sātvatas along with the Andhakas and Vṛṣṇis, which were Yādava tribes (I.14.25; III.1.29), and calls Vāsudeva Sātvatarṣabha (X.58.42; XI.27.5). From all these and other similar passages from Patañjali it appears that Sātvata was another name of the Vṛṣṇi race of which

---

[1] Quoted, Ibid.

[2] S. Radhakrishnan, *Indian Philosophy*, Delhi: Oxford University Press, 1991, Vol. I, 494ff.

[3] For a fuller discussion of the sequence and analysis see R.G. Bhandarkar, *Vaishṇavism, Śaivism and the Minor Religious Systems,* New Delhi: Asian Educational Services, 1983, 6-11.

Vāsudeva, Saṁkarṣaṇ, and Aniruddha were members, and that the Sātvatas had a religion of their own according to which Vāsudeva was worshipped as the Supreme Being, and thus the account given above from the Nārāyaṇīya is simply confirmed.'[1]

Worship of Vāsudeva-Kṛṣṇa is alluded to by Megasthenes, the Macedonian ambassador to the Mauryan court of Chandragupta in the last quarter of third century BCE. Kṛṣṇa in the Gītā too states that 'He who possesses knowledge gives himself up to me, believing Vāsudeva to be all' (VII. 19). There is reason to believe that when the Gītā was composed the identification of Vāsudeva with Nārāyaṇa or him being an incarnation of Viṣṇu had come to be acknowledged. During the *Viśvarūpadarṣana* (ch. 11), the best of the manifestations, he is twice addressed by Arjuna as Viṣṇu on account of his 'dazzling brilliance, which rendered everything hot, and filled the whole universe. Here Viṣṇu is alluded to as the chief of the Ādityas and not as the Supreme Being,' and Vāsudeva was Viṣṇu in this sense, as mentioned in ch. 10.

The Harivaṃsa, a supplement to Mahābhārata, contains materials from the Mahāpurāṇas. The Viṣṇu Purāṇa, which tells the story of Kṛṣṇa is the central part of the text in every sense. The Baviṣya Purāṇa has the ancestors and associates of Kṛṣṇa. Coming to the Bhāgavata itself, according to the tenth canto, Kṛṣṇa's main mission was to rid the country of the tyrant (yet his kinsman!) demon Kaṃsa, who usurped the throne of Mathura from his grandfather Ugrasena. At his birth, in order to escape the wrath of Kaṃsa, after many miraculous interventions, Kṛṣṇa was brought to Vraja (short form of Vṛndāvan) and raised by his foster parents, Nanda and Yasoda. The prince is brought among the gopīs, who came to love him more than their own children. After many miraculous exploits, when Kṛṣṇa was twelve the Rāsalīla took place.

---

[1] Ibid., 11ff.

Playful and Erotic

Kṛṣṇa or Viṣṇu, in the name and form of Kṛṣṇa, in the Bhāgavata is erotic and playful. Indeed, in the background, most significant is his playfulness or sportiveness. Another major deity in the pantheon, is Śiva who has been celebrated as sportive and dancer too. It indicates his independence, spontaneity and effortlessness. Out of this creative energy he created the world and maintains it. His famous posture Naṭarāja (king of dance) is associated with his creation, creativity and triumph. At the same time, the purāṇic Śiva is also the ascetic, mahāyogi and erotic. He lives in the constant tension between the two extremes – erotic and ascetic, a *coincidentiaoppositorum*. It is interpreted that as 'erotic ascetic' he represents the constant tension experienced by humans between tendencies to move towards extremes and check excesses.[1]

In the Bhāgavata, preceding the rāsalīla, Kṛṣṇa's mischievous playfulness is exemplified by the following acts: when he was born he attracted the gopīs of Vraja who visited the baby in costly costumes. During his boyhood they complained to his mother Yasodha about his antics:

> 'He unties the calves before milking time so they drink up all the milk.'
> 'If we scold him, he laughs in our faces.'
> 'He steels our butter and curd, swills all the milk in our vessels, and what he leaves he gives to the monkeys that follow him around.'
> 'When he is not in a mood to eat or drink he breaks our vessels so everything goes waste.'
> 'When he finds the vessels empty, when we hide our butter and curd he flies into a rage and stops out, pinching the little babies and smaller children on his way so they cry.'
> 'We hang our butter up, out of his reach, but he makes himself a ladder from our mortars and footstools and gets at them anyway.'

---

[1] See W.D. O'Flaherty, *Śiva: The Erotic Ascetic,* Oxford: Oxford University Press, 1981.

'When he still cannot reach he breaks a hole in the pots hung high with a stick and stands below eating and drinking whatever comes down.'
'He comes at dead of nights and the glow from his body gives him light enough to see the hanging pots!'
'He comes when we are out drawing water from the river or the well.'
'If we question him he answers as impudently and relieves himself in our yards!'
Yet they kept glancing him, because he was utterly beautiful and they could not help themselves because they were abused by the expression of fear that he assumed.[1]

In other times when Kṛṣṇa and his brother Rāma were playing with cowherd boys they rushed to Yasodha saying that Kṛṣṇa was eating mud again. His mother scolded. He denied. When he opened his mouth his mother saw the whole universe etc.[2] Once Kṛṣṇa stole the *gopīs'* clothes while they were bathing in a pool, thus exposing their private parts and embarrassed them.[3]

How on earth could the supreme God behave like this? This question has been asked by not only those outside the Vaiṣṇava tradition but those inside too. However, we have to recognize the fact that the tradition has come to terms with it in different ways. For some, however arbitrary, the acts of God cannot be questioned. For others, mischievous play of a divine boy is a mark of his transcendence. He cannot be bound by any human limitation. He is beyond the conventional norms of behaviour. Instead of trying to correct him, the devotees have to engage with such play and find joy and meaning in it. Hence, the enactment of Kṛṣṇa's plays in festivals. David Kinsley explains:

> Kṛṣṇa is the eternal child, the eternal adolescent and youth, whose pranks, uninhibited sporting, and wild

---

[1] Ramesh Menon, *Bhāgavata Purāṇa*, New Delhi: Rupa, 2011, 738, 752f.

[2] Ibid., 754.

[3] BhP. X. 22.

> gambols bear testimony, according to the Hindu tradition, to something essential in that other realm of the divine. What does Kṛṣṇa's youth reveal about the divine, what do his revels tell us about the Hindu vision of deity? Kṛṣṇa's life in the Vṛndāvana as a youth, first of all, suggests the freedom and spontaneity of the divine.[1]

The above portrayal and explanation are important to understand Kṛṣṇa's divinity and humanity in a distinction. We will come back to this theme in more detail when we deal with the nature of the divinity of Kṛṣṇa in the next chapter.

As portrayed, Kṛṣṇa is erotically playful and playfully erotic. But what we have here in the ecstatic play (*rāsalīla*) of Kṛṣṇa with the *gopīs* is an extremely complex story which can be understood on several levels. His dealing with the *gopīs* including caressing their breasts can easily raise eyebrows if not horrify. 'The story was scandalous to many Vaiṣṇavas. The redactor of the Bhāgavata apparently shared that scandal, though certainly not enough to suppress the story. The ambivalence is expressed through the comments that Śuka and Parīkṣit made during the narration of the story, where rationalizations are made for Kṛṣṇa's behaviour in committing adultery with the gopīs. These comments are not present in the version of the ecstatic dance in the Viṣṇu Purāṇa. The story in the Bhāgavata was intended to be taken as an allegory at least at a certain level of understanding. It was left for the scholars and devotees in future to interpret it in an acceptable way.

Caitanya (1485-1535), the founder of a Vaiṣṇava devotional sect in Bengal (Gaudia), for example, gives the following explanation:

> All the inhabitants of Vṛndāvana are parts of Kṛṣṇa (*svāṃśa*). They are all manifestations of the divine form. The cowherd girls, and especially Rādhā who is prominent in Bengal Vaiṣṇavism but not mentioned in the *Bhāgavata,*

[1] D.R. Kinsley, *The Sword and the Flute: Kāḷi & Kṛṣṇa – Dark Visions of the Terrible and the Sublime in Hindu Mythology*, Delhi: Motilal Banarsidass, 1995, 12f; for more such stories and explanations see 13ff.

> are powers *(śakti)* of Kṛṣṇa, who is the possessor of the powers (*śaktimat*). They are thus both different and non-different from Kṛṣṇa. The one single power of Kṛṣṇa is distinguished in three ways... (between the inner and outer powers)...is the expressive power (*taṭasthā*) which expresses itself in the individual selves....Kṛṣṇa is Bhagavān, not an *avatāra*. His descent at the end of the Dvāpara age, described in the *Bhāgavata,* is not properly a manifestation. The earthly Vṛndāvana, Mathurā, and Dvāraka are identical with their heavenly counterparts. At times the sports of Kṛṣṇa, which go on eternally in the heavenly cities, are not manifest in the earthly cities. What appears to be a descent of Kṛṣṇa is only a temporary manifestation for the sake of the devotees of what is really eternal in heaven.[1]

Consorts as personifications and expressions of divine power or grace are interpreted in this way in all the Hindu theistic traditions, especially the Śaiva and Vaiṣṇava. The gopīs as personification of the shared powers of Kṛṣṇa is a strange interpretation. That they represent his true devotees seems to be a more convincing interpretation as we will point out later.

A recent public reflection substantiates the continued popular imagination: 'The Rāsa Līla episode in the Bhāgavata Purāṇa highlights the Lord's compassion towards the Gopīs who proved to be the most staunch bhaktas for He provides them a taste of the bliss of union with Him, a state which even yogis and sages who are engaged in severe penance find it hard to attain.

The Gopīs are not learned; they do not know any philosophy. But they are strong in their single-minded devotion to Kṛṣṇa. This is the most important requirement for God realization. Kṛṣṇa's life among the Vṛṣṇis illustrates how He is the means and the goal for all the Jīvātmas keen on seeking salvation... In His own way, the Lord teaches them to shed their possessiveness towards the material and physical aspects of human existence and makes them

---

[1] Sheridon, Op. cit., 129f.

turn towards to understand the subtle essence of their selves which they have to offer to Him unconditionally. This spirit of surrender and yearning is the hallmark of a true bhakta. The soul has to long for union with the Lord and has to transcend the physical limitations of its embodied state. ..When the Gopīs revel in the dance with the Lord in the moon-lit night abandoning their hearth and homes, it is the cause of Viśeṣa dharma overriding Sāmānya dharma.'[1] Though this kind of *bhakti* is mentioned in other Vaiṣṇava texts, such as the Gītā, touching on different aspects, the erotic metaphor in the rāsalīla is unique.

Summary

Jesus was perceived and confessed using different titles and metaphors. He was a good Jew, religious teacher, prophet, king, Son of God, Messiah/Christ, Son of Man, Lord and Holy One. He was perceived and interpreted as the one who was with God in the most intimate sense and functional sense as well. All these do not permit single word confessions or even multiple word formulations. Plurality of perceptions and confessions is obvious. Through more than twenty centuries of existence, Christianity has not sealed with a final word about God and Christ. Such recognition, however, need not lead to throwing away the unique Christian vision of Jesus, the Son as part of a Triune God. St John's Gospel provides the ingredients to construct this vision which will be credible, clear and appealing enough to call for a new orientation in life and collaborative action with a view to transform the world.

Kṛṣṇa too is multifaceted with multiple identities. A survey of the occurrences of the name in Hindu scriptures, from Vedas through epics and purāṇas, to the Bhāgavata at the moment does not help to construct a history of the development of this fascinating deity. At the same time we have enough clues and particulars to suggest that he came from a warrior class, identified with a cowherd community and later was incorporated into the brāhmaṇic community not only as their spokesperson but also a

---

[1] "Unconditional Bhakti" in the column on 'Faith,' *The Hindu, India's National Newspaper since 1878,* 25 March 2014, 9.

rallying centre of diverse traditions in conflict. He was both an avatāra and non-avatāra. Surprisingly in the Bhāgavata he was Viṣṇu himself but retaining the name Kṛṣṇa. Then there was a retrospective vision to see him an extraordinary child and his exotic behaviour was seen as a sign of divinity. This provides erotic imagination to the rāsalīla which beautifully narrates the Lord's intimacy with his devotees even if they come from a low social strata.

Chapter 3

Jesus and Kṛṣṇa
Process of Ascendency to Supreme Divinity

In the last chapter we noted aspects of the multi-faceted personality and identity of Jesus and Kṛṣṇa. But their significance was quite inadequate for bhakti. For a truly religious bhakti experience there needs to be a vision of a transcendent force, rather a figure, who can attract devotion through his/her fascinating image, liberating activities and enlivening presence. In the last chapter, we also identified Jesus and Kṛṣṇa with titles and images of their respective traditions. In this connection we noted that their significance was gradually ascending. From human status and human-divine elevation, at the final stage, they were reigning supreme either as individuals or in association or unity with other figures or names. In this chapter we will trace the major stages of this ascendency in the persons of Jesus and Kṛṣṇa.

Jesus, from a Rabbi to the Son Component of the Triune God

According to John, Jesus of Nazareth, a devout Jew, called prophet, Lord (Master) and Rabbi, was given the confessional titles Son of God, (a great offence for Jews), Son of Man with a specific meaning, Messiah (in the context of many such claims) and interpreted as the enfleshment of the divine and eternal Word. There was an ambiguous controversy over his alleged claim that he was identical with God.

***Jesus as the Enfleshment of the Eternal Word*:** The first part of the 'Prologue' of St John's Gospel starts with the words: 'In the beginning was the Word, and the Word was with God, and the Word was God' (1. 1). After thirteen verses, it further describes the nature and function of the Word stating that 'The Word became flesh and made his dwelling among us' (1. 14). The usual term used for this act is incarnation. As this word is used in a loose manner with reference to great people both dead and living, 'enfleshment' seems to convey the original idea. We will point out later the limitation of the Sanskrit term *avatāra* which means the descent (of a god) in the Hindu pantheon.

It is held by scholars that the prologue was existing independently and later incorporated into the Gospel. It has been debated whether the 'word' (logos) came from the Hebrew tradition or the Greek tradition. In any case, the Word and its enfleshment add significance to the question who Jesus was. The answer is that he was the one time human expression of the eternal Word that coexisted with the Father God from eternity. Another eternally coexistent reality was the Holy Spirit or God's Spirit who filled the human form of the Word and then replaced Jesus when he went to heaven. Though not systematically constructed here, we have the three constituent realities (Father, Son and Holy Spirit) of a Triune God. We will elaborate this in a moment.

Can we say Jesus is God? We have already noted the difficulty of literally taking Thomas' exclamatory statement 'my Lord and my God.' Jesus' calling God his Father was seen by some Jewish leaders as making himself equivalent to God (5.18). A devout Jew would (just as a Muslim) never attribute divinity to a human being. At the same time, by all indications Jesus was not an ordinary person. In the efforts to find an adequate language there are few references in the New Testament that Jesus was equal to

God. Jesus claimed that even before Abraham he was (6. 58f). His identification with God was the greatest controversy between Jesus and his opponents. Jesus claimed that the lost sheep (marginalized people) were given to him by his Father. 'My Father who has given them to me, is greater than all; no one can snatch them out of my Father's hand. I and the Father are one' (10. 29f). When heard this, his opponents took stones and shouted blasphemy and said, 'because you, a mere man, claim to be God' (10. 33). Curiously, in response, Jesus quoted Psalm 82. 6 which, after a call to defend the cause of the weak and fatherless, maintains the rights of the poor and oppressed, and rescues the weak and needy, says, 'I said, 'You are "gods"; you are sons of the Most High.' This is followed by the words 'But you will die mere men.' Who are these gods? Are they angels or those giants called 'sons of God' as in Gen. 6: 2? Did Jesus or the writer really mean that he belonged to such extraordinary category of beings? Does this ambiguous reference attest that Jesus was God himself? Language stumbles; scholarly opinions widely differ. There are very few references to 'Jesus as God' in other books of the New Testament.[1]

The ambiguity and struggle to identify the true nature of Jesus in relation to God continued in the early Church as evident in the debates and formulations in the early Councils. Vempeny observes:

[1] Paul writes 'Christ who is God over all' (Rom. 9. 5). Tit. 2: 13: 'We wait for the blessed hope – the glorious appearing of our great God and Saviour, Jesus Christ' (Tit. 2. 13). Peter, at the beginning of his second epistle, after introducing himself as 'a servant and apostle of Jesus Christ' addresses his readers as 'those who through the righteousness of our God and Jesus Christ' and greets with grace and peace in abundance 'through the knowledge of God and of Jesus our Lord' (2 Pet. 1. 1-2). One may read 'God and Jesus Christ' as two persons. John in his epistle writes: 'We know also that the Son of God has come and has given us understanding, so that we may know him who is true. And we are in him who is true – even in his Son Jesus Christ. He is the true God and eternal life' (1Jn. 5.20). For a major study on the question see Larry W. Hurtado, *How on Earth did Jesus Become a God? Historical Questions about Earliest Devotion to Jesus*?, Cambridge: William B. Eerdmans Publishing Company, 2005.

The doctrine of incarnation has been approached since the earliest Christian tradition from two opposite directions, namely the humanity of Christ and his divinity. The Alexandrian and the Antiochian schools represented these two tendencies. Both had the burden of showing that *Christ is truly God, truly man and that He is one*. The Alexandrian trend followed a strict *descent* Christology starting from the '*Logos*'; but they mutilated the humanity of Christ. The Antiochian trend started from the true human nature of Christ, advocating a sort of ascent Christology, but it underplayed the divinity of Christ.[1]

Moving away from early and medieval mode of thinking, there have been unending pursuit of distinguishing between the Jesus of history and Christ of faith. Indigenous thinking is yet more challenging. For example, Chakkarai, one of the Indian Christian theologians of the early phase, affirms: 'To us He is the ineffable and adorable Lord, and no amount of historic criticism can rob us of Him realized by us in our experience.'[2] For him Rāma and Kṛṣṇa are dead and no more with us to experience. Later he elaborates this experience:

> The historical Jesus who may be discovered and paraded before our gaze may contain some outward historical features, but the inner life and secret are beyond the canons of criticism and have their fountain head in His heart as well as in ours. The quest of the historical Jesus is a necessary pursuit, and those who think that in bare facts lies the meaning of His life and its enigma would seek Him among the dead, but He is alive for evermore. Those who would know Him as He is and was must seek Him not in the tomb of forgotten facts and ancient circumstances but in the inner recesses of the *ātman*. This is the dominating

---

[1] Ishanand Vempeny, *Kṛṣṇa and Christ*, Anand: Gujarat Sahitya Prakash, 1988, 285. For details of other schools of thought see the ff.

[2] V. Chakkarai, *Jesus the Avatār*, Madras: CLS, 1926, 14.

> challenge of Indian religious experience and the guide that we shall follow in explicating the meaning and importance of Jesus. The Lord of the other world said to Nachiketa in the *Katha Upanishad* that the *Paramatman* is not to be sought among the perishable facts carried through the senses; even so the meaning of the person of Jesus is to be ultimately seen in the perception and experience of *bhaktas*, 'freed from passion and desire' as the same *Upanishad* says.[1]

Such explanation, however, does not solve the puzzle of Jesus' claim of oneness with God the Father, the Father of all. Appasamy, did an extensive study of this issue taking insights from Hindu bhakti. He observes: 'Jesus then had no experience of identity in His relation with God. He did say, "I and the Father are one", but in the light of the other statements in the Gospel, we cannot interpret these words to mean identity. They rather indicate a completeness of harmony between Him and God in thought and purpose. The Father's business was His; the Father's love impelled Him to action; the Father's house kindled His fervor; the Father's world revealed to Him goodness and love. It was in this sense that Jesus spoke of Himself as being one with God.'[2] By extension, for him there cannot be identity between God and Christian devotees. On the whole, the difference between ontological oneness and relational or moral oneness needs unpacking. We will have a chance to analyze the oneness between God the Father and Jesus his Son. It will include a new approach to the understanding of Trinity and enriching it with insights coming from the Rāsalīlā. With unwise reductionism of experience and of expression in missionary context, as observed in interfaith dialogue, Christians are both confused and confusing. What is most popular is a Jesus-cult in practice and Christo-monism in thinking. A rereading of the Gospels, particularly the Fourth Gospel, with new eyes and open mind, will certainly lead to accept a plurality of the facets

---

[1] Ibid., 126.

[2] Appasamy, *What is Moksha?*, 59.

and multiple identities of Jesus. As we noted earlier, there was an evolving process of perceptions. There is no reason to think that that process has ceased.

Jesus never claimed to be God or an avatāra of God. He did claim that he was one with God and this oneness was not ontological but relational. We will explain this oneness later. John's Gospel begins with the affirmation that Jesus was the enfleshment of the divine and cosmic Word. A great deal of discussion has taken place in the New Testament study and Christian theology. Particularly, discussions on proper understanding of it in a multifaith context is fascinating.[1] Basically, the Word was taken to be an interpretative symbol for enfleshment in the Hellenistic context.

J.A.T. Robinson refers to Whitehead in whose language,

> Jesus...is not the metaphysical exception, but the supreme exemplification – unique, but representative not exclusive. And this is what is implied by the climax of the Prologue, that the Logos, the self-expressive activity of God in all nature, history and humanity, finally comes to expression, not simply in a people, that refused (except partially) to receive him, but fully and utterly in a person, who perfectly reflected him as his very mirror-image... With him the boundary is crossed between inspiration and incarnation. The wisdom became person, not merely inspired, but became. A transition from 'impersonal personification to actual person...there is nothing in the Prologue that would have been strange to a Hellenistic Jew. The Word is the utterance of God personified and it is incidental that in Greek the word *logos* is masculine, rather than feminine like *sophia* (wisdom) or neuter like *pneuma* (spirit).[2]

---

[1] K. Cracknell, *Towards a New Relationship*, London: Epworth Press, 1986, 1-117.

[2] Robinson, Op. cit., 378f.

He also quotes J. Dunn who through a series of statements sums up the early church's understanding:

> Initially at least Christ was not thought of as a divine being who had pre-existed with God but as *the climatic embodiment of God's power and purpose...God's clearest self-expression, God's last word.*
> *The Christ-event defined God more clearly than anything else had ever been done.*
> 'Incarnation' means initially that God's love and power had been experienced in fullest measure in, through and as this man Jesus, that Christ has been experienced as God's self-expression.[1]

With reference to 1:18 Robinson gives his own interpretation. 'Jesus Christ as the Son of God has given an "exegesis."' There is a mythical element in the claim of a heavenly divine figure who becomes man, which, he observes that Dunn has not recognized. He continues saying

> What I believe John is saying is that the Word, which was *theos* (1.1), God in his self-revelation and expression, *sarx ageneto* (1.14), was embodied totally in and as a human being, became a person, was personalized not just personified. But that the Logos came into existence or expression as a person does not mean that it was a person before. In terms of the later distinction, it was not that the Logos was hypostatic (a person or hypostasis) and then assumed an impersonal human nature, but that the Logos was an hypostatic until the Word of God finally came to self-expression not merely in nature and in a people but in an individual historical person, and thus *became* hypostatic.' Such expressions seem to have no limit. 'Jesus is genuinely and utterly a man who so completely incarnates God that the one is the human face of the other' and Jesus is 'the wholly God's informed person',

[1] Quoted, Ibid., 380.

> 'a wholly human figure, without loss or compromise...to talk also of a wholly real presence of God so far as that nature...can be mediated to and through the process of a human life.[1]

Further he elucidates that 'the revelation of "the Son", a pre-existent heavenly being, later the Second Person of the Trinity, who became a man, was probably inevitable. The content of the Christian revelation of God in Jesus, in and as an individual person, was combined with the cultural transition in Judaism and Gnosticism to the notion of fully hypostatized celestial figure such Son of Man and Son of God, to produce this result.' Yet, as Dunn argues, this 'does not imply the personal pre-existence of a heavenly being in the theology of the Synoptic Gospels, let alone in the consciousness of Jesus. But when he comes to John he contends that the *combination* of the wisdom Christology of the Logos-hymn (which he thinks, I believe improbably, is pre-Johannine but agrees does not in itself require to be read as speaking of a pre-existent Person) with John's dominant Son of God Christology produces an entirely different situation. And in fact it is this latter Son of God language rather than the Logos language as such which compels him to this conclusion.'[2] One other opinion is that 'the Prologue at least had an independent existence (as was already widely recognized) before the evangelist took it over to serve as the introduction of the Gospel.'[3]

Robinson's following conclusion, following a fine scholarly discussion, gives a good summary of understanding Jesus as the enfleshment of the cosmic and divine Logos.

> For John, Jesus is not God *simpliciter*. Jesus is a man who incarnates in everything he is and does the Logos who is God. He is the Son, the mirror-image of God, who is God for man and in man. The 'I' of Jesus speaks God, acts

---

[1] Ibid., 380f.

[2] Ibid., 381ff.

[3] Ashton, Op. cit., 57; this was the view of Bultmann.

> God. He utters the things of God, he does the works of God. He is his plenipotentiary, totally commissioned to represent him – *as* a human being. He speaks and acts with the 'I' that is one with God, utterly identified and yet not identical, his representative but not his replacement – and certainly not his replica, as if he were God dressed up as a human being. He is not a divine being who came to earth, in the manner of Ovid's *Metamorphoses*, in the form of a man, but the uniquely normal human being in whom the Logos or self-expressive activity of God was totally embodied. As Cullmann sums it up, '*Jesus Christ is God in his self-revelation.*' But, to use the later distinction, he was *totus deus*, everything that God himself is, not *totum dei*, the whole of God. For there are greater things to come and to be revealed (14.12; 16.12f)...It is only as 'they are in us' 'just as thou, Father, art in me and I in thee' (17.21), and not *simply* as God is glorified (or vindicated) in the Son (12.28), that the divine love comes to its 'perfection' (1Jn. 2.5; 4.12, 17f). This is but another way of saying that the locus of the incarnation or the 'Christ-event' is not simply the one man Christ Jesus but, as John Knox has put it, 'the human community in which that event culminated and in which, in the measure of the Church's fidelity, it is perpetuated... "God was in Christ" but "Christ is a broader term than "Jesus."'[1]

The nature of God's and the divine word's relationship with Jesus was further discussed by Paul and others: e.g. For Paul, Jesus 'was in the form of God; yet he laid no claim to equality with God, but made himself nothing, assuming the form of a slave' (Phil. 2: 6f). 'He is the image of the invisible God; he is the primacy over all creation...the whole universe has been created through him and for him' (Col. 1: 15f). For the writer to the Hebrew, Jesus 'is the radiance of God's glory, the stamp of God's very being, and he sustains the universe by his word of

---

[1] Robinson, Op. cit., 393f.

power' Heb. 1: 3). All such efforts to clarify the fact appeared to culminate in the Nicene Council where the word *homo-ousios* (of the same substance shared by the Father and Son) was accepted. But it was gravely limited because the Hebrew idea of the Messiah and Jesus' indirect claim for it was not recognized and this may be attributed to the anti-Semitic attitude of the Church Fathers. And what was not clarified was the relationship between devotees who confessed Jesus as Christ, Lord and Saviour and Jesus' one of the last words 'your Father and my Father.'

Jesus was rather desperate to have some recognition, leave alone reception. Not only with his Jewish opponents but also with his own disciples he had discussion in order to make them understand who he was. When he was not able to persuade them in discussions and arguments, he declared himself as someone extraordinary, the one who came from heaven and the one who was very close to God. The famous 'I am sayings' in the Fourth Gospel have become assertive statements in the popular preaching circles. Jesus declared: I am the bread of life, gate, good shepherd, way-truth-life, even before Abraham, resurrection and life and so on. Do they imply that he was identical with God, the Yahweh of the Hebrews and heavenly Father of Jesus? Bishop Robinson answers, 'certainly do not imply that the subject is God. As Barret rightly says *ego eimi* does not identify Jesus with God, but it does draw attention to him in the strongest possible terms. "I am the one – the one you must look at, and listen to, if you would know God."'[1] Originally, the name Yahweh, enigmatic and holy to pronounce, meant 'I am' to be the liberating presence with the Hebrew community. In the context of a discussion on belief in resurrection Jesus referred to this revelatory declaration of 'Eternal I am' (Lk. 20: 37). But does this mean that Jesus' 'I am sayings' refer to Yahweh? It was impossible for a Jew to think so. For the Johannine scholar C.K. Barrett, they do not carry with them the implication that he is Yahweh but, in Johannine terms, 'the Christ, the Son of God.' Robinson observes that Barrett is unusually emphatic at this points out his comment on 8.28: 'It is

[1] Ibid., 385.

simply intolerable that Jesus should be made to say, "I am God, the supreme God of the Old Testament, and being God I do as I am told"; and on 13.19: 'I am God, and I am here because someone sent me.' The sole remaining instance is 8.58: 'Before Abraham was born'. 'This certainly asserts pre-existence.'[1] We should add, as the Word, not as Jesus, the particular manifestation of it. The difficulty to recapture the Johannine witness is caused by the over-clouding doctrines developed later. Today, in popular circles Christians vigorously propagate a kind of Jesus cult or Christo-monism that obscure the eyes of outsiders to have the vision of Jesus and understand the nature of his divinity.

How do we understand Jesus' Oneness with God? The famous saying of Jesus 'I and the Father are one' (10: 30) has been repeatedly quoted to establish the divine or ontological status of Jesus in relation to God the Father. We have already noted Appasamy's position that it was not ontological but relational/moral oneness. J.A.T. Robinson was one of the few who worked very hard to bring an understanding, approximately true and reasonably acceptable. He says: 'If then the "I" with which Jesus speaks is neither that simply of the individual ego nor of the divine name, what is it? I suggest that it is to be understood as the totality of the self, of which Jung spoke in contrast with the ego. As he saw it, the Christ-figure is an archetypal image of our being and with our own deepest existence. It is the "I" of the mystics, who make the most astonishing claims to be one with God, without of course claiming to be God, the "I" of Meister Eckhart and Angelus Silesius, or of the Sufis and the Upanishads, where *atman* and *Brahman* are completely "one", as in John 10.30. Such is Bede Griffiths' interpretation, born of long exposure to this tradition. In his latest book he says of Jesus,

> In the depths of his being, like every human being, he was present to himself, in relation to the eternal ground of his being. In most people this intuitive awareness is inchoate or imperfect, but in the great prophet and mystic, in the

[1] Ibid., 386.

> seer like Gautama Buddha or the seers of the Upanishads, this intuitive knowledge of the ground of being becomes a pure intuition, a total awareness. Such according to the tradition of John's Gospel (which in its origin is considered to be as old as that of the other gospels) was the nature of the knowledge of Jesus. He knew himself in the depth of his spirit as one with the eternal ground of his being.[1]

Robinson consults Martin Buber also: 'For it is the I of unconditional relation in which the man calls his *Thou* Father in such a way that he is simply Son, and nothing else but Son. Whenever he says I he can only mean the I of the holy primary word that has been raised for him into unconditional being.'[2]

Robinson concludes a long and comprehensive discussion on the nature of Jesus' oneness with God. 'There is nothing here that is not utterly and "superbly" human, as well as being totally transparent of God. To have seen the one is to have seen the other, without being dissolved in the other. The "I" that says "I and the Father are one" is an unequivocally human as the "I" that says "I thirst." There can be no residue or trace of a Christology that says that Jesus said or did some things as God and some things as man. That is wholly alien to the interpretation of John. He did everything as the integral human being who was totally one with his Father and with all other men, so that in him the fullness of deity as well as the fullness of humanity becomes visible. The distinctive thing about that "I" is that it was *not* human but that it was *wholly* one with the self-expressive activity of God, and thus *uniquely* human. What he was the Logos was and what the Logos was God was, so that in his 'I' God is speaking and acting. Bultmann in his commentary on John notes: 'In Jesus' words God speaks the *ego emi*. We should, however, reject the view that *ego emi* means "I, (Jesus) am God."'[3] For him this just like the great

[1] Ibid., 387; cf. Griffiths, *The Marriage of East and West*, London: SCM, 1982, 189.

[2] Quoted, Ibid., 388.

[3] Ibid.

missionary 'I' of the Synoptic Gospels as expressed in phrases such as 'I have come' (Mk. 2.17).

> In John this 'I' is portrayed and projected, backwards and forwards in terms of the pre-existence and post-existence of a heavenly person. But that is the language of myth, picturing the other-side, as Bultmann would put it, in terms of this side. It is pushing the truth of the sonship that Jesus embodied back to the very beginning of God's purpose – as well as, with the Synoptics, forward to its end. For John, as for the author to the Hebrews, it is through the Son and on account of the Son and the bringing of many sons to glory that all things are that are done. But all this is but drawing out to recognition the full cosmic significance of what was disclosed in the 'glory' of this utterly human life. John, again, differs only in the maturity with which he elicits and elaborates the 'initial' understanding of incarnation, common in principle to all the New Testament writers. He has not, I think, as Dunn suggests (even if only in the form of a question expecting the answer 'yes'), 'left behind the earlier idea of God acting in and through the Christ-event' by presenting 'Christ... conceived as a heavenly being distinct from God.[1]

As we have pointed out earlier, Indian Christian theologians such as A.J. Appasamy also have clarified that the oneness between Jesus and Father was not ontological but moral and relational. And New Testament scholars such as J.A.T. Robinson have gone deeper into the NT world, the context of the Johannine community and later deviation of doctrinal formulations. However, one may observe that in all such scholarly pursuits the 'functional centrality' has not adequately recognized and expounded. It was necessary for Jesus to explain who he was but he did not do it as an enlightened ascetic and scholastic philosopher but a devoted activist. The followings words recur in the Fourth Gospel: God

[1] Ibid., 389f.

loves and I love; my Father works and I work; what I see the Father doing I do; and so on. So, more than anything else the oneness between Jesus and his Father is a dynamic intimacy and functional oneness.

If Jesus had God for his Father as much as any other human being and he spoke of him as 'my God and your God' (20.17), how do we take Thomas' declaration 'my Lord and my God' (20.28)? In the context, as we noted earlier, it was an exclamatory confession of a peculiar kind but the dear disciple in response to the risen Jesus showing the wounds and calling him to come forward and touch as he had earlier wanted. Robinson says that Thomas, in his human friend and companion (cf. 11.16, 'let us go that we may die *with* him') 'recognizes the one in whom the lordship of God meets him and claims him, though not as a heavenly being but as a wounded yet transfigured man of flesh and blood, whose glorification lay in making himself nothing so that in him God might be everything. This is the language, not of ontological identity nor simply of functional equivalence, but of existential embodiment.'[1] We have sufficiently dealt with understanding Word and enfleshment and oneness between God and Jesus. Now we turn to look at some other titles.

Son of God-God, Blasphemy – 10: 34-36: The title 'Son of God' led to confusion and misunderstanding as much as to some Jews in Jesus' day as to the Muslims. We have noted earlier its non-physical connotation and defining the nature of the Messiah, and specially anointed ruler. We also, with reference to the verses 10: 34-36, noted the ambiguity of Jesus' answer. As Ashton has pointed out, 'On a superficial reading this passage appears quite innocuous: other men are called gods in Scripture; and since this is so, argues Jesus, why should not I, sanctified and sent, claim the title of Son of God? But if there were nothing more to his reply than this then it would be simply and solely a clever but otherwise undistinguished *argumentum ad hominem*, seemingly designed more to reassure his audience than to establish his own credentials as a messenger from heaven with a genuine claim to

[1] Ibid., 393.

divinity.' Further, he exegetes the passage: 'Much depends on the identification of those whom God is conceived to be addressing in the psalm that is being quoted (82.6). There are three candidates: (1) unjust judges; (2) Israel; (3) angels. The first two both have rabbinical support; but neither is really satisfactory, for it is hard to see in either case how Jesus could be making a strong enough claim to warrant the response he receives. One recent commentator, Jurgen Becker, points out that such a reading would make Jesus out to be a *primus inter pares*, a special case in relation to other men similarly addressed by God. This anticipation of Arius is not a theological position found elsewhere in the Gospel, and so Becker is inclined to regard the passage as an editorial intrusion, though he fails to explain why an editor should attempt to draw the truth of John's argument in this way. Surely it is preferable to look first for a reading strong enough to suit the context: another fierce and trenchant debate with the Jews that actually starts this time (10.31) with an allusion to their determination to see him dead. The suggestion that the *theoi* in this passage might really be angels was first made in 1960 by J.A. Emerton, who pointed out that in the Peshitta (Syriac) version of the psalm 'gods'...is rendered 'angels.'[1] Ashton takes further support from Targums and Qumran sources. In any case, Jesus' (or the editor's) incomplete response is confusing!

The Specific Meaning of Son of Man: As Ashton observes, 'Among the many puzzles presented by the Fourth Gospel one of the most intriguing is the paradoxical contrast between the titles 'Son of Man' and 'Son of God', originally at any rate, indicates a human being, the Messiah; whereas 'Son of Man' points to a figure whose true home is in heaven. Divine? Well, perhaps not necessarily, or not altogether, but certainly invested by God with an authority no ordinary human being would dare to claim. Why this should be so is a question whose answer revolves upon the interpretation of a single text – the famous vision of Daniel 7.'[2] For him the title as used in the Fourth Gospel also implies some

[1] Ashton, Op. cit., 147f.

[2] Ibid., 337.

sort of heavenly status also requires elucidation, since many of the passages in which it occurs are curiously opaque. He refers to some scholars. 'Rudolf Schnackenburg too believes that "all thirteen texts in John which speak of the Son of Man form a consistent and well-knit whole." What is more, he is convinced that "apart from the Son of Man logia themselves, there seems to be no grounds for assuming that the concept of the Son of Man has greatly influenced the Fourth Gospel."'[1] He points out that the reference to ascending and descending (1.51; cf. Gen. 28.12; 3.13; 6.62; though Jesus claims uniqueness) has close parallel to Mandaean writings connecting it to Gnostic mythology. He points out that Son of Man nowhere in the Gospel is associated with mission. 'If the Son of Man were indeed *sent* then he would have to be thought of as sent from heaven. But this point is not made. The Son of Man is first of all not an emissary but an intermediary.'[2] But the puzzle of his heavenly origin and human identification is not easily solved.

Morna Hooker in her book *The Son of Man in Mark* (London 1967) offers a closer exegesis of Son of Man verses in Dan 7: 13-14. She argues, 'the Son of Man can – and will – suffer when his rightful position and God's authority are denied: this is the situation in Dan. 7, where the 'beasts' have revolted against God and crushed Israel who, as Son of man, should be ruling the earth with authority granted by God. Given the situation of the nations' revolt and their rejection of the claims of the one who is intended to exercise authority, it is true to say that the Son of man not only can but must suffer.'[3]

Hooker's exegesis helps to perceive the unique position of Jesus as Son of Man, i.e., he is the representative of the victim community. He was sent by God to demonstrate this fact because in the situation of strained relationship and failed justice ultimately God is the victim. That he stood by the side of the victims of injustice and those vulnerable because of various impediments,

---

[1] Ibid., 339.

[2] Ibid., 348.

[3] Quoted, Ibid., 369.

and even acted as their representative in the face of unjust forces is demonstrated in the life of the Hebrew community (Exodus and Commandments) and their leaders (e.g. Jer. 8: 21f). Jesus' claim that he was from heaven found its most challenging expression in his death on the cross. Following an exposition of glory as to be dying like a single seed, Jesus said, 'But I, when I am lifted up from the earth, will draw all men to myself' (12: 32). This meaning fits well the distinctive version of the great commission recorded in John. Saying that he was sending his disciples just as the Father had sent him and showing the continuing wounds of his risen body and breathing the Holy Spirit, Jesus told them, 'If you forgive anyone his sins, they are forgiven; if you do not forgive them, they are not forgiven' (20: 23). Indirectly it implied that there was no extra or heavenly authority to forgive except by representing the victims and vulnerable even if the power and high position-mongering disciples did not understand such a sudden declaration. Obviously, the disciples were supposed to represent the victims just as was their Master. This profound idea in connection with the Son of Man is found in the last book of the Bible as well which is often connected with the Johannine literature (Rev. 1: 13; 14: 14).

Kṛṣṇa's Identity and Ascendency to Supreme Divinity

Kṛṣṇa's ascendency had an altogether different process. To start with, his association with the Vedic god Viṣṇu at a particular point was decisive. 'In the Rg Veda Vishnu is a benevolent, solar deity, often coupled with the warrior god Indra. The name Vishnu may be derived from the Sanskrit verbal root *viś* ("to enter"), so Vishnu is "he who enters or pervades the universe." In one hymn, Vishnu takes three strides thereby separating the earth from the sky, a story which forms the basis of the later myth in the Puranas where Vishnu, incarnated as a dwarf, covers the universe with three strides and destroys the power of the demon Bali."[1] Hymns like RV I. 154 describes Viṣṇu as the measurer of heaven and earth

[1] G. Flood, *An Introduction to Hinduism*, Cambridge: Cambridge University Press, 2008, 114.

and accomplisher of three mighty strides, wanderer at will as a savage beast and inhabitant of mountains, supporter of the three spheres of earth, sky and all living things, and his abode is full of abundance and splendor.

Later Viṣṇu was associated with sacrifice and Prajāpati. For instance, the Maitrī Upaniṣad VI.16 narrates him as priest, the enjoyer, the offering, the sacred word, the sacrifice itself, Viṣṇu and Prajāpati, the Lord, the Witness, the one who shines up yonder in the orb of the sun. From his right place in the system of Vedic sacrifice, he moved further to be along Brahman, the Upaniṣad's Supreme Reality. In the context of major deities contesting for supremacy, the Muṇḍaka Upaniṣad, after narrating the supreme qualities of Śiva, declares that Viṣṇu, Brahma, Śiva, Indra, while mentioning the Imperishable and the supreme Majesty, along with life, time, fire, and the moon (also see III.2.8). The transition from Viṣṇu's multiple identities to one Absolute Reality seems to have happened in the following way:

> Two Brahmans there are to be known; one as sound and the other Brahman supreme. Having known Brahman as sound one reaches Brahman supreme.
> Now this too has been said elsewhere: (Brahman as sound) and sound is the syllable OM. Its culmination is tranquil, soundless, free from fear and sorrow, full of sheer joy, lacking in nothing, steadfast, motionless, immortal, unfailing, and enduring forever. Its name is Viṣṇu the omnipresent. One should meditate on both to attain the supreme state (Mait. Up. VI.22f).

Now we move to an epic presentation. In the context of a decline and revival of the (c4-2cent BCE) Vedic religion there was fluidity and amalgamation of traditions and ideas. There was the incorporation of the ascetic practices of the śramaṇa such as interior path of devotion and ideals such as non-violence. Further, some independent divine heroes got fused with Viṣṇu and Kṛṣṇa.

> Vasudeva, who became identified with Krishna and Vishnu, was the supreme deity of a tribe called the Virshinis or Satvatas and may have originated as Vrishni hero or king, though it is impossible to trace a line back to an original Vasudeva. The Virshinis became fused with the Yadavas, the tribe of Krishna. The worship of Vasudeva is recorded as early as the fifth or sixth centuries BCE being mentioned by the famous grammarian Panini in his book of grammar the *Ashtadhyayi*. Here he explains the term *vasudevaka* as referring to a devotee (*bhakta*) of the god Vasudeva.[1]

When Vāsudeva was fused with Kṛṣṇa, the later already got the status of a deified king or divine hero. Though the historicity of Kṛṣṇa cannot be ascertained, "By the second century BCE Vasudeva-Krishna was worshipped as a distinct deity and finally identified with Vishnu in the Mahabharata, appearing, for example, three times in the Bhagavad Gita as synonymous with Vishnu."[2] The *Nārāyaṇīya* section of the Mahābhārata and *Mahānārāyṇa Upaniṣad* represent the fusion between Viṣṇu and Vāsudeva Nārāyaṇa, and then Kṛṣṇa.

Thus, the most visible form of amalgamation was between Brāhmaṇa and Bhāgavata traditions. Consequently, as we noted earlier, Kṛṣṇa from the Sātvata clan, shepherd community, after a struggle of entry (contest with Śiṣupāla) came to be the spokesperson of Brāhmanism. Subsequently, Kṛṣṇa gradually ascended from the position of a (divine) hero of a shepherd community to that of an avatāra of the supreme God or Brahman and, ultimately, the supreme God or Brahman himself. In Bhagavad Gītā which is part of Mahābhārata where Kṛṣṇa is presented as a kinsman, friend and charioteer of Arjuna, after mentioning his many births, (though otherwise unborn and imperishable), Kṛṣṇa talks about avatāra (the word not mentioned) or descents:

---

[1] Ibid., 119.

[2] Ibid., 119f.

> Whenever there is decay of dharma and rise of adharma, then I embody Myself…
> For the protection of the good, for the destruction of the wicked and for the establishment of dharma I am born age after age.
> He who thus knows My divine birth and action in true light, having dropped the body, comes not to birth again, but comes unto Me…(4: 7-9).

This text has become the key in the Vaiṣṇava tradition to expound the meaning of divine revelation, providence and grace. Also the *viśvarūpadarśana* in the 11th chapter of the Gītā almost sealed the unrivaled supremacy of Kṛṣṇa and the all-inclusive nature of his body.

The *Pañcarātra* Samhīta or Āgama (five nights or five nights sacrifices), part of the *Nārāyaṇīya* section, mentions the doctrine of 'the manifestations of the absolute through a series of emanations or *vyukas*. These begin with Vasudeva who manifests Samkarshana who in turn manifests Pradyumna, from whom Aniruddha emerges…This series of *vyuha* emanations comprise the highest level of the universe, the 'pure creation', while below this are intermediate or 'mixed' creation and the 'impure' or 'material' creation. Each *vyuha* has a cosmological function with regard to the lower creation, which manifests through Pradyumna.'[1] It is debated if the Pañcarātra tradition, texts and doctrine, are authentic. While orthodox Brahmins reject them, the Śrī Vaiṣṇava tradition accepts. Related yet distinct is Vaikhanāsa tradition which still directs the traditional ritual to Viṣṇu. Particularly in South India Vaikhanāsa priests have a stable standing.

From the epics to the Purāṇas there is no coherent and consistent development and this shows the continued fluidity of the traditions. Not only texts but also iconography played a role in depicting themes. Flood's following example is informative.

---

[1] Ibid., 121.

By the time of the Puranas (4th to 6th cent CE), Vishnu is iconographically depicted in two ways. Firstly as a dark blue youth, standing upright, possessing four arms and holding in each hand respectively, a conch, discus, mace and lotus. He wears the jewel called the *kaustubha* and has a curl of hair on his chest, the *srivatsa* ('beloved of the goddess Sri'). The second form is Vishnu lying asleep upon the coils of the great cosmic snake, Sesa ('remainder') or Ananta ('endless'), floating upon the cosmic ocean. When he awakes, he creates the universe. A lotus emerges from his naval, out of the lotus appears the creator god Brahma, who then manifests the universe which is maintained by Vishnu and then destroyed by Siva: Brahma is enfolded by the lotus which withdraws into Vishnu's naval who, finally, falls asleep once more. Vishnu is married to Lakshmi and Sri, who form a single being, though they were initially distinct goddesses. They appear in later Hinduism as other consorts of the god. He is also depicted riding, sometimes with Lakshmi, upon his mount, the large birdlike creature Garuda.'[1]

Already one would see the emerging sectarian nature of the traditions, particularly the Śaiva and Vaiṣṇava. In an explosive context of competing for supremacy, 'an ecumenism of the major gods' was worked out with assignment of particular work to each. Accordingly, Brahmā was the creator, Viṣṇu the sustainer and Śiva the destroyer. But it was short lived and later Brahmā receded to the background and Śiva and Viṣṇu were seen doing all the above three works and more by their respective devotees. Since then, there have been times of conflict, accommodation in the name of avatāra (although the Śaivas do not believe in it) and part of the framework of 'one and many.' In any case, while devotees of these two classical traditions extol their Gods as supreme, in dialogue some express the opinion that though the other is not invalid yet he is inferior.

---

[1] Ibid., 114f.

As we noted earlier, the Purāṇas provide different and overlapping lists of the avatāras. But as far as the Bhāgavata Purāṇa is concerned, Kṛṣṇa is not an avatāra of Viṣṇu, but the supreme God himself. At the same time, at least in one place the gopīs tell Kṛṣṇa, 'your incarnation is for the good of the universe and you remove the distress of Vraja' and later they declared that he was the unique embodiment of beauty and became manifest in as many forms as needed for their enjoyment with him (BhP. 31: 18; 32: 14; 33: 29). Towards the end he is called Viṣṇu and Vāsudeva! For new readers this might be confusing, because identifying with a shepherd community is the specific forte of Kṛṣṇa, either as their kinsman, divine hero, or the newly deified avatāra. There is no evidence that Viṣṇu has been closely associated with a shepherd community. Also, usually Rādha, the chief gopī used to be the consort of Kṛṣṇa, but here she is called Śrī (the goddess of fortune) and Śrī is famous as the consort of Viṣṇu. Here there is a riddle and it is not easy to resolve. In any case, it is not inconceivable to see Kṛṣṇa as the kinsman of the shepherd community of Vraja at one level and the lord of lords at another level. This is what we exactly see in the Gītā. And there are those (e.g. Chaitanya movement) who take Śrī here as none other than Rādha; take Kṛṣṇa as none other than Viṣṇu which may not be implausible although the occurance of the names Viṣṇu and Vāsudeva at the end is yet to be explained. Whatever may be the hidden motive of the authors, Kṛṣṇa as an erratic boy and erotic player and supreme Lord defines true bhakti the climax of which is found in the Rāsalīlā section.

Kṛṣṇa's achievements are recorded with reference to the defeat of his kinsman and demon king Kaṃsa who had usurped the throne of Ugrasena, the grandfather of Kṛṣṇa and his victory over Indra and liberation of cows and his victory over Śiśupāla which made him to be the promoter of bhāgavata-brāhmaṇa amalgamation and spokes person of the brāhmaṇic dharma. In a scheme of assimilating popular divine heroes and figures in the name of avatāra of God Viṣṇu, Kṛṣṇa was given a prominent place. At one level, like other gods, he had his own devotees, but at another level, whichever ways devotees approached whatever gods they in the end would come to Kṛṣṇa as mentioned in the Gītā. In the Bhāgavata, though he was both erratic and erotic thus transcending conventional norms, he is acclaimed to be the Supreme, self-content, playfully independent and bestower of grace and love to his longing devotees.

***The Concept of Avatāra*:** The use, overuse and even misuse of the term 'avatāra' has contributed to the complexity of understanding its meaning rather than clarifying it. Its literal meaning is "descent", but is often translated into English as 'incarnation.' It is misleading because it suggests too strong a resemblance to the incarnation of Christian theology. The Latin word *incarnation* or *incarnari* like the Greek *ensarkosis* which it translates, implies the divine Word 'in the flesh.' Christian theologians who use the word 'avatāra' take pains to distinguish between the occasional descent or visit of a god like Kṛṣṇa in strange forms for a momentary purpose and Jesus who was historical, fully human and decisive for the salvation of the whole world. We have already noted the interpretation of Chakkarai.

Sheridon notes, 'The word *avatāra* is itself rather late in the history of Vaiṣṇavism. It does not occur in the Bhagavad Gītā nor in the *Nārāyaṇiya* of the *Mahābhārata* nor in the *Harivaṁśa*, where such words as *janmam, sambhava, sṛjana* and *pradurbhāva* are employed.'[1] As Renou points out, 'The *avatāras* were originally independent legends which came to centre on Viṣṇu, perhaps because from the beginning Viṣṇu was the symbol of the propagation of the divine; they are legends for prowess over demons, of the usual type, which portray a hero.'[2] Though the history of the development of the concept of avatāra has yet to be constructed, it should be recognized that a hero deified and identified with a god or the supreme God is most phenomenal and decisive in the Vaiṣṇava tradition. But the word is not accepted in the Saiva tradition as, according to their belief, the supreme God Śiva does not incarnate which would involve him going through

---

[1] Sheridon, Op. cit., 60.

[2] L. Renou, *The Destiny of the Veda in India*, Delhi: Motilal Banarsidas, 1965, 113.

the process of *karmasaṃsāra* and instead he simply appears and disappears (theophany). However, at popular level the Saivas are not scrupulous to avoid using the term avatāra; so also other non-Vaiṣṇavas and now it is applied to any one if s/he is a famous thinker, political leader or guru in India.

There are different lists of different number of forms and names in the Mahābhārata, Purāṇas and the Bhāgavata. They are associated with other concepts such as the Sānkhyan category of triguṇa.[1] Every avatāra had a purpose and it reflected the gracious concern of Viṣṇu. The Bhāgavata projects him as the Supreme Being and mentions the following ten major avatāras:

(1) *Matsya*, the Fish, who saved Manu the progenitor of humankind from destruction by the Great Flood;
(2) *Kūrma*, the Tortoise who acted as the pivot underneath Mt. Mandāra which was the churning stick used by the gods to recover miraculous objects and divinities lost in the Ocean in the Flood;
(3) *Varāha*, the Boar who recovered the earth from the bottom of The Ocean, whither she had been dragged by a demon;
(4) *Narasiṃha*, the Man-Lion who slew the great demon Hiraṇyakāṣipu;
(5) *Vāmana*, the Dwarf, who delivered the Three Worlds from the dominion of Bali the demon-king;
(6) *Paraśurāma*, Rama with the Axe, who saved the Brāhmins from the arrogant dominion of the Kṣatriyas or warrior-caste;
(7) *Rāma*, the hero of Rāmāyaṇa, who delivered the world from the demon Rāvaṇa;
(8) *Balarāma*, elder brother of Kṛṣṇa, who together rid the world of the evil Kaṃsa;
(9) *The Buddha*, whom the Brāhmins incorporated quite late into Hindu tradition as an avatār of Viṣṇu incarnated to lead the evil men to despise the Vedas and the caste system and so destroy themselves; and

---

[1] See Sheridon, Op. cit., 60ff; Vempeny, Op. cit., 244f.

(10) *Kalki*, the future avatāra, who will come on a white horse at the end of this current age to destroy the wicked and reward the righteous. As an avatāra but a portion of the divine essence of Viṣṇu, it is Balarāma who is accounted as the eighth avatāra in the final authoritative list and not Kṛṣṇa who is Viṣṇu himself in all his divine splendor according to the Bhāgavata Purāṇa.[1] Then, how to work out a final tally of Kṛṣṇa's place and status in the scheme of avatāra? Freda Matchet, after a thorough study of the 'Kṛṣṇa Texts' identifies three perspectives.

1. Kṛṣṇa as one manifestation of many avatāra lists – he is 8th;
2. Kṛṣṇa as the focal point of a series, described in greater detail;
3. Kṛṣṇa as the source of the series. Kṛṣṇa here 'is not only acting out the human roles of a cowherd boy, householder and warrior chief. He is even playing at being an *avatāra*, allowing himself to be listed among the many and varied forms which he brings into being.'[2]

In the above lists the purpose of avatāra is not clear and consistent. In Mahābhārata (I. 54-61) it is stated that God's concern was to remove earth's burden. The Gītā, while not using the word avatāra, gives a succinct expression in Kṛṣṇa saying that he came to restore dharma and punish adharma (4. 7-8). In Harivaṃśa there are clues in 1.8.32-5. Most notably, Kṛṣṇa was a hero whose deeds increased the fame of his race and his associates, to help those gods who were in trouble and rescued the earth from destruction. In addition, the Bhāgavata notes welfare of the universe, defeating the asuras, providing means of liberation and sportive enjoyment. It is the last one we will concentrate with reference to the Rāsalīla. It was God's pastime with a group of chosen people.

---

[1] Jeremiah P. Losty, *Krishna: A Hindu Vision of God*, London: British Library, 1980, 5f.

[2] Freda Matchett, *Kṛshṇa: Lord or Avatāra?*, London: Curzon, 2001, 187.

However, the exact identity of Kṛṣṇa in relation to Viṣṇu, the Supreme God, is not clear. In many manifestations the former was subordinated to the latter. In *viśvarūpadarṣana*, a gracious manifestation of the charioteer Kṛṣṇa to his friend and devotee Arjuna, mentioned in the Gītā, Arjuna could see the whole universe with its multiplicity and splendor. Here Kṛṣṇa demonstrates himself as the supreme being without any connection with Viṣṇu. Understandably, the Viṣṇu Purāṇa presents Viṣṇu as the supreme God, identical with the Upaniṣad's supreme Brahman. Probably, the bhāgavata community worked hard to liberate their Lord Kṛṣṇa from his position of subordination to that of Viṣṇu. This is reflected in the Bhāgavata in which the supreme titles Brahman, Paramātman and Bhagavan refer principally to Krṛṣṇa. In this purāṇa there is a declaration: 'Kṛṣṇa is God himself' (BhP. I.3.27). It is extremely surprising that here Kṛṣṇa is the name of Viṣṇu! Viṣṇu's consort Śrī (the goddess of fortune) is Kṛṣṇa's consort, not Rādha, the foremost of the Gopīs and the beloved. What is behind this concealed identity? Was it because the popularity and appeal of the name Kṛṣṇa? Or, sociologically speaking, was there an intention of not polluting the brāhamaṇic Viṣṇu in association with the lower caste cowherd community? There is a scope for a separate research.

***Kṛṣṇa as Playing God*:** There is a reason to present this topic at the end of this section. Given the complexity of the process of Kṛṣṇa's ascendency to supreme God, it is difficult to imagine a history of his personal birth and growth. However, what is undeniable is that at a particular point in the theological imagination of the Kṛṣṇa community is the child image of their God became prominent. As a matter of fact, Bāla Kṛṣṇa (child Kṛṣṇa) is the image which is celebrated most enthusiastically and devotionally with colourful decorations and symbolic actions of cuddling the divine baby, rocking his cradle, reenacting his plays and pranks etc in the celebrations of Kṛṣṇa Jeayanti.

Earlier we noted the mischievous acts of Kṛṣṇa reported by the gopīs as recorded in the Bhāgavata. We also pointed out the meaning of independence, creativity and transcendence attached to those abnormal acts. David Kinsley seems to be a most prominent exponent of the child image of Kṛṣṇa and we have already quoted him to this effect in passing. After illustrating with stories of play as divine activity in Hindu traditions, Kinsley points out Kṛṣṇa's moments of comedy and laughter while he was seen as a divine child. In a section titled "The Frolicking Child and Adolescent God" he narrates the following:

> The play of Kṛṣṇa as a child is of three varieties, each more or less associated with a stage in his maturation. As an infant his play is highly unstructured. He moves his arms and legs erratically, wants one thing or another, crawls around aimlessly in his mother's yard, and covers himself with dirt. As a child his play centres around his tricks, the most common of which is his repeated theft of butter from his mother and other women of Vṛndāvana. As a boy or adolenscent his play is more varied. He plays games with his friends, teases the *gopīs*, imitates various animals, and gambols in the forest.[1]

He continues to list out Kṛṣṇa's other mischiefs as recorded in the Bhāgavata. They include untimely untethering of calves, laughing in the face of anger, inventing novel means of pilfering, distributing his drinks among monkeys, out of anger making other infants cry aloud, using precarious means to reach out hanging pots of butter, finishing his thefts by making the jewels of his person to serve the purpose of lamps and passing urine and leaving excretions in cleansed houses. The particular text ends with the words, 'In this way he commits vile deeds by thievish tricks, but when near thyself he lives like a very gentle boy.'[2]

As a carefree adolescent or youth Kṛṣṇa was sparkling and beautiful, 'the irresistible exhilarator and inebriator' who could

---

[1] D. Kinsley, *The Divine Player: A Study of Kṛṣṇa Līlā*, Delhi: Motilal Banarsidass, 1979, 62.

[2] Ibid., 65.

easily attract the gopīs. A passage from *Brahma-vaivarta-purāṇa* narrates his extraordinary beauty in the following way:

> The light of Lord Kṛṣṇa is circular and vies with millions of suns. The Yogis, adepts and gods adore this light. But the Vaiṣṇavas adore the indescribable, lovely image of Kṛṣṇa located in the centre of this light. He is blue like a new cloud; his eyes are like lotuses; his face is as graceful as the autumnal full Moon; his lips are like *bimbas*; the row of his teeth shames the pears. A gentle smile plays on his lips. He holds a flute in his hands....He is clad in yellow dress.[1]

This and other such mythical portrayals have been most valuable sources for poetic imagination of the Vaiṣṇava bhakti literature, Vedantic/theological interpretations and iconic representations in Kṛṣṇa temples.

Flute is of special significance in the playful image of Kṛṣṇa. Kingsley reflects that 'Kṛṣṇa's flute is an extension of his beauty. Not only is it the most beautiful sound imaginable, it imparts the essence of Kṛṣṇa's intoxicating nature. While Kṛṣṇa is also adept at singing, it is the sound of his flute, not his voice, that echos throughout Vṛndāvana, beckoning all to join him in the forest.... The flute gives forth a clear, pure, simple sound that can be both intensely melancholy and entrancingly sprightly. In either mood, haunting or haughty, its clear notes sound as if they come from a world beyond the din of the ordinary.'[2] Again, the music of the flute enchanted not only the gopīs of Vṛndāvan but it can beckon all those who struggle in the bewildering forest of the universe. Hindu worship and celebrations are spiritually sustained by all sorts of music though in the worship of Kṛṣṇa the flute is central.

Kinsley cites the Bengali verse 'without Kṛṣṇa, there is no song.' He adds saying that, 'of all the Hindu gods Kṛṣṇa expresses most completely all that is beautiful, graceful, and enticing in

[1] Quoted, Ibid., 76.

[2] Ibid., 95.

the other world of the divine...he sports as an equal with lowly cowherd women or plays with cowherd boys. His appearance is not mighty but almost rustic. He always smiles and never frowns. He is young, eternally young. He runs, jumps, scampers, and bounds through the forest in a constant display of irrespressible vitality and enthusiasm.'[1] Vṛndāvana, Vraja, Goloka or Kṛṣṇa 's 'Garden of Eden' was not only his abode, far above the abodes of other gods (including Śiva and Viṣṇu), but also his play ground where people in Vṛndāvana and Kṛṣṇa-bhaktas everywhere believe his sportive presence is still experienced. Kinsley consults the definition of play or the characteristics of play by J. Huizinga. They are primal, irreducible, voluntary act, an end in itself; superfluous and non-utilitarian; outside ordinary and non-serious; it has its own order, rules and limits of space and time; a kind of secrezy, otherness, leading to cohesive social groups; sense of make-believe or pretending; actualization and representation with imagination to create its own worlds; and a joyous mood.[2] This definition has been offered in general terms and also in some characteristics with reference to cult. And it is not difficult to apply most of them to the play of Kṛṣṇa. The following is a good summary of divine play which is applied to Kṛṣṇa:

Līlā is descriptive of divine activity in another way. The gods as players are revealed to act spontaneously, unpredictably, and sometimes tumultuously. To play is to be unfettered and unconditioned, to perform actions that are intrinsically satisfying, to sing, dance, and laugh. To play is to step out of the ordinary world of the humdrum, to enter a special, magical world where one can revel in the superfluous. To play is to display oneself aimlessly and gracefully. As player, then, the gods are revealed to be delightful, joyful, graceful beings whose actions are completely spontaneous, unconditioned, and expressive of their transcendent completeness and freedom. No Hindu deity

---

[1] Ibid., 120.

[2] Ibid., 123.

expresses this aspect of the divine more completely than the cowherd Kṛṣṇa.[1]

As we indicated before, Kṛṣṇa's play in Vṛndāvan continues with flute, song, dance with beauty, freedom and bounty. He is still flolicking and making love with his beloved gopīs, the modeling bhaktas, inciting them to frenzy and abandon the domestic chores, social responsibilities and moral restrictions.

Commenting on the recurring theme of divine sport in the Bhāgavata, Siddheśvara Bhaṭṭācārya writes:

> Divine Sport is the expression of the majestic independence of the Absolute, and so, it refuses to be conditioned by time and space or to be cast into a specific pattern. It bristles with infinite variety that baffles prediction or description of any kind....According to the Bhāgavata, the perpetual realization of its blissful nature makes the Absolute perpetually charged with free creativity. It is the spontaneous overflow of the Absolute to realize itself in all kinds of ideal possibilities.[2]

Such understanding seems to suggest a devotional commitment that can transcend sectarian identities. We should note, however, the Bhāgavata is solely confined to extol the greatness of Kṛṣṇa Bhagavān. Empirical studies alone will reveal how many Kṛṣṇa bhaktas are able to imagine the Absolute beyond Kṛṣṇa and how many non-Kṛṣṇites accept the vision of the Bhāgavata.

To conclude this discussion, apart from all such narratives as above, we need to recognize the instances in some purāṇas wheret Kṛṣṇa is clearly identified as supreme reality, identical with the Supreme Brahman of the Upaniṣads. Noel Sheth from his most thorough study of the divinity of Kṛṣṇa with special reference to Harivaṃśa, Viṣṇu Purāṇa and Bhāgavata Purāṇa (Harvard PhD), points out that he was not only as the rider of Garuḍa and a 'shamanistic heroe using magic and supernatural weapons' winning

---

[1] D. Kinsley, *The Sword and the Flute,* 74.

[2] Quoted, D. Kinsley, *The Divine Player*, 105f.

fights with gods and protecting the cowherd etc. Particularly according to Harivaṃśa, Kṛṣṇa is Brahman, the Ancient One, the Immeasurable, the highest, the undecaying, eternal, self-born, the mysterious self, the beyond of the beyond and the original creator.[1] He has the form of *sattva* and yet is beyong *prakṛti* and the *guṇas*. He is both the effective and material cause of the universe and it is from him and by him that the universe arises and perishes.[2] Sheth concludes his study with the following words:

> Thus, we witness an evolution in the understanding of the divinity of Kṛṣṇa ... not only through the many-faceted development in the philosophical and theological comprehension of Kṛṣṇa's divine nature, but also through the handling of various episodes in the life of Kṛṣṇa. Through the process of omission, transformation and removal of blemishes in the picture of of Kṛṣṇa, through hymns and spiritual discourses...present a progressively more divine portrait of Kṛṣṇa.[3]

The way the devotees and theologians of the later Kṛṣṇa tradition handle the episodes individually and in combination without worrying about the perceived evolution or progression is remarkable. The imagination is so creative that the Vaiṣṇava theologian Rāmānuja compares the brightness in the face of Brahman or God (with the names and forms of Viṣṇu, Vāsudeva-Nārāyaṇa and Kṛṣṇa) to that of a thousand suns!

Summary

Jesus was a devout Jew, a religious teacher and prophet, who was confessed to be Messiah (Christ), the symbol of the Jewish hope for a fulfilling future. The related confession was that he was the Son of God, being one in will and purpose with the heavenly Father. But none of these names suggested he was equivalent to or the

---

[1] Sheth, Op. cit., 69ff.

[2] Ibid., 81.

[3] Ibid., 164.

totlality of God. As the Son of Man he claimed to have come from heaven to be in solidarity with the oppressed and marginalized and to represent them before the oppressors. Here too he was not seen as God. However, his 'I am sayings', the saying 'I and the Father are one' and Thomas' exclamation before him 'my Lord and my God' have the potential for misunderstanding. Even in his time on earth Jesus had to clarify to his opponents who criticized him for having claimed to be God and the clarification (e.g. ref. to 'gods' or angels) was not convincing. The most thorough and careful interpretations of John's opening words that Jesus was the enfleshment of the divine Word too have not subscribed to the position that Jesus was simply God. But this is not to deny that he embodied the divine presence, manifested God's will to liberate the oppressed, his relational and moral oneness with God and his openness to the unfolding of new perceptions and experiences of the Godhead.

In the case of Kṛṣṇa the accounts are varied and complicated to the extent of some scholars suggesting that there are more than one Kṛṣṇa in the Hindu texts. However, if we start from Mahābhārata, we get glimpses into his development from a hero of the Sātvata clan of the Yādava tribe with the bhāgavata cult, belonging to the cowherd community of Vṛndāvana. At a decisive movement, not without struggle and tension, he was incorporated into the Brāmaṇic fold as their spokesperson and adorable Lord. In the Bhagavad Gītā he appears to be multifaceted as the kinsman of both Pāṇdavas and Kauravas, charioteer of Arjuna, descent of God and the Lord of the universe. Of the different lists of the avatāras found in the purāṇas one or two mention him. Nevertheless, as far as the Bhāgavata Purāṇa is concerned, Kṛṣṇa is God supreme identical with Viṣṇu and Vāsudeva and there is some confusion about this identity. Combining in himself Supreme God (or incarnation of God) and the kinsman of Vṛndāvana as well as the lover of the gopīs, he appears to be youthful, beautiful, attractive, playful and having love games with the gopīs, thus supreme and intimate.

Chapter 4

Selections from St John's Gospel Pertinent to Kristu Bhakti

Introduction to the Fourth Gospel

The idiosyncratic St John's Gospel is among the best known, most extensively studied books in the New Testament. 'It became customary to describe the Fourth Evangelist as "the greatest of the followers of Paul," and his work "deutro-Pauline". Yet it was original and creative.'[1] It has 'stirred minds, hearts, and imaginations from Christianity's earliest days.'[2] And the 'Christology and theology of the Gospel provided the raw material out of which the great Christian doctrines were forged.'[3] More significantly, it has been suggested to take the Gospel of John as parallel to the Hindu bhakti literature as evident in Johannine scholar B.F. Westcott's wish and Indian theologian A.J. Appasamy's pioneering fulfillment. Its nature and history

[1] C.H. Dodd, *The Interpretation of the Fourth Gospel*, Cambridge: At the University Press, 1963, 4, 6.

[2] Francis J. Moloney, *The Gospel of John*, Minnesota: The Liturgical Press, 1971, xi, 5.

[3] Ibid., 20.

have been hotly debated. Its priority, posteriority or simultaneity in relation to the Synoptic Gospels – Matthew, Mark and Luke – is still argued for.[1] It is commonly held that much of the Gospel's material was written by John, the beloved disciple of Jesus, to address the particular context of a Jewish-Christian community situated in a Greek milieu. It faced the dual challenge of persecution and harassment of a section of Jews on the one hand, and misunderstanding by Greeks about Jesus and his message, on the other. The conservative side of Rabbinic Judaism with Hellenistic influence continued to struggle about the exact nature and stature of the anticipated Messiah. At the same time the higher universalist religion of Hellenism expounded in the Hermetic literature, attributed to *Hermes Trismegistus,* was best suited to receive the gospel and later influence it. To address the new situation, Jesus is presented as making profound claims, giving long discourses and encouraging vulnerable folk, his disciples and those who believed the disciples' witness. It is held that the Fourth Gospel was written towards the end of the first century of the Christian era.[2]

John's Gospel follows neither a historical or chronological order, nor does it have a conceptual construction with sequential progression. Certain events are narrated in unexpected moments and locations. For example, the event of Jesus cleansing the temple at Jerusalem is recorded at the beginning of the Gospel following the miracle at Cana in Galilee of changing water into wine, which is reported only in John's Gospel, whereas the other three Gospels place the events in the temple towards the end of his ministry, following the dramatic procession into Jerusalem. Similarly, there are factual inconsistencies in certain popular narratives. For example, in the twelfth chapter, it is written, Jesus was anointed by his friend Mary at Bethany and she poured an expensive perfume

---

[1] For a detailed discussion see John A.T. Robinson, *The Priority of John*, London: SCM, 1985, 3ff.

[2] It was written 'not earlier than AD 90.' Jose Maniparampil, *The Gospel According to the Beloved Disciple*, Bangalore: Claretian Publications, 2011, 27f; 'was probably written at the turn of the century,' Francis J, Moloney, Op. cit., 5.

on his feet and wiped his feet with her hair. This event precedes the triumphal entry in which palm branches were used. In the case of the other three Gospels, it succeeds the entry where 'palm' is not mentioned and Matthew and Mark simply note 'a woman' and she poured the perfume on Jesus' *head* and Luke 'a sinful woman' poured the perfume on his *feet*. Above all, the lengthy debate with some hostile Jews and long discourses in order to comfort and instruct his disciples occur only in John's Gospel.

We carefully make selections from the fourth Gospel that will compare to the Rāsalīla section of the Bhāgavata Purāṇa regarding the nature and function of bhakti.

Cosmic and Creative Word

Unlike any of the other Gospel writers, John opens his Gospel with a metaphysical affirmation: 'In the beginning was the Word, and the Word was with God, and the Word was God. He was with God in the beginning. Through him all things were made; without him nothing was made that has been made. In him was life, and that life was the light of men. The light shines in the darkness, but the darkness has not understood it' (1: 1-5). The immediate continuation is interrupted by a note on John the Baptist's witness to the Word as light and a clarification that he himself was not the light. The affirmation continues: 'The true light that gives light to every man was coming into the world' (1: 9). The affirmation continues: 'He was in the world, and though the world was made through him, the world did not recognize him. He came to that which was his own, but his own did not receive him. Yet to all who received him, to those who believed in his name, he gave the right to become children of God – children born not of natural descent, nor of human decision or a husband's will, but born of God' (1: 10-13).

'The Word became flesh and made his dwelling among us. We have seen his glory, the glory of the one and only Son, who came from the Father, full of grace and truth' (1: 14). 'Out of his fullness we have all received grace in place of grace already given. For the law was given through Moses; grace and truth came through Jesus

Christ. No one has ever seen God, but the one and only Son who is himself God and is in the closest relationship with the Father, has made him known' (1: 16-18). Later, it is clarified that those who hate light and love darkness, is evil and exposed (3: 19-21). The whole affirmation is made in the context of a concept held as potent, dynamic, creative and eternal by either the Jews or the Greeks or both.

The Witness of John the Baptist

Confessing his own inferior status, John the Baptist, seeing Jesus coming toward him, declared 'Look, the Lamb of God, who takes away the sin of the world! This is the one I meant when I said, "A man who comes after me has surpassed me because he was before me." I myself did not know him, but the reason I came baptizing with water was that he might be revealed to Israel' (1: 29-31). 'Then John gave this testimony: 'I saw the Spirit come down from heaven as a dove and remain on him. I would not have known him, except that the one who sent me to baptize with water told me, "The man on whom you see the Spirit and remain is he who will baptize with the Holy Spirit." I have seen and I testify that this is the Son of God' (1: 32-34). At one point it appeared that Jesus was gaining and baptizing more disciples than John, although, as clarified, it was not Jesus who baptized, but his disciples. When Jesus learned of this, he left Judea and went back once more to Galilee' (4: 1-3). When, after escaping from those hostile Jews, Jesus went to where John was baptizing, and the people said, 'Though John never performed a miraculous sign, all that John said about this man was true and in that place many believed in Jesus' (10: 41f). The introduction of John the Baptist suggests that members of his movement or his disciples tended to claim that their master was superior to Jesus. However, John, the Gospel writer, seems to have settled the matter by presenting the Baptist affirming himself as only the forerunner of Jesus.

Born of the Spirit

In his conversation with Nicodemus, a Pharisee and member of the Jewish ruling council, who came to Jesus at night, Jesus made a distinction between a member of a religious tradition and being born again or born from above to see the kingdom or reign of God (3: 3). It was not a physical birth but a spiritual one, the total transformation or a new orientation in life (3: 5). It is being caught up by the Spirit who like the wind blows wherever it pleases. We hear its sound, but cannot tell from where it comes or where it is going. So, it is with everyone born of the Spirit' (3: 8). It implies a commitment on the part of someone who has been allowed to be led by the cosmic Spirit but without knowing the future of the journey. Jesus' own disciples too were expected to join this journey though there were moments of confusion and tension.

The Disciples

One day two unnamed disciples of John the Baptist stood with their leader as Jesus was passing. John exclaimed 'Look here is the Lamb of God', whereupon the two disciples followed Jesus. They called him 'Rabbi' and wanted to know where Jesus was staying. Continuing to follow Jesus the two stayed with him (not noted where!). One was Andrew who brought his brother Simon (Cephas or Peter) to Jesus. The following day Jesus called Philip and Philip found Nathaniel in the context of a dialogue (1: 35-49). The call of all the twelve is not mentioned. Following Jesus' teaching on the bread of life, finding it hard, many of his disciples left him, never to return (6: 60, 66). Jesus asked if the 'Twelve' (first time this number) also wanted to go. Peter said, 'Lord to whom shall we go? You have the words of eternal life. We believe and know that you are the Holy One of God' (6: 68f). There is a note that Jesus chose the twelve but one of them (Judas) was a devil who would later betray him (6: 70f).

To the Jews who believed him, Jesus said: 'if you hold on my teaching you will be my disciples. And then you will know the truth, and the truth will set you free' (8: 31f). The 'truth' of course was not the pleasures and fancies of the world but experiencing the cost of discipleship in the context of struggling against the powers of evil and injustice, both religious and secular.

When the time of his cruel death was approaching, Jesus comforted his disciples: 'Do not let your hearts troubled. Trust in God; trust also in me. In my Father's house are many rooms; if it were not so, I would have told you. I am going there to prepare a place for you. And if I go and prepare a place for you, I will come back and take you to be with me that you also be where I am. You know the way to the place where I am going' (14: 1-4). When Thomas said they did not know the way, Jesus answered, 'I am the way and the truth and life. No one comes to the Father except through me. If you really know me, you will know my Father as well. From now on you know him and have seen him' (14: 6-7). Philip asked him to show the Father. After chiding him Jesus said, 'anyone who has seen me has seen the Father...Don't you believe that I am in the Father, and that the Father is in me? The words I say to you are not just my own. Rather, it is the Father, living in me, who is doing his work. Believe me when I say that I am in the Father and the Father is in me; or at least believe on the evidence of the miracles themselves. I tell you the truth, anyone who has faith in me will do what I have been doing. He will do even greater things than these, because I am going to the Father. And I will do whatever you ask in my name, so that the Son may bring glory to the Father. You may ask anything in my name, and I will do it' (14: 9-14). 'Peace I leave with you; my peace I give you. I do not give to you as the world gives. Do not let your hearts be troubled and do not be afraid' (14: 27). We will come back later to the intimacy between the Father God and Jesus and between them and the disciples in connection with transformation activities.

Jesus also told his disciples, 'If you love me, you will obey what I command. And I will ask the Father, and he will give you another Counselor to be with you for ever – the Spirit of truth. The world cannot accept him, because it neither sees him nor knows him. But you know him, for he lives with you and will be in you. I will not leave you as orphans; I will come to you. Before long the world will not see me anymore, but you will see me. Because I live you also will live. On that day you will realise that I am in my Father, and you are in me, and I am in you. Whoever has my commands and obeys them, he is the one who loves me. He who loves me will be loved by my Father, and I too will love him' (14: 15-21). The vulnerability and promise of discipleship stated here was experienced by the disciples in complex stages.

Separation was unavoidable in the life of discipleship but there was ample scope for hope. Jesus said, 'I am going away and I am coming back to you. If you love me, you would be glad that I am going to the Father, for the Father is greater than I. I have told you now before it happens, so that when it does happen you will believe. I will not speak to you much longer, for the prince of the world is coming. He has no hold on me, but the world must learn that I love the Father and that I do exactly what my Father has commanded me' (14: 28-31). Even at the emotional points of realising the separation and reunion Jesus seems to have no doubt about the love with God, obedience to commands and action for transforming the world should continue to be the connecting links.

In his long prayer Jesus expressed his concern about his disciples when he said to his Father God: 'I have revealed to those whom you gave me out of the world. They were yours; you gave them to me and they have obeyed your word. Now they know that everything you have given me and they accepted them. They knew with certainty that I came from you, and they believed that you sent me. I pray for them. I am not praying for the world, but those you have given me, for they are yours. All I have is yours, and all you have is mine. And glory has come to me through them. I will remain in the world no longer, but they are still in the world, and I am coming to you. Holy Father, protect them by the power of your name – the name you gave me – so that they may be one as we are one. While I was with them, I protected them and kept them safe by that name you gave me. None has been lost except the one doomed to destruction so that Scripture would be fulfilled' (17: 6-12).

'I am coming to you now, but I say these things while I am still in the world, so that they may have the full measure of my joy within them. I have given them your word and the world has hated them, for they are not of the world. My prayer is not that you take them out of the world but that you protect them from the evil one. They are not of the world even as I am not of it. Sanctify (*set apart for sacred use or make holy*) them by the truth. As you sent me into the world, I have sent them into the world. For them I sanctify myself, that they too may be truly sanctified' (17: 13-19). Not to be corrupted by the evil forces of the world, was Jesus' main concern about his disciples.

Apart from the twelve disciples, there were some other kind of disciples: four women at the cross including Mary his mother who was entrusted to his beloved disciple John (19: 25-27). Joseph of Arimathaea was a secret disciple, accompanied by Nicodemus, who arranged for burial with spices (19: 38-40). We will note later the risen Jesus appearing to his disciples and commissioning them for continued mission.

Eternal Life

What is the goal of life? More than any other, John's gospel uses the term 'eternal life' while using the expression 'kingdom of God' as well. To see the kingdom of God (3:3) and to enter it (3. 5) one has to be born again. Everyone who believes in the Son of Man may have eternal life (3: 15). The principal verse that is repeatedly quoted is: 'For God so loved the world that he gave his one and only Son, that whoever believes in him shall not perish but have eternal life' (3: 16).

In response to the Samaritan woman's surprising question Jesus said, 'Everyone who drinks this water will be thirsty again, but whoever drinks the water I give him will never thirst. Indeed, the water I give him will become in him a spring of water welling up to eternal life' (4: 13f). The Father loves the Son and shows him all he does. He will show him greater things. Just as the Father raises the dead and gives them life, even so the Son gives life to whom he is pleased to give it. The Father honours the Son and has entrusted all judgment to the Son (5. 20ff).

To a group of Jews Jesus said: 'You diligently study the Scriptures because you think that by them you possess eternal life.

These are the Scriptures that testify about me. Yet you refuse to come to me to have life' (5: 39f). When crowds approached him for miraculous food for the body, Jesus asked them to work for food for eternal life (6: 27). He claimed that those who believed in him had eternal life and Peter once confessed saying, 'You have the words of eternal life' (6: 47, 68).

Using the images of shepherd and sheep, Jesus said, 'My sheep listen to my voice; I know them, and they follow me. I give them eternal life, and they shall never perish; no one can snatch them out of my Father's hand' (10: 27f). The man who loves his life will lose it, while the man who hates his life in this world will keep it for eternal life (12: 25). 'I know that his command leads to eternal life. So, whatever I say is just what the Father has told me to say' (12: 50). Jesus prayed to God: 'Father, the time has come. Glorify your Son, that your Son may glorify you. For you granted him authority over all people that he might give eternal life to all those you have given him. Now this is eternal life: that they may know you, the only true God, and Jesus Christ, whom you have sent' (17: 1-3). This seems to have been one of the confessions of the early church as Jesus places himself in the third person.

Believing, Having Faith and Trusting Jesus or his Name, what do they Mean?

We have already noted the word 'believe' as a necessary condition for one to get eternal life. When Jesus spoke of earthly things (bird, wind, spirit) and his audience did not believe, he asked how they would believe if he spoke of heavenly things. Everyone who believed would not perish but have eternal life. But those who did not believe they were condemned, because they did not believe in the name of God's one and only Son (3: 12-18).

Jesus asked the Samaritan woman to believe him that the time was coming when all people everywhere will worship God in spirit and truth (4: 21-24). By her testimony many of the Samaritans believed in Jesus and because of his own word many more became believers (4: 39, 41). Before healing a royal official's son Jesus said: 'Unless you people see miraculous signs and wonders you will never believe' (4: 48). After the healing the official and all his household believed (4: 53). To believe the word of Jesus was to believe God who had sent him, and thus to escape condemnation (5: 24, 38). Those who were religious and honoured one another would make no effort to receive the praise from God (5: 44). If they believed Moses they would have believed Jesus too (5: 46).

Jesus appeared to be weary of getting people to believe. In response to people's question about what they should do, Jesus insisted that they believe in the one God had sent (6: 29). 'He who believes in me will never be thirsty...you have seen me but still you do not believe' (6: 35f). 'I tell you the truth, he who believes has eternal life' (6: 47). To the arguing Jews about his mention of (the symbolic) eating his flesh, Jesus said, 'unless you eat the flesh of the Son of Man and drink his blood, you have no life in you. Whoever eats my flesh and drinks my blood has eternal life, and I will raise him up at the last day' (6: 53f).

Whoever believed in him, with scriptural authority Jesus said that streams of living water will flow from within him. By this he meant the Spirit, whom those who believed in him were later to receive (7: 37-39). Once some Pharisees asked the temple guards, 'Has any one of the rulers or of Pharisees believed in him?' (7: 48). If they did not believe that he was the one he claimed to be, Jesus warned saying that 'they would die in their sins' (8: 24). To the Jews who believed him, Jesus said that if they held on his teaching they would be his disciples (8: 31). A passionate plea: 'I am telling the truth, why don't you believe me?' (8: 46). To the one whom he healed of his blindness and who was thrown out by the religious authorities Jesus asked, 'do you believe in the Son of Man? The man wanted to know who he was and Jesus 'the one who speaks to you' and immediately he said, 'Lord I believe' and worshipped him (9: 35ff).

Once a group of Jews asked Jesus to tell them plainly if he was the Christ. He answered, 'I did tell you, but you do not believe. The miracles I do in my Father's name speak for me, but you do not believe because you are not my sheep' (10: 25f). When, after escaping from the hostile Jews, Jesus went to where John was baptizing. 'And in that place many believed in Jesus' (10: 41f).

Before raising Lazarus Jesus said, 'I am the resurrection and the life. He who believes in me will live, even though he dies; and whoever lives and believes in me will never die. Do you believe this (Martha)? (11: 25-26). "I believe that you are the Christ, the Son of God, who was to come into the world" (11: 27). To Martha: 'Did I not tell you that if you believed, you would see the glory of God? Following the raising of Lazarus, and many put faith in Jesus, the Pharisees called a meeting of the Sanhedrin and said, 'If we let him go on like this, everyone will believe him, and then the Romans will come and take away both our place and our nation' (11: 48). Even after many miraculous signs, the Jews did not believe in him (12: 37). They did not believe because as the prophet said 'who shall believe?'(Is. 53:1) and 'he has blinded their eyes' (6: 10; Jn. 12: 37-40). Isaiah spoke this because he saw Jesus' glory (12: 41) 'Yet at the same time many even among leaders believed in him' (12: 42). Yet they would not confess fearing their excommunication. Jesus cried out that those who believed in him believed in the one who had sent him (12: 44f). 'Don't you believe that I am in the Father, and that the Father is in me? The words I say to you are not just my own. Rather, it is the Father, living in me, who is doing his work. Believe me when I say that I am in the Father and the Father is in me; or at least believe on the evidence of the miracles themselves. I tell you the truth, anyone who has faith in me will do what I have been doing' (14: 10-11). Similar occurrences of the word 'believe' are many more (14. 28f; 16. 9, 27, 30; 17. 8, 20f; 20. 29). In almost all the cases the insistence is that people should believe that Jesus was sent by God, used by God and raised by God.

The concluding words of the Gospel itself states that 'these are written that you may believe that Jesus is the Christ, the Son of God, and that by believing you may have life in his name' (20: 31).

In a context of controversy over Jesus as Christ and of his enemies trying to seize him, it is noted, 'Still many in the crowd put their faith in him' (7: 31). Even as he spoke, many put their faith on him (8: 30). Many of the Jews who witnessed Jesus raising his friend Lazarus from the dead put their faith in him (11: 45; 12: 11). 'I tell you the truth, anyone who has faith in me will do what I have been doing' (14: 12). Here 'faith' is not radically different from 'belief.' It is a sure confidence and concrete commitment.

The word 'trust' occurs very rarely. After talking about walking in light and darkness, Jesus said, 'Put your trust in the light while you have it' (12: 36). In his farewell address Jesus told his disciples, 'Trust in God; trust also in me' (14: 10).

Believing or belief is more used by religious communities but less understood. When we start the classical creeds with the words 'we believe' we mean 'we affirm.' In the comparative religion the real meaning of 'belief' is not defined to the satisfaction of all.[1] In the above section, Jesus appears to struggle rather desperately to be believed in the sense of having his claims that he was from God and though he was not God himself came very close to that position accepted. This confused the Jews who were strictly monotheistic; so also his disciples some of whom left him. The words 'faith' and 'trust' seem to be identical with 'belief' as far as the fourth Gospel is concerned. In the Synoptic Gospels 'faith' also had the meaning of being able to move on, to swim against the currents, and to change though it was implied in John (e.g. Mtt. 8: 10; 15: 28; Mk. 2: 5; 5: 34; Lk. 17: 19; 18: 42). Jesus found this 'great' faith in certain individuals outside the Jewish fold. We may understand what Jesus practically meant by these words when we deal with them in connection with other events and words.

---

[1] Wilfred Cantwell Smith (1916 – 2001), a Canadian missionary, theologian and promoter of the comparative study of religion with a dialogical openness, proposed a distinction between belief and faith. For him, belief is part of the cumulative tradition but faith is the fundamental ability, even an urge, shared by all humans, including religious persons, to transcend. See W. C. Smith, *Towards a World Theology*, London: Macmillan, 1981, p. 190ff. However, there are difficulties to accept his distinction between belief and faith with reference to the use of these terms which have particular meanings in different religious traditions. Therefore, his assertions have not been accepted by many scholars.

The Transcendent Power of Jesus

We have already noted some of the claims of Jesus in relation to his disciples, Jewish enemies and the words belief, faith and trust. Though he looked ordinary, at times he made extraordinary claims. For example, he said: 'I have food to eat that you know nothing about…My food is to do the will of him who sent me and to finish his work' (4: 32, 34). Also he performed some miracles as signs of the new dispensation of God being inaugurated by his ministry. They are, changing the water into wine in Cana (2: 1-11), healing an official's son (4: 46-53), healing a 38 years paralytic at the pool of Bethesda in Jerusalem (5: 1-14), feeding the five thousand (6: 1-13), walking on the stormy water (6: 16-21), healing a man born blind (9: 1-41) and raising Lazarus from dead out of compassion for his sisters (11). Healing the paralytic and the blind man took place on a Sabbath and hence raised a controversy.

When people saw the miraculous sign that Jesus did, they began to say, 'Surely this is the Prophet who is to come to the world.' Jesus, knowing that they intended to come and make him king by force, withdrew again to a mountain by himself' (6: 14f). When his heart was troubled, he wanted to glorify the Father by fulfilling the purpose and said, 'Father glorify your name.' Then a voice came from heaven saying 'I have glorified it, and will glorify again.' The crowd that was there and heard it said it had thundered; others said an angel had spoken to him. Jesus said, 'This voice was for your benefit, not mine. Now is the time for judgment on the world; now the prince of this world will be driven out. But, I, when I am lifted up from the earth, will draw all men to myself. He said this to show the kind of death he was going to die' (12: 28-33). Later, at the time of his arrest, when the authorities and soldiers said that they wanted Jesus of Nazareth, he said 'I am he' but they drew back and fell to the ground (18: 6). But he did not escape the arrest, trial and crucifixion!

The resurrection was the greatest miracle. After his resurrection Jesus had the ability to get into a locked room (20: 19). Also a miraculous catch of one hundred fifty three fish is noted in the last, appended chapter (21: 7-10).

Claims of Jesus

Because of his having healed on the Sabbath some Jews hated Jesus. He said to them: 'My Father is always at work to this very day, and I, too, am working.' For this reason the Jews tried all the harder to kill him; not only was he breaking the Sabbath, but even was calling God his own Father, making himself equal with God. Jesus spoke to them: 'I tell you the truth, the Son can do nothing by himself; he can do only what he sees his Father doing because whatever the Father does the Son also does. For the Father loves the Son and shows him all he does. Yes, to your amazement he will show him even greater things than these. For just as the Father raises the dead and gives them life, even so the Son gives life to whom he is pleased to give it. Moreover, the Father judges no one, but has entrusted all judgment to the Son, that all may honour the Son just as they honour the Father, who sent him' (6: 19-23). He also told the truth that 'a time is coming and has now come when the dead will hear the voice of the Son of God and those who hear will live. For as the Father has life in himself, so he has granted the Son to have life in himself. And he has given him authority to judge because he is the Son of Man' (5: 25-27). The following verse notes that the time is coming when those in grave will hear his voice and they will be judged according to good and evil. Jesus claims that his judgment will be just as he seeks to please him who sent him. He refers to the testimony of John the Baptist and his Father himself (5: 31ff).

While teaching in the temple, following a controversy over 'Christ' Jesus cried out, 'Yes, you know me, and you know where I am from. I am not here on my own, but he who sent me is true. You do not know him, but I know him because I am from him and he sent me' (7: 28f). On the last and greatest day of the festival (Feast of Tabernacles) Jesus stood and said in a loud voice: 'If anyone is thirsty, let him come to me and drink. Whoever believes in me, as the Scripture has said, streams of living water will flow from within him.' By this he meant the Spirit, whom those who believed in him were later to receive (7: 37-39).

Jesus spoke again to the people and said: 'I am the light of the world. Whoever follows me will never walk in darkness, but will have the light of life' (8: 12). The Pharisees challenged his self-witness and testimony. Jesus answered: 'Even if I testify on my own behalf, my testimony is valid, for I know where I came from and where I am going. But you have no idea where I come from or where I am going. You judge by human standards; I pass judgment on no one. But if I do judge, my decisions are right, because I am not alone. I stand with the Father, who sent me. In your own Law it is written that the testimony of two men is valid. I am one who testifies for myself; my other witness is the Father, who sent me' (8: 14-18). When they asked 'where is your father?' Jesus answered 'You do not know me or my Father… If you know me, you would know my Father also' (8: 19f). Where is the location of the Father? Jesus said that they cannot come there. When he said that he was going away his opponents wondered if he would kill himself (8: 21f).

Jesus continued saying, 'You are from below; I am from above. You are of this world; I am not of this world. I told that you would die in your sins; if you do not believe that I am the one that claim to be, you will indeed die in your sins' (8: 23-24). When they asked again, 'Who are you?' he answered, 'Just what I have been claiming all along…I have much to say in judgment of you. But he who sent me is reliable and what I have heard from him I tell the world' (8: 25-26). When they said they did not understand about Father, Jesus said, 'When you have lifted up the Son of Man, then you will know that I am the one I claim to be and that I do nothing on my own but speak just what the Father has taught me. The one who sent me is with me; he has not left me alone, for I always do what pleases him' (8: 28-30). Even as he spoke many put their faith in him (8:30).

In the controversial debate with a group of Jews who judged him to be a Samaritan and demon-possessed, Jesus said: 'I am not possessed by a demon…but I honour my Father and you dishonor me. I am not seeking glory for myself; but there is one who seeks it and he is the judge. I tell you the truth, if any one keeps my word, he will never see death' (8: 49-51). 'If I glorify myself, my glory means nothing. My Father whom you claim as your God, is the one who glorifies me. Though you do not know him, I know him. If I said I did not, I would be a liar like you, but I do know him and keep his word. Your father Abraham rejoiced at the thought of seeing my day; he saw it and was glad' (8: 54-56). When the Jews questioned his age and claim of knowing Abraham, Jesus continued saying, 'I tell you the truth…before Abraham was born, I am' (8: 58).

'I am the gate for the sheep. All who came before me were thieves and robbers, but the sheep did not listen to them. I am the gate; whoever enters through me will be saved. He will come in and go out, and find pasture. The thief comes only to steal and kill and destroy; I have come that they may have life, and have it to the full' (10: 7-10).

'I am the good shepherd. The good shepherd lays down his life for the sheep. The hired hand is not the shepherd who owns the sheep. So, when he sees the wolf coming, he abandons the sheep and runs away. Then the wolf attacks the flock and scatters the sheep. The servant runs away because he is a hired hand and cares nothing for the sheep' (10: 11-13). 'I am the good shepherd; I know my sheep and the sheep know me - just as the Father knows me and I know the Father – and I lay down my life for the sheep. I have other sheep that are not of this sheep pen. I must bring them also. They too will listen to my voice, and there shall be one flock and one shepherd. The reason my Father loves me is that I lay down my life – only to take it up again. No one takes it from me, but I lay it down on my own accord. I have authority to lay it down and authority to take it up again. This command I received from my Father' (10: 14-18).

Understandably, Jesus' claim to special knowledge of and intimate relation with God bewildered his Jewish partners in debate. For them Jesus was blasphemous as he claimed to be God. Did he really make that claim? In any case, to make them more bewildered, Jesus, referred to Ps. 82: 6, ('I have called them gods'). As we remarked in the last chapter, the reference is irrelevant here because the context is God's judgment of those 'gods'(or 'rulers' or 'angels'?) who defended the unjust, wicked and victimizers and though they claimed to be 'gods and sons of the Most High', they will die like mere men and fall like every other ruler. If they said: 'to whom the word of God came – and the Scripture cannot be broken – what about the one whom the Father set apart as his very own and sent into the world? Why then do you accuse me of blasphemy because I said, "I am God's Son?" Do not believe me unless I do what my Father does. But if I do it, even though you do not believe me, believe the miracles, that you may know and understand that the Father is in me, and I in the Father' (10: 35-38).

'I am the resurrection and the life. He who believes in me will live, even though he dies; and whoever lives and believes in me will never die. Do you believe this (Martha)?' (11: 25-26).

Responding to the Greeks who came to the Feast Jesus said: 'The hour has come for the Son of Man to be glorified. I tell you the truth, unless a kernel of wheat falls to the ground and dies, it remains only a single seed. But if it dies, it produces many seeds. The man who loves his life will lose it, while the man who hates his life in this world will keep it for eternal life. Whoever serves me must follow me; and where I am my servant also shall be. My Father will honour the one who serves me' (12: 23-26).

Then Jesus declared: 'When a man believes in me, he does not believe in me only, but in the one who sent me. When he looks at me, he sees the one who sent me. I have come into the world as a light, so that no one who believes in me should stay in darkness' (12: 44-46). 'As for the person who hears my words but does not keep them, I do not judge him. For I did not come to judge the world, but to save it. There is a judge for the one who rejects me and does not accept my words; that very word which I spoke will condemn him on the last day. For I did not speak of my own accord, but the Father who sent me commanded me what to say and how to say it. I know that his command leads to eternal life. So, whatever I say is just what the Father has told me to say' (12: 47- 50).

In his farewell speech Jesus comforted his audience saying he was going and his disciples knew the way. When Thomas said they did not know the way, Jesus answered, 'I am the way and the truth and life. If you really know me, you will know my Father as well. From now on you know him and have seen him'(14: 7). A detailed exegesis[1] reveals that, as we briefly indicated in the last chapter, 'the way' here is not a shortcut nor easy nor broad nor implying any distance between two locations but the way of the cross, a guidance to the crucified mind of the Father God. Truth, for Jesus, is not a speculation, nor a package, nor a conceptual capsule but a pilgrimage of the Spirit with commitment and openness. The 'life' does not suggest a luxurious and carefree life but a life in its fullness which can be sustained only by sharing it with others at even the cost of sacrifice.

In the 15th chapter, Jesus compares his relationship with his disciples to that between the vine and the branches (vs1-8). There is deep intimacy and perpetual pruning but those branches that do not remain in Jesus and bear no fruit will be cut down and thrown into fire. Subsequently, Jesus speaks the finest verses in the Gospel. It is about love, love for God and love for each other. But to avoid any sentimental connotation, Jesus clarifies that this love requires obedience to the commandments and bearing fruit. It is like the love between close friends without having any secret between them. Going a step further, Jesus asserts there is no greater love than one lays down one's life for friends (vs 9-17). Further, forecasting persecution, Jesus comforts his disciples saying that 'the world' will hate and persecute them just as it has done to him and in turn to the Father as well. This hating is unjustified and throughout the history most righteous people have experienced this (vs 18-25; cf. Ps. 35: 19; 60: 4).

The Holy Spirit

At Jesus' baptism the Spirit came down as dove, as witnessed by the Baptist (1: 32-34). Later, Jesus promised that in the life of s/he

---

[1] See I. Selvanayagam, *Relating to People of Other Faiths: Insights from the Bible*, Thiruvalla: CSS-BTTBPSA, 2004, 228ff.

who believed in him 'streams of living water, the Spirit, will well up from him' though up to that time the Spirit in a special way had not been given, since Jesus had not yet been glorified (7: 39). In his farewell address, Jesus told his disciples that if they loved him and obeyed his commandments he would ask the Father, and he would give them another Counselor to be with them forever – the Spirit of truth. Not the non-accepting and non-obeying world but they knew him, 'for he lives with you and will be in you' (14: 16f). The Counselor, the Holy Spirit, 'who the Father will send in my name, will teach you all things and will remind you of everything I have said to you' (14: 25f). The Counselor, the Spirit of Truth, 'will testify about me. And you also must testify, for you have been with me from the beginning' (15: 26f).

Jesus said, 'It is for your good that I am going away. Unless I go away, the Counselor will not come to you; but if I go, I will send him to you. When he comes he will convict the world of guilt in regard to sin and righteousness and judgment: in regard to sin, because men do not believe in me; in regard to righteousness, because I am going to the Father, where you can see me no longer; and in regard to judgment, because the prince of this world now stands condemned...when the Spirit of truth comes, he will guide you into all truth. He will not speak on his own; he will speak only what he hears, and he will tell you what is yet to come. He will bring glory to me by taking from what is mine and making it known to you. All that belongs to the Father is mine. That is why I said the Spirit will take from what is mine and make it known to you' (16: 15). The moment of the Spirit's coming is unclear and is subjected to scholarly debate. However, finally at the end of his presence on the earth, the risen Jesus breathed on the disciples and said 'receive the Holy Spirit' (20: 22) and sent them on a mission. On the whole, the Spirit is internally present and externally manifests at particular occasions in different measures.

The Bread of Life

After feeding the 5000, when people sought after him, Jesus told them that they were not concerned about the miracle but wanting to eat in an easy way. 'Do not work for food that spoils, but for food that endures to eternal life, which the Son of Man will give you. On him God the Father has placed his seal of approval' (6: 27). People looking for a sign asked about the manna that their ancestors ate in the desert. Jesus answered: 'I tell you the truth, it is not Moses who has given you the bread from heaven, but it is my Father who gives you the true bread from heaven. For the bread of God is he who comes down from heaven and gives life to the world' (6: 32f). Jesus' denial of the manna feeding under the leadership of Moses is difficult to understand. Does he mean that living on the memory of the past without being open to the present amounts to the invalidity of a past tradition? Or does Jesus mean that it was his Father who enabled Moses to give the 'bread from heaven'? Besides, Jesus gives a long discourse on bread of life: 'I am the bread of life. He who comes to me will never go hungry, and he who believes in me will never be thirsty' (6: 35). Those the Father gives him Jesus will accept and he will never turn anyone away (6: 37). 'For my Father's will is that everyone who looks to the Son and believes in him shall have eternal life, and I will raise him up at the last day' (6: 40).

How could Jesus claim that he came down from heaven since his father Joseph and mother Mary were well known? Jesus said: 'No one has seen the Father except the one who is from God; only he has seen the Father. I tell you the truth, he who believes has everlasting life. I am the bread of life. Your forefathers ate the manna in the desert, yet they died. But here is the bread that comes down from heaven. I am the living bread that came down from heaven. If anyone eats of this bread, he will live forever. This bread is my flesh, which I will give for the life of the world…I tell you the truth, unless you eat the flesh of the Son of Man and drink his blood, you have no life in you. Whoever eats my flesh and drinks my blood has eternal life, and I will raise him up at the last day. Whoever eats my flesh and drinks my blood remains in me, and I in him. Just as the living Father sent me and I live because of the Father, so the one who feeds on me will live because of me. This is the bread that came down from heaven. Your forefathers ate manna and died, but he who feeds on this bread will live forever.' He said this while teaching in the synagogue in Capernaum' (6: 46-59). For some Jews the language of 'eating my flesh and drinking my blood' was disgusting. Here creative imagination is required to discern the relational language of the poor. Even today such people in communities such as in slums and hills are addressed as 'flesh of flesh and blood of blood' which signifies close intimacy and solidarity. Moreover, Jesus' denial in this debate of Moses' bringing down bread from heaven is most interesting. One perception is that Jesus struggled with his religious community to convince them about something new happening in their history and in the pursuit of this new truth clinging to past stories can be not only doubted but also denied!

Separation/Disappearance

When some Pharisees sent temple police to arrest him Jesus said: 'I am with you for only a short time, and then I go to the one who sent me. You will look for me, but you will not find me; and where I am, you cannot come' (7: 33f). The leaders raised questions about this. Will he go to the Jews scattered among the Greeks? Following the claim of light and owning the Father's testimony, Jesus said to the Pharisees: 'I am going away, and you will look for me, and you will die in your sin. Where I go you cannot come' (8: 21). 'Is he going to kill himself?' the Jews asked. But the message of separation and reunion was meant for his disciples. 'My children, I will be with you only a little longer. You will look for me, just as I told the Jews, so I tell you now: Where I am going you cannot come' (13: 33). The same he had to repeat when Peter asked him along with warning of his denial (13: 36-38). Jesus promised: 'I will not leave you as orphans; I will come to you. Before long the world will not see me anymore, but you will see me. Because I live you also will live. On that day you will realize that I am in my Father, and you are in me, and I am in you. Whoever has my commands and obeys them, he is the one who loves me. He who loves me will be loved by my Father, and I too will love him' (14: 18-21).

Jesus further clarified: 'If you love me, you would be glad that I am going to the Father, for the Father is greater than I. I have told you now before it happens, so that when it does happen you will believe. I will not speak to you much longer, for the prince of the world is coming. He has no hold on me, but the world must learn that I love the Father and that I do exactly what my Father has commanded me' (14: 28-31). He expressed his concern about the possibility of his disciples going astray. 'I have told you all this to guard you against the breakdown of your faith. They will put you out of the synagogue, in fact, a time is coming when anyone who kills you will think he is offering a service to God' (16: 1-2). They do such things because they do not know the Father or me. I say this so that when time comes you will remember I warned you. 'I did not tell you this at first because I was with you' (16: 4). Now I am going to him who sent me but none of you have asked where I am going. You are filled with grief. It is good that I am going so that the Counselor can come (16: 5-6, 12). 'In a little while you will see me no more, and then after a little while you will see me' (16: 16). What is this 'little while'? The disciples kept asking about the character of his going away and coming back (16: 17-18). Knowing this Jesus told: 'I tell you the truth, you will weep and mourn while the world rejoices. You will grieve but your grief will turn to joy. A woman giving birth to a child has pain because her time has come; but when her baby is born she forgets the anguish because of her joy that a child is born into the world. So, with you; now is your time of grief, but I will see you again and you will rejoice, and no one will take away your joy. In that day you will no longer ask me anything. I tell you the truth, my Father will give you whatever you ask in my name. Until now you have not asked for anything in my name. Ask you will receive, and your joy will be complete' (16: 20-24).

Realising the difficulty of his disciples' understanding his speaking figuratively Jesus spoke plainly. 'That day I will not need to ask the Father on your behalf. He himself loves you' (16: 25f). The disciples responded saying 'now you speak plainly and we understand and believe you are from God' (16: 29f). Jesus retorted: 'at last you have believed, but the time is coming when you will be scattered each to his own home and you will leave me. Yet I am not alone, for my Father is with me' (16: 32). 'I have told you these things, so that in me you may have peace. In this world you will have trouble. But take heart! I have overcome the world' (16:32f). This part of a long discourse was reassuring and comforting for his disciples.

The Oneness between Jesus-the Father God-Disciples and Believers

We have already noted the close and concomitant relationship between Jesus and his heavenly Father in various contexts some of which became controversial, particularly on the question if he was God. We earlier discussed in detail the nature of the relationship and even 'oneness' between Jesus and his Father. Here we will consult the key supplementary verses. Leaving the task of judgment for the Father, Jesus said, 'For I did not speak of my own accord, but the Father who sent me commanded me what to say and how to say it. I know that his command leads to eternal life. So, whatever I say is just what the Father has told me to say' (12: 48- 50). 'I am telling you now before it happens, so that when it does happen you will believe that I am He. I tell you the truth, whoever accepts anyone I send accepts me; and whoever accepts me accepts the one who sent me' (13: 19-20). There was a claim of sharing in the glory of God: 'Now is the Son of Man glorified and God is glorified in him. If God is glorified in him, God will glorify the Son in himself, and will glorify him at once' (13: 32).

Philip asked Jesus to show them the Father. After chiding them he said, 'anyone who has seen me has seen the Father… Don't you believe that I am in the Father, and that the Father is in me? The words I say to you are not just my own. Rather, it is the Father, living in me, who is doing his work. Believe me when I say that I am in the Father and the Father in me' (14: 8f). The language of sharing the same concern, representating the Father, mutual glorification, remaining with the Father yet going to him etc suggests a plurality of meanings and a fixed doctrine is impossible. But more remarkably, the Father-Son intimacy is extended to the disciples and explained as mutual love in which obeying commandments takes place (14: 17-21). Responding a disciple's question about not showing his own self, Jesus said, 'If anyone loves me, he will obey my teaching. My Father will love him, and we will come to him and make our home with him. He who does not love me will not obey my teaching. These words you hear are not my own; they belong to the Father who sent me' (14: 23f). 'If you loved me, you would be glad that I am going to the Father, for *the Father is greater than* I. 'I love the Father and that I do exactly what my Father has commanded me' (14: 31).

We have already noted the simile of vine branches bearing fruit, which is followed by obedience to the commandments and the intimacy of deep friendship. The key is love shared between Jesus and his Father as also between Jesus and his disciples (15: 1-17). There was a limited time that Jesus had to intercede with his Father for his disciples, but he wanted to see a stage to the effect of him saying 'I will not ask the Father on your behalf. No, the Father himself loves you because you have loved me and have believed that I came from God' (16: 27). This was particularly important as Jesus was going to the Father.

Later, Jesus prayed to God: 'Father, the time has come. Glorify your Son, that the Son may glorify you. For you granted him authority over all people that he might give eternal life to all those you have given him. Now this is eternal life; that they know you the only true God, and Jesus Christ, whom you have sent. I have brought you glory on earth by completing the works you gave me to do. And now, Father, glorify me in your presence with the glory I had with you before the world began' (17: 1-5). 'Holy Father, protect them by the power of your name – the name you gave me – so that they may be one as *we are one*' (17: 11). Going a step further, Jesus said: 'My prayer is not for me alone. I pray also for those who will believe in me through their message, that all of them may be one. Father, just as you are in me and I am in you. May they also be in us so that the world may believe that you have sent me. I have given them the glory that you gave me that *they be one as we are one*: I in them and you in me. May they be brought to complete unity to let the world know that you sent me and have loved them even as you have loved me' (17: 20-23).

Just like love, knowledge also leads to oneness. Jesus prayed: 'Father, though the world does not know you, I know you. I know you, and they know that you have sent me. I have made you known to them, and will continue to make you known in order that the love you have for me may be in them and that I myself may be in them' (17: 25-26).

The resurrection of Jesus presented yet a new dimension of oneness. The risen Jesus told Magdalene Mary asking her to tell his disciples: 'I am returning to my Father and your Father, to my God and your God' (20: 17). Seeing the wounds of the risen Jesus Thomas exclaimed, 'My Lord and my God' (20: 28).

What kind of oneness do the above verses present? Is it an ontological oneness or identity of substance as claimed in Christian circles for a long time? We have already discussed in detail. Some Indian Christian theologians suggested different explanations. For example Keshub Chunder Sen clarified that it was not a material or a metaphysical oneness but a deep inner communion. Challenging the Calcedonian formula of *homoousios* (of the same substance) Appasamy holds that 'the union of Father and Son is rather a *moral* unity' as ultimately in eternity the Son conforms to the will of the Father. Appasamy also refutes the explanations in the monistic or non-dual (*advaita*) sense. He stresses that Jesus and the Father were in complete harmony in thought and purpose, or a union of love and work.[1] Then logically, the Holy Spirit should also have the same kind of relationship contributing to a dynamic and creative life of the Trinity, a vision which was yet tobe shaped fully.

It is not my purpose here to expand a discussion but to make a few observations. First, there is no fixed doctrine of oneness in the fourth Gospel; the descriptions are fluid and flexible. Second, the descriptions help us to be pluralistic in understanding oneness

---

[1] See Robin Boyd, *An Introduction to Indian Christian Theology*, Delhi: ISPCK, 2004 (first published in 1969), 119ff.

taking the dialogical context seriously. It makes sense that at some point Jesus says that he and the Father God are one, but at another point 'My Father is greater than I.' Third, the most distinctive vision of this oneness is functional, concurrent and collective. In the same understanding the oneness can be extended to the Holy Spirit as well. There is a chain of shared identity – Father God, Son Jesus, Guide Spirit and the disciples and those who believed the words of both Jesus and his disciples, which was in effect accepting the Father and the Spirit. What Jesus saw the Father doing he did with the help of the Spirit and the disciples had to follow the line. All of them were to join a mystical union which need not be construed as a static and ontic union, but dynamic and functional union.

Power and Servanthood

Countering a perception of authority ('the last temptation'), when the devil prompted Judas to betray him (13: 3), Jesus in the midst of his last dinner, stood up and began to wash the feet of his disciples. He showed them the full extent of his love (13:2). First it was not comprehensible for the disciples, but, as Jesus foretold, later they will understand. Jesus told Peter who refused to be washed, 'Unless I wash you, you have to part with me' (13: 8). That means, it was not a mere ritual wash. 'You call me "Teacher and Lord" and rightly so, for that is what I am. Now that I, your Lord and Teacher, have washed your feet, you also should wash one another's feet. I have set you an example that you should do as I have done for you. I tell you the truth, no servant is greater than his master, nor is a messenger greater than the one who sent him. Now that you know these things, you will be blessed if you do them' (13: 13-17). Jesus' dramatic event of washing the feet of his disciples as an antidote to being tempted by power (see 13: 2) and his exhortation to follow that in their ministry, suggests that the function of the churches and their members is not in the fashion of superficial humility and moral nicety but in the manner of challenging every kind of the domination and exploitation of power and authority. As the early Christians understood, it was the incarnational principle to be a slave or servant (Mk. 10: 45; Phil. 2: 5-11) and to disarm the powers and authorities (Col. 2: 15).

Love is still central to all that Jesus did and taught. John's preamble of Jesus' feet washing is indicative: 'Having loved his own who were in the world he now showed the full extent of his love'(13: 1). 'A new command I give you: Love one another. As I have loved you, so you must love one another. By this all men will know that you are my disciples, if you love one another' (13: 34-35). 'If you love me, you will obey what I command' (14: 15).

The Crucified and Risen Jesus

For Jesus love did not mean uncritical acceptance of all that happened to him and to others. His sharp criticism of the conservative religious leaders who forgot their origin of liberation and new life attracted enmity. The accusations in the trial such as that he said he would destroy the temple, spoke against paying tax to Rome and claimed to be the king of Jews, did not unnerve him to deviate from the truth. For instance, when one of the officials struck him on the face he did not turn the other cheek but asked him, 'If I said something wrong testify as what is wrong. But if I spoke the truth, why did you strike me?' (18: 23). He did not want an official to behave in such a way in a public place. While hanging on the cross, possibly in order to draw the attention of the indifferent soldiers, he said, 'I am thirsty' (19: 28). Finally, having received the drink, saying 'it is finished' Jesus 'bowed his head and gave up his spirit' (19: 30).

Of all the accounts of Jesus as risen only in John's Gospel does Jesus appear first to a woman and after that to others. Remarkably, John's accounts of the risen Jesus are rather obscure: as gardener (20: 15) and a stranger standing on the shore (21: 4). However, his appearance in the room behind the locked doors (20:19ff) was almost in a clear form which preceded to giving the Great Commission. Compared to the versions of the Great Commission found in other Gospels John's was the most dramatic and moving. Showing the wounds and breathing the Holy Spirit, he sent the disciples just as he had been sent by the Father. They had to go as representatives of victims with the inalienable right to forgive or not to forgive (20: 21-23). Thus, mission continued, not with a 'crusading mind but a crucified mind.'

In the final chapter which was obviously a late addition, the risen Jesus had a personal dialogue with Peter in which he pointed out that loving him more than others should find expression in taking up responsibility, i.e., feeding Jesus' lambs (21: 15-18). Though his end could be a martyrdom the final call too was 'Follow me' (21: 19).

Summary

St. John depicts Jesus in a unique manner in order to make an appeal to a particular context. The context was marked by a Christian community as persecuted by certain Jewish leaders who were surrounded by Hellenists. Jesus and his disciples came from a low stratum of the society, but they felt they had a mission to transform the society. The sign of this transformation was Jesus' miracles and his challenge to a conservative wing of the Jewish community. Jesus claimed himself to be the good shepherd and the gatc which was accessible and attractive to the lost sheep meaning those scattered or oppressed. He was the resurrection and life. He was the way, truth and life. Also he was the enfleshment of the eternal cosmic Word. He was one with the Father and did his will. Yet the Father was greater whom he obeyed and glorified. Love and liberative action by obeying the commandments alone can attest the loving intimacy with God. Jesus was unjustly crucified and vindicated by being raised from the grave by God the Father. The greatest point in the Gospel is the intimate relationship between God the Father and Jesus, the Holy Spirit and Jesus, Jesus and his disciples and finally a vision of a divine commune constituted by all of them.

Chapter 5

Highlights of the Rāsalīlā

Introduction

There can be little doubt that the Rāsalīlā (dance or play of divine love) is the finest section of the preeminent purāṇa (i.e., Bhāgavata) of the eighteen Mahāpurāṇas. Its description of the nature of Kṛṣṇa with enchanting beauty, the immense bhakti of the gopīs and their sporting with their Lord cannot but inspire an engaged reader. It is the 'sporting experience' that is central to the narrative. The section does not require the overall background of the whole purāṇa[1] and as a piece of literature it is wholesome in itself, though it might have an indirect appeal to a dying king.

---

[1] '*The recitation of the Bhāgavata is set in the forest of Naimiṣha. Because of the onset of the inauspicious age of Kaliyuga, which had begun after Kṛṣṇa had returned to his own divine abode, the sages were performing a 1,000-year sacrifice in order to attain Viṣṇu's divine abode. During the proceedings, they invite the sage Sūta to relate to them narrations concerning the appearance and activities of Lord Kṛṣṇa, since one is liberated even by uttering his name. Sūta narrates the Bhāgavata Purāṇa, which he had heard from the lips of Śuka when the latter had related it to king Parīkṣit, grandson of Arjuna and grand-nephew of Lord Kṛṣṇa...the last surviving member of the Yadu clan after the carnage of the Mahābhārata war, but had been cursed by a brāhmaṇa boy to die within seven days.' Having renounced the kingdom etc he was asking questions about*

In the last chapter we presented a summary of selections from St. John's Gospel with a rough classification. It was necessary because compared to the Rāsalīlā section, the Gospel is much longer with many details of activities and discourses much of which are not directly related to bhakti. But in the case of Rāsalīlā the material is shorter, coherent and progressive. Therefore we simply follow its narrative summarizing where the details are not necessary.

An Enchanting Atmosphere and Emotional Movement

The Rāsalīlā section of the Bhāgavata Purāṇa starts with a description of the blossoming of the autumnal jasmine, the moon arising in the east, covering the face of heavens with its copper-colored soothing rays, herald of the white night-lilies reddened with fresh vermilion powder, its splendor like the face of Lakṣmī, the goddess of fortune, and seeing a forest cloured by its silky rays. Kṛṣṇa plays his flute softly, capturing the hearts of the beautiful-eyed women (29: 1-3). God, the Bhagavān, decided to enjoy his pastime.

'The music aroused Kāma (god of love). When they heard it, the women of Vraj, enchanted by Kṛṣṇa, came to their lover, their earrings swinging in their haste, and unknown to one another' (29: 4). Some who were milking cows, putting milk on fire, serving food, attending to their husbands, eating, others putting on make-up, washing, applying mascara, feeding their babies, they all went to be near Kṛṣṇa, their clothes and ornaments being in disarray (29: 5-7). 'Their hearts had been stolen by Govinda, so they did not turn back when husbands, fathers, brothers and relatives tried to prevent them. They were in a state of rapture' (29: 8). Some gopīs, unable to go out, remained at home, completely absorbed in meditation. '(Their karma) from their impious deeds was destroyed by the intense and intolerable pain and separation

---

the ultimate duty, things to be done and remembered. In response, Śuka recited to him the Bhāgavata in the assembly of sages. Edwin Bryant, *Krishna: The Beautiful Legend of God (Śrīmad Bhāgavata Purāṇa Book X),* London: Penguin Books, 2003, 8.

from their lover, and their auspicious deeds were diminished by the complete fulfillment resulting from the intimate contact with Acyuta that they obtained through meditation. Their bondage was destroyed, and they immediately left their bodies made of the *guṇas*.[1] Uniting with the supreme Soul, they considered him their lover' (29: 10-11).

Kṛṣṇa as Supreme

Parīkṣit the Kuru king, asked Śuka: 'O sage, they related to Kṛṣṇa as their supreme lover, not as *brahman*, the absolute truth. So, how did the flow of *guṇas*, in which their minds were absorbed, cease for the *gopīs*?' (29:12). The answer: as previously explained with reference to how Kṛṣṇa's enemies attained perfection. What then of those dear to him? 'God appears for the supreme good of humanity…He is immeasurable and eternal. As the controller of the *guṇas*, he is beyond the *guṇas*. Those who always dedicate their desire, anger, fear, affection, sense of identity and friendship to Hari enter for certain into his state of being. You should not show such surprise at Lord Kṛṣṇa. He is unborn and the master of all masters of *yoga*. From him the whole universe attains liberation' (29: 14-16).

Kṛṣṇa's Initial Response to the Gopīs

Seeing the gopīs from Vraj who just arrived in his presence, Kṛṣṇa 'addressed them, captivating them with the charm of his words.' Welcoming them, asking about the wellbeing of the people in Vraj, he asked them what he can do to please them and what was the purpose of their coming. With a caring pastoral concern he warned

---

[1] The passing mention of the idea *guṇa* seems to be interrupting. However, the Sāṃkhya darśan which was associated with the Bhāgavatā as evident in the Bhagavad Gītā, is partially attested. According to Sāṃkhya, the three *guṇas* – *sattva*, *rajas*, and *tamas*, meaning respectively, pure and bright, energy and passion, darkness and dullness – are inherent in *prakṛti* and in the process of evolution of the universe they become the inhibiting and even impelling traits of the human mind. This will explain the question posed in 29: 14. But as far as God, the supreme Puruṣa, is concerned, he is not only immeasurable and eternal, but also the controller of the *guṇas* and beyond the *guṇas* as noted in 29: 14.

about the danger of the dark nights and ferocious creatures, noting, 'O slender-waisted ones, this place is not fit for women.' With a further note on the worry of their family and in any case that they had seen the beauty of the forest on the bank of Yamuna, he asked them to 'hurry now to the cow-pen and serve your husbands – you are chaste ladies. The babies and calves are crying; suckle them and milk them' (29: 17-22).

Kṛṣṇa stated further: 'Or perhaps your hearts are captivated, and you have come out of love for me. This is commendable of you - living beings delight in me. The highest *dharma*[1] (duty) of a woman is to serve her husband faithfully, to ensure the well-being of the relatives, and to nourish her children. A husband who is not a sinner, even though he be of bad character, ill-fated, old, dull-headed, sick or poor, should not be abandoned by women who desire to attain heaven. Without exception, the adultery of a woman of good birth does not lead to heaven. It is scandalous, fear-laden, worthless, fraught with difficulty and abhorrent. Love for me comes from hearing about me, seeing me, meditating on me and reciting my glories – not in this way, by physical proximity. Therefore return to your homes' (29: 23-27).

The gopīs found themselves unwelcome, dejected and their aspirations dashed, were inconsolable in their distress. 'They stood silently, their red *bimba*-fruit-coloured lips faded by their sighs, and the vermilion powder on their breasts smeared by the mascara carried by their tears. Casting down their faces out of sorrow and scratching the ground with their feet, they were weighed down by extreme unhappiness. Wiping their eyes and having checked their tears somewhat the *gopīs* spoke to Kṛṣṇa, their beloved, with voices faltering with agitation. They were utterly devoted, and had sacrificed all desires for his sake, but had replied to them as if he were anything but their beloved' (29: 28-30).

---

[1] In the Hindu tradition the Sanskrit term dharma is an extremely complex one for which there is no single English equivalent. It signifies behaviors that are considered to be in accord with rta, the cosmic order that makes life and universe possible, and includes duties, rights, laws, conduct, virtues and 'right way of living.'

The *gopīs* spoke to Kṛṣṇa: 'You should not speak to us in such a heartless fashion, O Lord. Renouncing all enjoyments of senses, we are devoted to the soles of your feet. Reciprocate, you obstinate one, just as the Lord, the original being, reciprocates with those who desire liberation. Do not reject us. You, the knower of *dharma*, have declared that the occupational *dharma* of women consists of attending to friends, husbands and children. Then let this be our *dharma* when it comes to you, the source of this advice, O Lord – after all, you are the soul within all relatives. Indeed, you are the most dear of all embodied beings. You are the eternal beloved, O soul of all, and so the learned place their affection in you. What is the use of husbands and children who simply cause problems? Therefore, O supreme Lord, be pleased with us. Do not dash our hopes. They have been sustained by you for such a long time, O lotus-eyed one. Our hearts which were absorbed in our households, have been stolen away with ease by you, as our hands from domestic chores. Our feet cannot move one step from the soles of your lotus feet. How can we go to Vraj? And, besides, what would we do there? (29: 31-34).

The gopīs continued: 'O beloved, pour the nectar of your lips on the fire dwelling in our hearts which has been kindled by your musical harmonies, your glances and your smiles. If you do not, we will traverse the path to your feet through meditation, our bodies consumed by the fire born of separation. Lotus–eyed Kṛṣṇa, you are dear to the forest-dwelling hermits. Somewhere or other, for a moment, we providentially touched the soles of your feet, which belong to the goddess of fortune. Alas, from that moment, instantly enamoured of you, we became incapable of remaining in the presence of any other man. The goddess of fortune aspires to the dust of those lotus feet which is worshipped by your servants, even though she has obtained a place on your chest along with Tulasī (holy basil). Other gods, even, strive to attract her personal glance. In the same way, we solicit the dust of your feet (29: 35-37). Acclaiming Kṛṣṇa as the banisher of distress, compassionate and worthy of worship, and acknowledging his beautiful feet, ornaments, strong arms, fearlessness, smiles and glances, the women of Vraj asked him to allow them to be at his feet. They asked him, 'what women in the three worlds would not stray from the behaviour proper to Āryans, when thrown into turmoil by the melodies of your flute, which vibrate harmoniously? And what woman would not stray after seeing this, your form, which brings good fortune to the three worlds and causes the hair of cows, birds, trees and deer to stand on end with bliss? It is clear that you have accepted birth to remove the tribulations and fear of Vraj just as the Lord, the primeval person, protects the denizens of heaven. Therefore, since you are the friend of the afflicted, place your lotus hands on the burning breasts and heads of your servants' (29: 38-41).

Kṛṣṇa, hearing their despairing words, 'laughed and engaged in amorous pleasures from compassion, even though his satisfaction is self-contained. Kṛṣṇa, the infallible one, whose conduct is upright, shone forth with the assembled *gopīs,* who were dazzling with jasmine teeth and broad smiles. As the *gopīs*' faces blossomed from the glances of their beloved, Kṛṣṇa appeared like the moon surrounded by stars. Praised in song, and singing loudly himself, the Lord of hundreds of women, wearing a garland of *vaijayantī* flowers (*a mythical flower offered as a garland to Kṛṣṇa and Viṣṇu in worship*), frolicked in the forest, making it beautiful. Accompanied by the *gopīs*, Kṛṣṇa approached the bank of the river. Its cool sand was swept by a wind bearing the scent of *kumuda* flowers and refreshing from its contact with the waves. Having aroused Kāma in the young women of Vraj with jokes, smiles and glances, playfully scratching their breasts, girdles, thighs, hair and hands with his nails, and embracing them with outstretched arms, he gave them pleasure' (29: 43-46). Because of such treatment of the supreme soul made the women proud. They thought of themselves as the best women in the world. In order to balance their pride Kṛṣṇa vanished from the spot of their first encounter.

Separation and Searching for Kṛṣṇa

When their Bhagavān suddenly vanished, the gopīs became filled with remorse and felt like female elephants having lost sight of the leader of the herd. Intoxicated by the overwhelming memory of the great time they had with their lover imitated what happened in their fellowship with him, smiles and movements, to the extent of saying 'I am he.' Becoming mad, they searched from grove to grove and asked the trees, plants, and even the wife of a deer about the whereabouts of Kṛṣṇa (30: 1-14). They were crazy acting like Kṛṣṇa taking different roles of acting including the infant Kṛṣṇa and playing flute and calling, another claiming to look like Kṛṣṇa, another offering protection from wind and rain, another climbing upon one, yet another one claiming that she incarnated and so on (30: 15-23). 'Inquiring thus after Kṛṣṇa from the creeping plants and trees of Vṛndāvana, the *gopīs* noticed the footprints of the supreme soul in a certain part of the forest.' 'These footprints are certainly those of the great soul, the son of Nanda (Kṛṣṇa's stepfather according to the Bhāgavata Purāṇa),' they said. 'They are recognizable from such marks as the flag, the lotus flower, the thunderbolt, the goad and the barley' (30: 24-25). Then they identified the footprints of a young woman and discussed about her and said 'She has worshipped Bhagavān Hari, the Lord. Consequently, Govinda (another name for Krsna, he pervades the world) was pleased, and so has abandoned us and led that *gopī* to a secluded place' (30: 26-28). There have been discussions about the unknown woman. One opinion is that she was Rādhā, the most beloved gopī of Kṛṣṇa. One of them said, 'Just see, O friends, how fortunate are of these particles of dust from the lotus feet of Govinda. Brahmā, Śiva and the goddess of fortune, Ramā (Śrī), place them on their heads to remove their sins' (30: 29). The purāṇic sectarianism is reflected here.

There is an internal dialogue among the women who wanted to investigate the identity of the strange footprints. 'The footprints of that woman causing us great distress because she alone of the *gopīs* is enjoying the lips of Acyuta (another name for Kṛṣṇa) in a secluded place. Now, right here her footprints are no longer visible:

the lover has lifted up his beloved, whose feet with their delicate soles are bruised the blades of grass. Look, *gopīs,* at these deeper footprints of lusty Kṛṣṇa weighed down by carrying the young woman. And here the beloved has been put down by that great soul in order to (gather) flowers. Look, here the lover has plucked flower for his beloved: 'these two footprints are incomplete because he stood on tip-toe. Here, lusty Kṛṣṇa decorated that lusty woman's hair. Surely he sat here making his lover a crown with those (flowers)' (30: 30-33).

'Kṛṣṇa took pleasure with that *gopī*, although he is complete, content within himself and delights in his own self. He was displaying the wretchedness of lusty men and women because of their depravity. The dispirited *gopīs* wandered about pointing (things) out in this way. The *gopī*, whom Kṛṣṇa had taken to the forest after abandoning the other women, then thought she was the best of all women: 'Kṛṣṇa, my beloved, has abandoned the (other) *gopīs* who were impelled by Kāma and dedicated himself to me.' Then, after going to a spot in the wood the proud woman spoke to Keśava (Kṛṣṇa): 'I am unable to walk any further. Take me wherever your mind (desires).' At this request Kṛṣṇa told his beloved that she should climb on his shoulder, but then he disappeared. The young woman was filled with remorse: 'O Lord, lover, dearest! Where are you? Where are you, mighty-armed one? Reveal your presence to me, friend - I am your miserable servant!' (30: 34-39).

'The *gopīs*, searching for the path of the *Bhagavān*, saw a distressed girl not far away who was disorientated by the separation from her beloved. Hearing the story of how she had first received respect from (Kṛṣṇa), and then humiliation because of her bad faith, they were astounded' (30: 40f). Then they went into the forest where there was moonlight and when darkness descended they returned. Their minds absorbed in Kṛṣṇa, the women's conversation again focused and activities centred on him, and they dedicated their hearts to him. 'Simply by singing about his qualities they forgot their own homes. Meditating on Kṛṣṇa, they reached the bank of the Kālindī (Yamunā) river again.

Gathering together they sang about Kṛṣṇa, longing for his arrival' (30: 42-44). A new experience was to dawn on them.

A Psalm of Praise and Prayer by the Gopīs (Ch. 31)

The gopīs said: 'Vraj has become preeminent because of your birth; indeed, Indrā (Lakṣmī) resides there permanently. O loved one, show yourself! Your devotees, whose lives are sustained you, are searching for you everywhere. You are taking our life, O Lord of autumn; your glance excels in beauty the heart of a beautiful lotus perfectly born in autumn from a pool of water. We are your maidservants (and do not ask for) any payment. Isn't this killing us, O bestower of favours?' (vv 1-2). The prayer continues to mention his protection from poisonous water, from wicked demon, winds, rains, fire, lightning, bull Ariṣṭa, son of Maya (Vyomāsura) and from fear from all sides (31:3). They continue:

'You are not, in fact, the son of a *gopī*. You are the witness of the inner self of all embodied beings. Being petitioned by Brahmā, you become manifest in the family of the Sātvatas (a tribe of Kṛṣṇa bhaktas descendent from the mythical King, Yadu), O friend, for the protection of the universe. Place your lotus hand on the head of those who have approached you of fear of the material world, O foremost of the Vṛṣṇi clan. Your hand, which holds the hand of Śrī (Lakṣmī), bestows fearlessness and fulfils desires, O lover' (31: 4-5).

They describe him as hero of women, who takes away the pain of the people of Vraj, who annihilates the pride of his devotees by his smile, to accept his maidservants and show them his beautiful lotus face. 'Place your lotus feet upon our breasts. Your feet have been placed on the hoods of the serpent (Kāliya) and follow the animals to the pasture. They are the abode of the goddess of fortune, Śrī, and they remove the sins of submissive embodied beings. Excise Kāma, who dwells within our hearts. O hero, these women obedient to your will are stunned by your sweet voice, your charming words which please the mind and the intelligence, and your lotus eyes. Reinvigorate us with the intoxicating liquid of your lips'(31: 6-8).

'Those who repeat the sweetness of your words in this world are munificent. These words are praised by poets, spread abroad, and are auspicious to hear. They are life-giving for those who are suffering. They remove sins and bring good fortune. Your bursts of laughter, pleasing looks of love, and pastimes are auspicious to contemplate. Those meetings in secret places touch our hearts, you cheater, and perturb us thoroughly. When you go out of Vraj for grazing you are distressed by grass that troubles us. You possess a lotus face surrounded by blue locks of hair which you constantly display covered with thick dust at the end of the day. You arouse Kāma in the heart, O hero. O lover, place your most magnificent lotus feet on our breasts. They fulfill the desires of the humble and should be meditated upon in trouble, O destroyer of anxiety. They are worshipped by the lotus-born Brahmā and are the ornament of the earth. Bestow upon us the nectar of your lips, thoroughly kissed by the flute as it plays music. It destroys sorrow, increases the pleasures of love, and cause men to forget other passions' (31: 9-14).

'When you, Lord, go to the forest during the day, a moment becomes a *yuga* (an epoch in a four age cosmic cycle) for those who do not see you. He who created eyelashes is dull-witted, from the perspective of those beholding your beautiful face, with its curled locks of hair. Acyuta, you are the knower of (people's) movements. Bewildered by your song, we have thoroughly neglected our husbands, sons, family, brothers and kinsfolk, and come before you. Who would abandon women in the night, you rogue? We have become unsettled from contemplating your broad chest, the abode of Śrī, the goddess of fortune, as well as your looks of love, your smiling face and the meetings in secret places which aroused Kāma. We long for you intensely all the time' (31: 15-17).

'Your incarnation is for the good of the universe, and dispels the distress of the people of Vraj. Deliver a little of that (medicine) which removes the ailment from the hearts of your devotees to us. Our hearts yearn for you. We gently place your tender lotus feet on our rough breasts with trepidation. You wander in the forest on them and our minds are disturbed: what if they have been hurt by small stones? Your Lordship is our life' (31: 18- 19).

Kṛṣṇa's Reappearance and the Gopīs' Reaction (Ch. 32)

The gopis sang and spoke incoherently, and longing for Kṛṣṇa, they wept loudly. 'Kṛṣṇa, the descendent of Śūra, bewilderer of mind of the mind-bewilderer Kāma himself, appeared in their midst, his lotus face smiling. He was wearing yellow garments, and bore a garland. Seeing that their beloved had returned, the women, their eyes wide with love, sprang up simultaneously as if the vital air of the body had returned' (32: 2-3).

Each one responded differently: one ecstatic woman caught hold of Kṛṣṇa's hand in her folded hands, placed his arm on her shoulder, accepted his chewed betel nut with folded hands, placed his feet on her breast, bit her lips with her teeth with her brows knitted in a frown and she glared at him 'as if she could strike him with a look of rebuke', another dwell on his lotus face with unblinking eyes, though drank not satisfied just as a saint is not fully satisfied with meditation, drew him in her heart, through the apertures of her eyes and then sealing them shut 'like a *yogī* immersed in bliss.' 'All rejoiced at the wonder of seeing Keśava (one of 24 names of Viṣṇu) and let go the distress they had felt at separation, as people are joyful after encountering a wise man' (32: 4-9).

'Bhagavān, Acyuta, surrounded by women who had shaken of their sorrow, shone brilliantly, like the supreme being surrounded by his *śakti* powers'. The supreme ruler took the women to the bank of the Yamuna River where there were six-legged bees and fragrance of blossoming jasmine and mandara (hibiscus) flowers; lapping of waves like hands of Kṛṣṇa; the darkness was dispelled by the full rays from the autumn moon. The headache of the women was replaced by the bliss of seeing Kṛṣṇa, just like the Vedas attained the culmination of the hearts' desire. The *gopīs* made a seat for the friend of their heart with their outer garments, which were smeared with the *kuṅkum* powder (made from either turmeric or saffron to be used for social and religious markings) from their breasts. '*Bhagavān*, the Lord, whose seat is fixed within the hearts of the masters of *yoga*, sat down there. He was worshipped as he sat in the company of the *gopīs*, and revealed himself in a form that was a unique embodiment of beauty in the three worlds. The women worshipped that inciter of Kāma by massaging his hands and feet, which they had placed on their laps. They praised him their eyebrows quivering, with playful looks and laughter. Then they spoke somewhat angrily'(32: 10-15).

Stating that some serve those who serve them and others in the opposite but some never serve, the *gopīs* asked their Lord if he could explain. *Śrī Bhagavān* said: 'Friends, there are those who serve each other reciprocally but their exchange is exclusively out of self-interest; there is no *dharma* or friendship there. Personal gain and nothing else is the motive. Those, like mothers and fathers, who serve those who do not serve (them) are truly compassionate. There is perfect friendship and *dharma* in this, O slender-waisted ones. Some do not serve even those who serve (them), let alone those who do not serve (them). They include those who take pleasure in their spiritual self, those whose desires are fulfilled, the ungrateful and the *guru*-haters. I do not serve even those beings who serve me to enhance their devotional state of mind, O friends. The case is like that of the poor man who is not conscious of anything else when the wealth that he had gained is lost, but continues to contemplate that wealth obsessively. In this way, O women, when I disappeared from your presence – you who had abandoned relatives, the (injunctions of the) Vedas, and the world for my sake – it was really to further (your dedication) to me. I was serving you. Therefore, beloved ones, you should not be displeased with your beloved. You have broken the enduring shackles of the household, and have served me. You are full of goodness and without fault, and I am unable to reciprocate, even in the lifetime of a god. Therefore, let your reward be your own excellence' (32: 17-22).

Moving Towards the Climax (Ch. 33)

Hearing the Lord's winning words, the gopīs relinquished their distress of separation and aspired to touch his limbs (33: 1). Govinda began his pastime there and the women linked arms happily together (33: 2). 'The festival of the *rāsa* dance began, featuring a circle of *gopīs*. The Lord of all *yogis*, Kṛṣṇa, inserted himself between each pair of *gopīs*, and put his arms about their necks. Each woman thought he was at her side only. Meanwhile, the sky was crowded with hundreds of the vehicles of the gods, who were accompanied by their wives and carried away with excitement (33: 3). Kettledrums resounded then, streams of flowers fell, and the chiefs of the *gandharvas* (celestial singers) and their wives sang of Kṛṣṇa's spotless glories' (33: 4). With tumultuous sound of bracelets etc the young women danced with their beloved (33: 5). 'Kṛṣṇa, *Bhagavān*, the son of Devaki was radiant in their company, like a great emerald in the midst of golden ornaments' (33: 6). It was a vigorous dancing with braids and belts fast secured, faces sweating and smiling, garments on their breasts slipping, waists bent, shining like a lightning in the clouds (33: 7). 'They were intent on amorous pleasure and overjoyed by Kṛṣṇa's touch. Their throat decorated with dye, they sang loudly as they danced, and the world reverberated with their songs' (33: 8). One *gopī* sang a duet in harmony and he praised her. Another was tired and her jasmine flowers and bracelets got loosened. Kṛṣṇa was standing by her side. He put his arm around one woman and smelt her blue lotus and sandal fragrance. Kṛṣṇa gave his chewed betel nut to another who kissed him next to his cheek. Another, fatigued, placed his hand on her breast (33: 9-13). 'The *gopīs* won their lover Acyuta, who is the exclusive beloved of Śrī, the goddess of fortune. Their necks encircled by his arms, they delighted in him as they sang' (33: 14). The *gopis* danced with glowing faces, adorned locks, to the musical accompaniment of bees and complimented by the sound of their bracelets and anklets; wreaths of flowers fell down from their hair (33: 15). 'Thus Kṛṣṇa, the Lord of Lakṣmī, sported with the beautiful girls of Vraj with freely playful smiles, amorous glances and with caresses and embraces. He was like a child enraptured by his own reflections' (33: 16). The women had pleasure by touching his limbs and they could not keep their garments (covering breasts) and hair intact. The celestial women travelling in the air were stricken with desire at seeing Kṛṣṇa's pastime and became entranced. The moon and stars were full of wonder. Content with himself the Lord became manifest as many forms as the *gopīs* and enjoyed with them his pastime (33: 17-19). 'With great compassion, Kṛṣṇa lovingly caressed with his very soothing hands the face of those *gopīs* who were exhausted from the pleasures of love' (33: 20).

The *gopīs* paid homage to their hero with sideways looks and honeyed smiles. Their ornaments made their cheeks glow. Thrilled by his touch of finger nails they sang of his auspicious deeds. Just like the chief elephant Kṛṣṇa went with them to the water followed by bees etc and enjoyed without any inhibition (33: 21-22). 'With looks of love, the young women around him laughed and splashed him vigorously...Worshipped with showers of *kusuma* (large deciduous tree) flowers by the celestial beings in their aerial chariots, Kṛṣṇa disported himself like an elephant in *līlā* pastimes, even though he is content within himself.' Later he strolled around the banks of Yamuna, surrounded by groups of young women and bees. He went to the farthest corner of the river surrounded by wind bearing fragrance of flowers, was exhilarated like an elephant in the company of female elephants. Though content himself and desires fulfilled within, in those nights Kṛṣṇa participated in the company of young women with brilliant rays of moon, which was the setting for his pastime (33: 23-25).

The attentive king Parīkṣit said: 'God, the Lord of the universe, has descended into the world along with his bodily expansion (Balarāma) for the establishment of *dharma* (here, all that is in accord with cosmic order) and for the suppression of *adharma*, non-dharma. He is the original speaker, exemplar and protector of the injunctions of *dharma*. How could he behave in a manner contrary to *dharma*, O *brāhmaṇa*, by touching the wives of others?' How can he (the Lord of the Yadu dynasty) do such abhorrent act? Clear my doubt' (33: 26-28). Śrī Śuka[1] said: 'Just as fire consumes everything (without being polluted), so it is seen that the blatant transgressions of *dharma* by the more powerful of rulers are not faults. One who is not a powerful being should certainly never behave in the fashion, not even in his mind. Otherwise, acting out of foolishness, he will be destroyed, just as one who is not Śiva will be destroyed (by drinking) the poison churned from the ocean. The words of powerful beings are truth, and so is whatever is performed by them. The wise will act in accordance with their words. O master, those who are devoid of personal ego do not accrue benefit for themselves through appropriate behaviour, nor undesirable results through its opposite. What then of the applicability of auspiciousness and inauspiciousness to the supreme being of all supreme beings and of all living entities, whether celestial, human or animal? Satisfied by worshipping the dust of Kṛṣṇa's lotus feet, even the sages act according to their own free will. The bondage of all their *karma* has been destroyed through the power of *yoga,* and so they are never bound. How, then, can one speak of bondage for Kṛṣṇa, who accepts forms according to his own will? He lives within the *gopīs*, their husbands and all living beings. He is the supreme witness who has assumed a form in this world for the purpose of sport. Manifest in a human form, he indulges in such pastime as a favour to the devotees. Hearing about these, one becomes fully devoted to him. Confused by his power of illusion, the menfolk of Vraj were not resentful of Kṛṣṇa; each thought his own wife was present at his side' (33: 29-37).

'The *gopīs* held the Lord dear. When the duration of Brahmā's night had expired, they went home unwillingly with the approval of Vāsudeva. The sober person who is endowed with faith should hear and describe these pastimes of Viṣṇu with the maidens of

[1] Śuka, the son of the sage Vyāsa, credited as the organizer of the Vedas and Purāṇas, is the main narrator of the Bhāgavata Purāṇa. Most of the purāṇa consists of Śuka reciting the story to the dying king Parīkṣit. Śuka is depicted as a sannyāsin, renouncing the world in pursuit of mokṣa (liberation), which most narratives assert he achieved.

Vraj. Achieving supreme devotion to the Lord, one quickly frees oneself from lust, the disease of the heart' (33: 38-39).

Some Highlights

Kṛṣṇa appeared as a most pleasant presence with his attractive physical features, attachment to the beauty of the nature and flute music. The *gopīs*' 'mad rush' to his presence, leaving the dear ones at home, narrates a particular aspect of bhakti. But interestingly, those left at their homes did not miss the gopīs as they felt the presence of these ladies with them. And some of them who remained at home did not miss the invigorating experience with their Lord as they too were absorbed with him in meditation. There is mention of *dharma*, its parameters and flexibility to accommodate the Lord's occasional pastime with the women of Vraj.

Just like the intense pain of separation, viraha, experienced devotees of all bhakti traditions, here also the women after an initial phase of blissful fellowship with their Lord, experience his unbearable absence. Perhaps it is unique here that the experience is by a group, not individuals as is the case of other traditions, particularly the mystical traditions. Their expression of remorse and despair is moving with no human solution readily available. Later, Kṛṣṇa explains that just like a person's concentration is focused on the wealth he lost, so also those devotees who feel the absence of God concentrate fully on him. In other words, separation intensifies love.

Following the deadening separation between Kṛṣṇa and the young women from Vraj, their dance symbolized resurrection and new life. Their dance is the most beautiful one ever recorded in the Hindu Sanskrit literature. There was no room for aspiration and competition to take the left side and right side of the Lord. All of them had equal share of the bliss. The musical accompaniment was from the nature, bees etc. The whirlpool dance creates a distinctive oneness. The faster the movement less obvious is the individual identity. The divine deity and the devoted partners engage in love, mutually giving and receiving, sharing in the bliss that is uniquely experienced in that particular moment.

Just as in the Gītā here also yoga is given a new meaning. It is neither illusion nor forced control. As the Lord of all yogis, Kṛṣṇa appeared in the forest on the banks of Yamuna and played his flute which enchanted the maidens of Vraj, the short form of Vṛndāvana. It was the same yogic power which suddenly took him away without preparing the consorts who were engaged in sharing love. When the maidens reached a moment that impressed upon them the reality that this close intimacy with their Lord could not be taken for granted, and at the moment when they felt the helplessness and total inadequacy of their love for him Kṛṣṇa reappeared shining and smiling even more intensely. He inserted himself between each pair of *gopīs* and there is no mention of their number. The mystery of the unknown woman whose footprints they saw is still unknown.

The ecstatic height achieved in the dance was the expression of the intense love of the *gopīs* for their Lord Kṛṣṇa. Throughout the Rāsalīlā, to avoid any misunderstanding of his romantic dalliance, the text affirms that Kṛṣṇa's desires are always fulfilled, as is his propensity for enjoyment. He is content in himself. His participation in the sportive pastime with the *gopīs* was exceptional in a special season when nature appeared in her most radiant glory. The splendor increased when nature, Kṛṣṇa and *gopīs* collaborated to display oneness in a most distinctive way.

The erotic symbolism may lead to sexual arousal within a reader who not experienced in deep intimacy with God, which is sometimes called bridal mysticism. The narrative no doubt seems obscene when we read of Kṛṣṇa caressing with his soothing hands the faces, breasts and thighs of the women, thus arousing kāma in them. At the same time Kṛṣṇa calls them 'chaste women.' His own divine consort Lakṣmī is remembered. He carefully differentiated their love for him from the adultery of a woman of good birth which, without exception does not lead to heaven. 'It is scandalous, fear-laden, worthless, fraught with difficulty and abhorrent' (29: 26). Finally, when the duration of Brahmā's night

(4320 million years!) had expired the cowherd maidens went home unwillingly with the approval of Vāsudeva. The last verse mentions the true identity of God and the true meaning of lust in relation to devotion: 'The sober person who is endowed with faith should hear and describe these pastimes of Viṣṇu with the maidens of Vraj. Achieving supreme devotion to the Lord, one quickly frees oneself from lust, the disease of the heart' (33: 39).

What is the ultimate goal of the bhakti between Kṛṣṇa and the *gopīs*? It is affirmed that the incarnation of Kṛṣṇa 'is for the good of the universe, and dispels the distress of the people of Vraj.' Part of that medicine removes the ailment from the hearts of his devotees whose hearts yearn for him (31: 18). It is noted that sages, satisfied by worshipping the dust of Kṛṣṇa's lotus feet, act according to their own free will. Through the power of *yoga* all their *karma* has been destroyed and so they are never bound (33: 34). Earlier, it was stated that their (those maiden who remained at home) *karma* from their impious deeds was destroyed by the intense and intolerable pain of separation from their lover (29: 10). It may look that attachment to Kṛṣṇa also may be a kind of bondage, but he lives in all living beings including the maiden and their husbands. 'He is the supreme witness who has assumed a form in this world for the purpose of sport' (33: 35). In human form he indulges in a romantic pastime as a favour to the deities. Though not explained thus, it is right to assume that the message is that all those who join in a loving pastime with the Lord experience their bondage to *karma* as either broken or already broken.

What are the existential implications of bhakti to Kṛṣṇa? It is noted: 'The words of powerful beings are truth. And so is whatever is performed by them. The wise will act in accordance with their words...those who are devoid of personal ego do not accrue benefit for themselves through appropriate behaviour, nor undesirable results through its opposite' (33: 31f). We will come back to some of these issues when we make a comparative analysis in the next chapter.

Summary

The Rāsalīlā section of the Bhāgavata Purāṇa seems to be the finest of any sections of any other purāṇas. Particularly, it has been interpreted to be the greatest bhakti text in the Gaudia Vaiṣṇavism and the International Society for the Kṛṣṇa Consciousness (ISKCON). It starts with Kṛṣṇa's enchanting music on his flute that aroused kāma within the women of Vraj. They rushed to meet him in the forest in a state of rapture forgetting or ignoring their household duties. Unexpectedly their Lord chided them for daring to rush to see him in the frightening forest leaving their dear ones at home and this appeared to dash their aspiration and made them inconsolable. Then their praise of Kṛṣṇa and despairing words made him laugh and engage in amorous pleasures from compassion though his satisfaction was self-contained. When the gopīs became proud, Kṛṣṇa disappeared from their midst and their searching involved questions, lamentation, doubts and despair. Kṛṣṇa's instant return revived their spirit and they praised his glory. It was explained that the separation intensified their love for the Lord (varaha bhakti). There was the element of some women trying to possess the Lord. The culmination was a dynamic and whirlpool dance in Yamuna, near the forest, in moon light. To avoid any quarrel and competition Kṛṣṇa multiplied himself and placed in between two gopīs. The main story is mixed with descriptions of the beauty of nature, Vedic gods and sages, yoga and erotic behaviour. But as if giving a warning not to take Kṛṣṇa's (Viṣṇu's) behaviour with the maidens of Vraj the final words give a succinct meaning of devotion: 'Achieving supreme devotion to the Lord, one quickly frees oneself from lust, the disease of heart.'

Chapter 6

Kristu Bhakti and Kṛṣṇa Bhakti
A Comparative Analysis

What We Compare and for What?

The word 'comparative' in religious studies has been used in several senses. At a base and apologetic level it means comparing and scoring more points for a particular position over against other(s). What is known as comparative religion – also called comparative study of religion, or questionably, science of religion, scientific study of religion, history of religion, religious studies and sometimes phenomenology of religion – has taken various methodological routes and even the conclusions of the study of a particular data, object or phenomenon are not the same. Even in the case of the classical phenomenology of religion in general, with the emphasis on the value free and objective outlook, typological classification of the data and eidetic vision, the essence of religion was proposed to be 'Mana' or sacred power (E. B. Tylor), Holy as both terrifying and fascinating (R. Otto) and Prayer (F. Heiler). Though the conclusions are not totally different to each other, one may view the reason for the difference being the different contexts the study was carried out or different source materials consulted. Since then, after mammoth efforts to understand religion, recognizing the amazing complexity and variety of religious visions, traditions and experiences, the study of religion has reached a stage in which it is convincingly declared *Religion Beyond a Concept.*[1] However, certain old slogans continue and a typical slogan recited by Hindus is that the essence of all religions is the same without taking any pain to study the religions and expound the nature of the so called essence. This comparison is specific taking the narrative of two texts (selections from St. John's Gospel and the Rāsalīlā section of the Bhāgavata Purāṇa), juxtaposing them, picking up identical themes and pointing to missing ideas or emphases.

Francis Clooney defines comparative theology as reflection on practice.[2] There are other comparative theologians too such as John Thattamanil, Robert Neville, James Fredricks, and Michelle in the USA, Keith Ward in the UK and Indian Christian theologians of the early phases and Dayanandan Francis and Thomas Thangaraj in the Tamil context. It might be a useful exercise to compare the definitions of comparative theology of these theologians. As far as we are concerned, the specific purpose is to study Kristu bhakti and Kṛṣṇa bhakti in comparison with the limited scope of taking two texts with a probing approach to find new aspects to be added to the already existing views and definitions of bhakti and suggesting if hybridization is possible or not, or an alternative may be possible.

'Bridal mysticism' is a phrase which has been already used in bhakti studies. There have been women saints most of whom had a failed marriage came to see in God, the most durable loving husband, the source of fulfillment of all their longing for affection and passion. Thus, Āṇḍāḻ, one of the twelve Tamil Vaiṣṇava Āḷvārs, Kāraikkāl Ammaiyār, one of the sixty-three

---

[1] See particularly the long hundred page introductory essay by the editor, *Religion: Beyond a Concept*, ed. by Hent de Vries, New York: Fordham University Press, 2008.

[2] See F. Clooney, *Comparative Theology: Deep Learning Across Religious Borders*, Oxford: Wiley-Blackwell, 2010, 21.

Tamil Śaiva Nāyanmārs, Akkammādevi, a Vīra Śaiva saint and Mirabai, a Kṛṣṇa devotee, use imagery and imagination of the passionate and even conjugal love between a lover and the beloved. The only exception in this pattern was the Tamil Śaiva saint Māṇikkavācakar's *Tirupperuntokai* (part of the eighth of the twelve canonical texts of the Tamil Śaiva tradition) in which Śiva is depicted as bride and the devotee the groom. Of course no one has suggested literal meaning but the profound nature of bhakti is observed.

In the New Testament references are scanty to the imagery of romantic love. Jesus did apply the image 'bridegroom' to himself but called his disciples the 'best men' (Mk. 2: 18-20). One of his parables was ten virgins waiting upon the arrival of the bridegroom (Mtt. 25: 1-13). Paul applied the relationship between a husband and wife to Christ and the Church but amorous behaviour and romance he viewed negatively (Eph. 5: 21-33). There are few hymns, lyrics and popular songs that mention passionate and even romantic love with a view to express the devotee's love for God or Christ (e.g. Jesus as rose of Sharon and lily of valley). Nevertheless any idea of God having a romantic relationship is unthinkable!

The Hebrew poetry *Song of Solomon* (or Song of Songs) baffled the early church fathers when they considered its status in the canon. Finally they settled with the idea that it was an allegorical description of the love and relationship between Christ and the Church. At the same time, it is not a wonder that the poetry caught the imagination of scholars to compare it with the Rāsalīlā. As Schweig observes, expression of passion presented in two very different scriptural texts, the first biblical and the second purāṇic: 'Let him kiss me with the kisses of his mouth' (Song of Solomon 1:2), and 'Please bestow upon us the nectar of your lips!' (Rāsa Līlā 31:14). But he adds that 'These explicitly romantic expressions have been perceived as the voice of the soul in its passionate yearning for the divine.'[1] Further, he observes:

---

[1] G. Schweig, *Dance of Divine Love*, Princeton University Press, 2005, 6.

> In the Western world, the biblical book of Solomon, also known as the Song of Songs, relating the passionate love between a king and queen, has been regarded by many as a sacred love story. This story has become foundational for various forms of Jewish mysticism such as Kabbalah. The rich and erotic words of the Song reveal the union of lover and beloved who symbolize, for these traditions, the divine 'queen' and 'king' within the godhead. Additionally, the Song of Solomon has been a profound source of inspiration for Catholic love mysticism and Christian piety in general. The feminine and masculine voices of the text have represented the loving relationship between the soul and God, respectively, in which the soul becomes the 'bride' and Christ the divine 'bridegroom.'[1]

The phrase 'divine queen and king in the godhead' needs to be explained with reference to the mainstream piety and literature of the Jewish and Christian traditions in order to understand the nuances.

Stories of divine-human encounter do not happen in a vacuum. The geographical ambience, literary genre, purpose and terminology need to be given due attention.

Distinctive Backgrounds

As we noted earlier, Jesus was identified with Nazareth, an insignificant hamlet in the region of Galilee where poor peasants and those marginalized lived. His parables were mostly about shepherds, gardeners, peasants, tenants, labourers, shepherds etc. He said that he came to seek the lost, least and last. It was not new for those who are familiar with the Hebrew tradition. The root story of liberation from Egypt, covenant and prophetic challenges stressed again and again that though God was the God of all, God had a special eye on those who were vulnerable as victims of injustice or physical and mental impediments. He visited Samaria and Judea and encountered individuals and groups and his talks

---

[1] Ibid., 7.

and few miracles expressed his focused concern about the poor and the vulnerable. He visited the holy city of Jerusalem, the hub of Jewish religious, political and economic activities within the rule of Rome. Jesus' criticism of the Jewish leaders there for forgetting their root story and prophetic tradition invited trouble and hostility. He was arrested and killed. When he rose again from dead he rushed to Galilee and renewed fellowship with his dear ones and his giving of Great Commission and ascension also took place in this region.

Kṛṣṇa was associated with a number of spots such as Kuruśetra and Dvāraka, but in the Bhāgavata, Vṛndāvana, the short and popular name of which was Vraja, where he was a member of the shepherd community. It was 'Kṛṣṇa's Garden of Eden' (Kinsley). 'The sacred realm also imprints itself onto part of our world as the earthly Vraja, a rural area known as Vraja Maṇḍala ("the circular area of Vraja") in northern India, about eighty miles south of the modern capital city of Delhi. It is the celestial abode (Goloka) of Kṛṣṇa, which is said to be located above Viṣṇu's Vaikunta and Śiva's Kailāṣ. Vraja is described as a land of idyllic natural beauty, filled with abundant foliage, heavy with fruit and bloom, roaming cows, and brightly colored birds singing melodiously. The Rāsa Līlā takes place in the earthly Vraja during the bountiful autumn season, when evenings abound with soothing scents and gentle river breezes.'[1] The Rāsalīlā section presents the forest and banks of Yamuna River and the surrounding with stunning beauty and enchanting sight, sound and smell.

It has been pointed out by Asian theologians that particular geographical locations affect moods and attitudes: e.g. the 'hot and zealous God of Mount Sinai versus the cool *arhants* (Buddhist monks on the way to liberation) of Mount Fuji – K. Koyama; 'desert religions (Semitic, often intolerant) versus riverside religions (Indian religions), tolerant in general) – S.J. Samartha. One may argue that such assessments betray generalization, but it is hard to deny the influence of geographical locations on religious life and articulation, particularly the bhakti experience.

[1] Ibid., 2.

Both Jesus and Kṛṣṇa were associated in different measures with the shepherd communities. Obviously this community lived on the fringes of the society. Jesus was born in a carpenter family but shepherds appeared in his birth narrative, parables and imagery. He claimed to be the Good Shepherd who was willing to give his life for his sheep. The other and back door shepherds (leaders), he said, had the hidden plan to exploit and devour the sheep. Kṛṣṇa was fondly owned by the gopīs as their dear most. He was born and grew up in their community before his wanderings and assuming different status.

Jesus was a devout Jew, teacher and prophet who was fond of the liberation values of his tradition but agonizing for its erosion that left several people vulnerable. Using the titles, popular in his tradition, such as Messiah, Son of God and Son of Man, he presented himself as very significant for a hope in the future. All the same time he confronted the conservative and narrow minded persons and authorities of his own religious tradition and asked them to be open to the 'Eternal I am' and participate in God's continuing mission for humanizing the world. Kṛṣṇa's tradition(s) and challenges were different. The situation was very fluid and more complex as we will explain later. The key word *dharma* is used and though it came to assume different meanings, where it was specifically the Ārya dharma, its enduring features recur in texts. Thus, Kṛṣṇa, a brahmaṇised divine hero of a shepherd clan, tells the gopīs that the highest dharma for a woman is to serve her husband, even if he is a rogue and for Āryans it is proper to remain at his feet (BhP. 29: 23ff). And one can argue that Kṛṣṇa bhakti and cult was a deviation from the Āryan dharma though later it was accommodated. Just before the climax of dance, Kṛṣṇa speaks of joy 'just like the Vedas attained the culmination of the heart's desire' (32: 10f); adds, 'you left not only the relatives but also (injunctions of) the Vedas' (32: 21). There are questions about Kṛṣṇa's amorous behaviour with the gopīs and its compatibility with the Vedic dharma. For example, the maiden ask, 'what women in the three worlds would not stray from the behaviour proper to Āryans, when thrown into turmoil by the melodies of your flute, which vibrate harmoniously?' (29: 38). Suffice to say at this point that the Rāsalīlā section of the Bhāgavata Purāṇa reflects the tension accrued in the amalgamation of two traditions while the John's Gospel reflects an intra-Jewish confrontation with the addition of non-Jewish ideas and elements.

Purpose and Literary Genre

John's Gospel seems to be an apologetic tract with didactic flavor. There are in it theological interpretations, parables, miracles and actions, arguments and long discourses. Its purpose is stated towards the end: 'Jesus did many other miraculous signs in the presence of his disciples, which are not recorded in this book. But these are written that you may believe that Jesus is the Christ, the Son of God, and that by believing you may have life in his name' (20: 30-31). Ashton observes that, 'no other passage in the Fourth Gospel lends more plausibility to the thesis that the Gospel was designed as a missionary tract to draw Jews of the diaspora to the new faith. For here we have Jesus who is *presented* to the Jews as the one who has come to fulfill all their hopes: he is the promised Messiah, he is Elijah returned to earth, he is the eschatological prophet foretold by Moses, he is the Chosen One, the Son of God, the King of Israel.'[1]

The Bhāgavata Purāṇa is set in the background of performing a magnificent sacrifice in order to attain the abode of Viṣṇu and Kṛṣṇa's manifestation. Further, the story is told in response to the request of the dying king Parikṣit (a relative of Arjuna and Kṛṣṇa) for fulfilling the dharma of his remaining few days. Of course, like any other purāṇa the Bhāgavata contains several stories and sub-stories. As far as the Rāsalīlā section is concerned, there is a sharpened focus, the love of God and souls, which is portrayed with romantic embellishment. Does it connect with king Parikṣit's quest? It does not seem directly. But indirectly, the unreserved love of God can be the answer for a dying person. It may be compared to the encounter of Kṛṣṇa and Arjuna in the battle field of Bhārata

[1] Ashton, Op. cit., 264.

in which the former declared that leaving all dharmas a devotee could surrender to him as recorded in the *Carama Śloka* of the Gītā (18: 66). In both cases it is life in its fullness and love in its intensity, but the application of the details in concrete context is different.

The common terms 'life' and 'love' are not used consistently. This fact creates difficulty for simple and direct comparison. Jesus used words such as children of God, glory, salvation, being born again, eternal life, the Spirit, God the Father, Son of Man, Son of God, Messiah, belief, living and dying for others and truth. More than everything, he was in confrontation with a conservative leadership and fiercely critical of his tradition having deviated from its original vision. Without knowing the Hebrew tradition one cannot understand the full connotation of these terms. None of these are evident in Kṛṣṇa's discourses and the gopīs' responses. In their speech the most popular terms are love, contentment, dharma, karma, beauty, music, dance, duty, jasmine, other flowers and joy. The difference is not only because of the literary genres but also the particular tradition in which the narrative is set. It may not be a gross exaggeration to say that the bhakti-related passages of John offer a wholesome view of life with all its complexity whereas Rāsalīlā focuses on a fascinating expression of romantic love which explains the most profound love between divine and human. Without realizing this fact, to rush to the conclusion that 'Jesus and Kṛṣṇa were parallel figures teaching the same message' is misleading.

Disciples and Devotees

Though God is universal, both transcendent and immanent, capable of revealing divine glory and will in many ways, it is common in religious traditions holding a special person and close circle as locus of enjoyment of close intimacy and sending guidance. As was the custom, Jesus chose twelve disciples and they all were male although there were female disciples too belonging to a different category. Compared to the disciples of great teachers who were intellectual giants, the twelve disciples of Jesus were a laughing stock! They were dull-headed, silly and power-mongering. They were 'wholly fools' who needed rigorous training to become 'holy fools.'[1] It is not explained why Jesus, who was chiding and reprimanding them very often, chose them in the first place. Obviously, most of them came from insignificant strata of society, i.e. uneducated fishers. God's choice of the powerless and numerically weak to be his people who would play the role of being instruments in the hands of God was already underlined in the Hebrew scripture (Deut. 7: 7) and this extraordinary notion continued in the New Testament. Paul says:

> Not many of you were wise by human standards; not many were influential; not many were of noble birth. But God chose the foolish things of the world to shame the wise; God chose the weak things of the world to shame the strong. He chose the lowly things of this world and the despised things – and the things that are not – to nullify the things that are so that no one may boast before him (1 Cor. 1: 26-29).

There is no evidence in all these cases that the instruments lived up to the ideal and in the course of the history Christianity connected with power centers and thus the original vision of their choice was forgotten though today Christians are reminded of it by sermons and study programs.

According to John Jesus called his disciples directly or through the first ones to follow him even if where he lived was not known (1: 35-50). There were many surprises and learning moments for the disciples. For instance, they were surprised to find Jesus talking to a Samaritan woman (4: 27). But the climax was to share in the suffering of their Master. At a time when Jesus' enemies waiting to stone him in Judea, where he was going again to raise his friend Lazarus, the probing Thomas said to rest of the disciples, 'Let

[1] See, I. Selvanayagam, "Theological Education and Regeneration of the Church in India", in *Communion on the Move: Towards a Relevant Theological Education* (Essays in Honour of Bishop John Sadananda), ed. by Wati Longchar & P. Mohan Larbeer, Bangalore: BTESSC, 2015, 37-49.

us also go, that we may die with him' (11: 16). Following Jesus' triumphal entry into Jerusalem, there is a note which says, 'At first his disciples did not understand all this' (12: 16). Soon they were told that the only antidote to the temptation of power was washing one another's feet as their Master demonstrated (13: 1-17). Even the betrayer and denier among them were not excommunicated! There was no compulsion and in fact many disciples deserted Jesus as they found his life style and teaching to be very hard to emulate (6: 60ff).

Jesus' comforting farewell speech to his disciples points out a poignant moment and the intimate relationship between them (ch. 14-16). He promised them that whatever they asked in his name they would get so that the Father's name was glorified. If they loved him they would obey his command. The Father would send the Spirit of truth as their counselor, internal presence and guide and he would not leave them orphans. 'On that day you will realize that I am in my Father, and you are in me, and I am in you. Whoever has my commands and obeys them, he is the one who loves me. He who loves me will be loved by my Father, and I too will love him and show myself to him...and we will come to him and make our home with him' (14: 20-23). He was leaving unworldly peace with them and their hearts needed no trouble and fear. Like a vine and branches if Jesus and disciples were united they would bear fruit. He calls them friends, so intimate that there is no secret between them. There is no greater love than one giving life for his/her friend. Jesus commented: 'You did not choose me, but I chose you and appointed you to go and bear fruit – fruit that will last...This is my command: Love each other' (15: 16-17). He warned them that they would be hated by the world just as he himself was; also he would disappear for a while.

In his long prayer mainly for his disciples for their protection, unity, freedom from evil, sanctification by the truth and greater unity within the unity of the Father, Son and those who believed Jesus by their word.

Apart from the twelve male disciples, Jesus had many women disciples who served him with their wealth, time and hospitality.

Particularly he often visited Martha and Mary, the sisters of Lazarus in Bethany. According to John, Mary Magdalene was the first to see the empty tomb of Jesus and then ran and told Peter and John, the two cardinal disciples. Also she was the first to have the vision of the risen Jesus and shared her experience with the other disciples.

On the whole, Jesus' disciples were too ordinary and weak yet Jesus chose and called them to follow him, to provide company and learn about the ethos of the heavenly life on earth. The greatest new lesson they learned was the greatest command, 'love each other.' Life for them was full of challenges and surprises yet they were assured of God's abiding presence and guidance. Finally, just like the Son of Man they were sent on a mission to represent the victims of society with the discretionary power, either to forgive or not to forgive, perhaps depending on the response of those who needed forgiveness.

The gopīs with Kṛṣṇa were of a different category though they had similar experiences of the disciples of Jesus. Excluding the beloved favorite Rādha who is normally depicted as standing with her lover Kṛṣṇa in the centre of the dance circle of the Rāsalīlā, tradition holds there were eight topmost gopīs who participated in dance.[1] They were teenage, beautiful with fair complexion, talented in different arts with rare skills and fascinatingly loving by nature. They were special among hundreds of gopīs who in various ways were serving Kṛṣṇa-Rādha in their 'palace' or garden.

The initial moment in Rāsalīlā is the flute music of Kṛṣṇa which once again aroused passion in the hearts of the gopīs and they rushed to meet their beloved Lord. Nothing else appeared to them more important, even their cows, husbands and children. Even Kṛṣṇa chides them for this but they argue that he was their choicest and best who can fulfill their desires and aspirations. This single minded love is different from following, believing, trusting,

[1] 1. Lalita-devi, 2. Viṣaka-devi, 3. Campakalata, 4. Citra-devi, 5. Tungavidya, 6. Indulekha, 7. Rangadevi, 8. Sudevi; from Google search on 'Gopis', http://www.vrindavan.de/varistha.htm; http://www.vrindavan.de/othergopis.htm (accessed, 13/4/2015).

obeying the command of loving one another, demanded of Jesus' disciples.

Friendship is said to be the highest form of relationship which can be incorporated into all forms of relationships. As we have noted above, Jesus called his disciples friends. Lazarus and his sisters also were known as Jesus' friends. But Jesus gave a definition of genuine friendship, that is, there is no secret kept in between friends; there is no greater love than one giving his life for his friend. The gopīs made a seat of their garments for their friend. Kṛṣṇa too addressed them his friends (BhP 32: 17). Just like Jesus was very concerned about the wellbeing and future of his disciples, Kṛṣṇa was concerned about the wellbeing of his devotees. He says, even in separation he was serving them as it intensified their love for him. He broke the enduring shackles of household life and rewarded with excellence (32: 22). There are emotions running through at the sight of the Jesus in a crisis. We may recall that Martha and Mary wept bitterly on the arrival of Jesus when their brother died, and similarly the gopīs wept loudly longing for Kṛṣṇa when he left them instantly. Human emotion and passion mix with longing or waiting upon the beloved Lord.

The disciples of Jesus and the gopīs of Vraja have been taken as pioneers and paradigmatic figures of the future adherents of the respective communities of devotees. Originally members of the Jesus' movement were simply called disciples. 'The disciples were called Christians first in Antioch' (Acts 11: 26). Though their identity and self-understanding had complicated turns in history, in the present situation there is a perpetual need to remind Christians of their original call, commitment and identity. In the Vaiṣṇava bhakti movements the Kṛṣṇa-Gopīs encounter is reenacted in festivals and other special occasions. Particularly, in the ISKCON temples their iconic presentation is the focal point thus inspiring and evoking the spirit of devotees. The question, 'can the disciples of Jesus and devotees of Kṛṣṇa today worship and work together?' is important and we will come back to it later.

Aspects of Bhakti Experience

Bhakti as expressed in the chosen texts does not confine to a transcendental plane or esoteric enclosure. It happens in the context of an ordinary yet purposeful living. Jesus' disciples were called for a risk-involved journey. They witnessed their Master's compassion that found concrete expression in healing the disabled and sick and identifying with the least, last and lost in the society who were the victims of a deviation from a vision and tradition of liberation and fulfillment. At the same time they themselves were taken care of in matters of physical needs, being prepared for a moment of great pain and promised for a life of fulfillment. Kṛṣṇa also was concerned about the welfare of his devotees. He asked the gopīs, 'how people are in Vraja?' He pointed out their risk-taking journey in frenzy to the forest in the dark where there were wild animals. To their frustration he even asked them to hurry back to take care of their husbands, babies and cows that were crying for suckling (BhP. 29: 21f). The gopīs also included ordinary facts connected with bhakti. For example, they told Kṛṣṇa, 'after seeing your form animals stand with hair on end in bliss' (BhP 29: 40).

Love and grace of God is both attractive and activating in a bhakti experience. In John this manifested in Jesus Christ not only for his disciples and friends but for the whole world. The intimacy of love is compared to that between a good, live saving and life giving shepherd and lost sheep; between a vine and the branches; and between close friends. The intensity of this love could be realized not only in loving one another but also willing to give up the life for others. Kṛṣṇa-Gopīs' encounter is love-play defining pure love and one requires a loving-eye to interpret it correctly. Schweig makes a pertinent observation:

> ...traditions tell us that the true interpretation of the story requires a certain type of vision, the "eye of pure love," *premā-netra*, which sees a world permeated by supreme love constantly celebrated by all beings and all life. This eye beholds a realm of consummate beauty and bliss, in which both the soul and intimate deity lost themselves in

> the eternal play of love. *Premā-netra* is said to be attained when the "eye of devotion" is anointed with the "mystical ointment of love," an ointment that grants a special vision of the "incomprehensible qualities" of the essential form of Krishna.[1]

One can reasonably revise some of the above phrases in the light of John's presentation of God's love with special reference to the person and ministry of Jesus. Then *premā netra* may be followed by *seva netra* and *tyāga netra* and these are attained when the eye of devotion is anointed with the 'practical ointment of love.' Here the language is not the soul and deity getting lost themselves in the 'eternal play of love' but maintaining intimate relationship in the bond of love and working together for the transformation of the world. The sense here is one of primacy and emphasis, not of exclusive uniqueness.

Unless the vision and experience of divine grace and love are focused on liberation and transformation in various spheres of life it remains a spiritual sentiment. God is specially concerned about the suffering. Kṛṣṇa is called the friend of the afflicted (BhP. 29: 41). The *karma* of those focused on him in meditation and the bondage of their *guṇa*-bound (as explained earlier) bodies are destroyed (29: 10-11). The terms in John's Gospel are different. When they encountered a man born blind from birth the disciples asked Jesus if it was due to his parents' sin or his own sin. The belief here seems to reflect the opinion of a fringe group in Judaism, perhaps influenced by Greek belief. In any case Jesus said, 'neither this man nor his parents have sinned, but this happened so that the work of God might be displayed in his life.' The second part of this saying is not very clear; it seems to suggest that instead of wasting time for probing into the the moral cause of a problem, try to solve it taking it a chance and opportunity to demonstrate the fact that God is able to work through such a crisis so that God's glory will be displayed in an unusual way. Then Jesus healed him and this created a fierce controversy on sin and spiritual blindness of the

---

[1] Schweig, Op. cit., 4.

religious (Jn. 9; see also 8). Jesus refused to a narrow and moral understanding of sin and declared those conservative religious sinners or slaves to sin because they were not open to the signs of the time and to move on in faith. In Christian-Hindu dialogue understanding of sin, karma and grace needs to go deeper and more comprehensive. Particularly the unconditional acceptance of any one irrespective of one's moral condition and social standing, leading to a new life led by the Spirit, a life for others, should be clarified. A realization that there can be a 'sinful religiosity' which can be overcome by transformation or a born again experience with permanent well-spring of the Spirit within may lead to newer perceptions of bhakti.

Casual intimacy in bhakti expression is often forgotten and this is because the prose narratives are limited to convey friendly and casual communication. There was humour, sarcasm and engaging questions in the conversation between Jesus and disciples. Elements of this kind of intimacy are evident in Jesus' friendship with his disciples (Jn. 15: 15). His conversation with Nathanael has humorous and telling notes (1: 1: 47-51). The disciples' surprising questions about his conversation with a Samaritan woman, alone in a public place, was casual (4: 27). Other such moments had mutual questioning and chiding (6: 66ff;), poignant sharing of affection and solidarity in believement (11: 11: 17ff), dealing humanly yet religiously with two women friends, Mary and Martha (12:1-11), friendly yet serious dialogue between Jesus and Peter during washing the disciples' feet (13: 1-17) and questions and answers about the future (14: 1ff). However, in Jesus''highpriestly' prayer to the heavenly Father there are most positive references to their acceptance, obedience, experience of sanctification and commitment to mission (17:6-19). This looks exaggerated and this may reflect the later claim of the early Christians. Similarly, Kṛṣṇa and the gopīs chide one another. In response to his comment on their leaving the dear ones, they said, 'you should not speak to us in such a heartless fashion; what is the use of husbands and children who cause problems? You only developed the hope and our hearts were stolen by you'

(BhP. 2931ff). Their reaction when their lover disappeared and then reappeared has many such spontaneous expressions.

Feeling of separation from the divine or deity for a while or of unbearable absence has been expressed in different magnitude and duration, with analogous imageries and poetic imagination, abound in theistic bhakti literature across the traditions. John notes that Jesus explicitly tells of his going away and then returning. It is debated if Jesus means his going and returning as his parousia in clouds at the end time or his resurrection after death.[1] Ashton observes:

> Given the setting of the whole discourse, as Jesus prepares his disciples to face up to their imminent loss, the promise that in 'a little while' his disciples will see him again cannot but remind the Christian reader (and also of course the Johannine prophet's original audience) of the appearances to the disciples 'on the first day of the week' (20.1) and again 'eight days later' (20.26). Here too we are concerned with private rather than public manifestations: unless those to whom Jesus appeared after his death could respond with faith, the term 'resurrection' would have no meaning and the Christian proclamation no content.[2]

Jesus compares his disciples' pain of separation to that of childbirth and the reunion to the joy of the birth of a child (16: 16ff). He prepares them, encourages them and comforts them, as well as promises them expectant joy.

---

[1] Especially see Jn. Chapter 14 and Ashton, Op. cit., 462.

[2] Ibid., 463; Ashton also refers to the following: "Barret is right here to speak of 'a studied ambiguity'; 'The sayings about going and coming can be interpreted throughout of the departure and return of Jesus in his death and resurrection; but they can equally well be interpreted of the departure to the Father at the ascension and his return at the parousia.' All agree that there is a reference to the resurrection; but our attention is also directed to signs of an imminent end, partly by the image itself, the woman in travail, partly by the use of the significant term…(anguish, tribulation) in 16.21. So, Barret rightly dismisses Bultmann's suggestion that 'Easter and the Parousia are interpreted as one and the same event.', 464.

In the case of Kṛṣṇa and gopīs the former's disappearance was sudden and the response of the latter was abnormal speech and behaviour as they were so devastated. It is explained that to balance the pride of his devotees thinking they were the greatest women he vanished. This was the fate of a mysterious woman that Kṛṣṇa accompanied in lonely places for some time during his absence with the gopīs (30: 28ff). Further, separation also prompted creative thinking and new realization. For example, the gopīs in their frenzy expressed expectant praise for their Lord and some imitated him to the extent of saying 'I am he.' Finally, Kṛṣṇa told them that the separation was to intensify love; when someone has lost his wealth his/her focused attention was on the lost. The idea that separation intensifies love is quoted in many other texts too.

The Climax

In spite of all preparatory talks Jesus' disciples, following their Lord's death, found themselves in a locked room. Mary Magdalene first saw the empty tomb and reported to Peter and John. Then she had the obscure vision of the risen Jesus who appeared to be a gardener. His calling her name uplifted her spirit and she ran to share the experience with other disciples. In a locked room Jesus appeared to his disciples and showed them his hands and side. 'The disciples were overjoyed when they saw the Lord' (Jn. 20: 20). Further they received the greeting of peace and gift of the Holy Spirit, but they could not remain in that blessed mood for long; they were sent out on a mission which had been explained as that just as the Father had sent him Jesus sent his disciples into the world (17: 18). Here, as we have already noted, the distinctive emphasis was on forgiving or not forgiving as representatives of the victims of injustice. A further emphasis is found in a poignant dialogue between Jesus and Peter in the appended chapter 21: if you really love me more than others, feed my lambs. Thus, the climax of a bhakti encounter is not only joy, peace and power of the Spirit but also participating in God's continued mission following the model of Jesus who was the good shepherd willing to die for the vulnerable lambs.

In Rāsalīlā the climax is Kṛṣṇa's whirlpool dance with his loving gopīs who have had an experience of renewal. Unlike yogic elation and mystic meditation here dancing in joy is presented in a spectacular manner. Kṛṣṇa's presence and connection is equal to all the participants. He is inserting himself between each pair of the maidens whose hands are locked (BhP. 33: 1f). As we noted before, two of Jesus' disciples aspired for his left side and right side in his glorious reign which created tension among the disciples. Jesus could not think of the solution provided by Kṛṣṇa! Further, gods with their consorts and vehicles appeared in the sky and were carried away in excitement. Resounding of kettledrums, showers of flowers, celestial choir singing Kṛṣṇa's spotless glories, laughing, touching with playful smiles, amorous glanzes and caressing breasts, splashing, Kṛṣṇa putting his arm around certain gopī and smelling her blue lotus and sandal fragrance and being kissed by her next to his cheek, claiming to have won him from Śrī, delighting in him as they sing praises to him and so on. The whole nature including moon, star, flowers and bees are full of wonder. The girls give sideway looks, honeyed smiles and are thrilled by the touches of their Lord. In the vigorous movement of a hilarious dance in circle there is a flash of unity in which differences are obscured if not absent. In spite of this vigorous movement Kṛṣṇa does not fail to notice the individuals in trouble. One *gopī* ... was tired and her jasmine flowers and bracelets got loosened. Kṛṣṇa was standing by her side. ..Another, fatigued, placed his hand on her breast (33: 9-13). 'With great compassion, Kṛṣṇa lovingly caressed with his very soothing hands the face of those *gopīs* who were exhausted from the pleasures of love' (33: 20). Thus, Kṛṣṇa's compassion and care for his devotees are never absent.

It is interesting that the role of the goddess is absent in the sportive dance. In an earlier dialogue, the gopīs told Kṛṣṇa: 'we providentially touched the soles of your feet, which belong to the goddess of fortune... The goddess of fortune aspires to the dust of those lotus feet which is worshipped by your servants, even though she has obtained a place on your chest along with Tulasī (holy basil). Other gods, even, strive to attract her personal glance. In the same way, we solicit the dust of your feet. Having heard this Kṛṣṇa laughed (29: 35-37). There is praise with a stint of jealousy about Śrī but the idea of a paradigmatic figure for the devotees as we find in other devotional texts such as Māṇkkavācakar's Tiruvācakam is absent here. There are different interpretations about the invisible goddess in relation to the gopīs. Particularly, the Caitanya school identifies the chief and central gopī with Rādhā.

> Put in the simplest term here, the school explains that the Vraja Gopikās who make up the circle of female dancers are but the embodiments of Rādhā's emotions. Thus, the whole Rāsa Maṇdala is simply a portrait of both Rādhā and Krishna: the Vraja Gopikās, each as a particular embodiment of Rādhā's emotions, are themselves partly duplicate forms standing with each one of the Gopīs are, of course, ways in which Krishna lovingly attends to each and every emotional display of Rādhā. While the narrative of the sacred text centrifugally sends multiple duplications of Krishna out into the circle of female dancers, the interpretive eye of the Caitanya theological school centripetally projects from the Vraja Gopikās into the very centre of the circle with Krishna the goddess Gopī, Rādhā, from whom all the other Gopīs originate.[1]

The logical conclusion of this interpretation should be that the present day devotees of Kṛṣṇa are the continued embodiments of Rādhā's emotions. This may raise questions about the identity of Kṛṣṇa and his new devotees at every bhakti relationship. It will

---

[1] Graham Schweig "The Crucifixion and the Rāsa Maṇdala: A Comparative Sketch of Two Great Symbols of Divine Love," *Journal of Vaishnava Studies*, 20/2 2012, 180.

be a fruitful study in comparison with different schools of Kṛṣṇa bhakti.

Bhakti and Sexuality

Can bhakti and sexual passion go together in a positive way? It should be admitted that, at least in India there are ambiguity, confusion and even hypocrisy! The Bible contains sexual imagery of God and God's people as lovers, bride and groom, and husband and wife. Adulterous deviation with obscene language is described to indicate faithlessness. As we pointed out earlier, the erotic poetry of the Song of Songs was under the scrutiny of those who canonized the scriptural books and it was finally accepted with the allegorical interpretation of speaking about the relationship between Christ and his bride, the Church. In John's Gospel we have the record of Jesus' encounter with a few women. In his conversation with the Samaritan woman (ch. 4) Jesus predicted about her five husbands before and that the present one too was not her husband. Traditional interpretation is that she was a loose woman, even a harlot. Today, those who look at her from the experience of several women in India, suggest that she was already a victim of five irresponsible or violent men and the present one too looked unpredictable. And Jesus' approach to a woman caught up in adultery and put forward for stoning to death (ch. 8) showed how comprehensive he was to point out the initiating and integral role of men in adultery, and how compassionate he was to forgive the woman and send her away with a note of warning. Jesus' close relationship with Mary, Martha and Mary Magdalene is read with extra-biblical conjectures that he had a love affair with them. But confining to the evidence within the Gospel all one can say is that Jesus had compassion towards female victims caught up in the cross currents of unjust traditions and exploiting men. Also some women friends and disciples who played an important part in his ministry, but there is no erotic behaviour either in actual practice or allegorical/symbolic sense.

Christians on the whole continue to be hesitant to talk about sex publicly and especially in the bhakti context. The idea of divine presence in which the genuine sexual acts including intercourse can take place with a reverential mood has not got into their thought while they call the matrimony holy! They have struggled with connecting sex as a positive instinct, and even a great gift of God, with bhakti. Anders Nygren (1890-1977), a Swedish Lutheran theologian, published his best-known classic, *Agape and Eros* (1932-39). For him the first one is unmotivated and self-giving love and the other, love that desires to attain a higher good.[1] It appeared to be clarifying the clear distinction between supernatural love and natural or erotic love. But no one can argue this clarification has settled the issue. If sexuality is part of the original blessing in creation, how can it be abominable and secretive with shame while treacherous misconducts including 'beastly rapes' happen within and without wedded relationship? There was a time in the Christian tradition when celibacy was glorified beyond proportion but recent reports of sex-scandals make sensitive persons raise questions about the nature of sexuality and celibacy. Needed is not only simple sex education and safeguards, but also thorough reflection on the relationship between attitude to sex, sexual activity which could be an expression of pure love, and deep intimacy with God.

In the Hindu religious traditions there is more positive view of sexuality. Texts like *Kāmasūtra*, stories of wedding between Gods and Goddesses, sleeping rooms in temples, phallic-yoni symbol, and sculpted and artistic representation of postures of sexual intercourse in certain temples are examples. Though the extreme and excessive sexual activity as represented in certain Tantric tradition is not appreciated by those associated with male dominant traditions and practices of purity-pollution divide, one may like Hindus to be more open speaking about sex than others. Do all these mean that the erotic encounter and dance of Kṛṣṇa with the gopīs is taken plainly and positively? Not at all. In the text itself a pertinent question is posed. The attentive king Parīkṣit said: 'God, the Lord of the universe, has descended into the world along with his bodily expansion (Balarāma) for the establishment

[1] A. Nygren, *Agape and Eros*, London: ET, 2 Vols., 1932-1939.

of *dharma* (here, all that is in accord with cosmic order) and for the suppression of *adharma*, non-dharma. He is the original speaker, exemplar and protector of the injunctions of *dharma*. How could he behave in a manner contrary to *dharma*, O *brāhmaṇa*, by touching the wives of others?' How can he (the Lord of the Yadu dynasty) do such abhorrent act? Clear my doubt' (33: 26-28). Śrī Śuka said:

> Just as fire consumes everything (without being polluted), so it is seen that the blatant transgressions of *dharma* by the more powerful of rulers are not faults. One who is not a powerful being should certainly never behave in the fashion, not even in his mind. Otherwise, acting out of foolishness, he will be destroyed...The words of powerful beings are truth, and so is whatever is performed by them. The wise will act in accordance with their words... He lives within the *gopīs*, their husbands and all living beings. He is the supreme witness who has assumed a form in this world for the purpose of sport. Manifest in a human form, he indulges in such pastime as a favour to the devotees. Hearing about these, one becomes fully devoted to him. Confused by his power of illusion, the men folk of Vraj were not resentful of Kṛṣṇa; each thought his own wife was present at his side...The sober person who is endowed with faith should hear and describe these pastimes of Viṣṇu with the maidens of Vraj. Achieving supreme devotion to the Lord, one quickly frees oneself from lust, the disease of the heart' (33: 33ff).

The answer is not simple and straightforward. It has many layers that include Kṛṣṇa's supremacy, commitment to wise behaviour, divine favour to the devotees, the whole episode being illusion and in supreme devotion there is freedom from lust.

There have been consistent efforts in the tradition to justify the erotic play of Kṛṣṇa with the gopīs. We consult one example:

> It is not surprising that the flood of eroticism in Krishnaite literature and life has caused some outsiders to see these worshipers as a libertine community, praising and probably practicing promiscuity in sexual matters. It is indeed to be observed that the orthodox Hindu society was, after the triumph of caste in the Gupta age, one of the most restrictive in the world in sexual matters, and that, by the time of the *Bhāgavata Purāṇa*, tantric groups had arisen that were in rebellion against the severe moral codes. In secluded places they were said to hold lawless congress in meetings comparable in some ways to the gathering for the Rāsa. Were these Bhāgavatas not social rebels of the same kind? Not at all. No report is known, made by either friend or foe, that Bhāgavatas ever performed the Rāsa carnal act, either as holy rite or in folk festivals. The *Bhāgavata's* prohibition appears to have been observed. Even in the gossip of outsiders these believers are never connected with the tantrics. From the time of the *Bhagavad Gītā,* civic concern had been prominent in their literature. Their relationship with the dominant Brahmins and kshatriyas, arbiters of Hindu society, were not hostile.[1]

At the same time, there seems to be a view that in a complete and true incarnation the supreme deity goes through all human experiences. The allegory of romantic love is to be read by the bhaktas in the scripture but sexual promiscuity should be kept away! If the process of kissing, caressing the breasts, massaging the thighs etc are pushed to the logic limit it will culminate in actual sexual intercourse and orgasim. And for the right-minded it should be laudable as long as it is done out of pure love with adequate preparation jist as their Lord which is contrary to the manipulative romance and beastly rape of which many men are guilty.

Commentaries on the Rāsalīlā do not clarify the hairline between romantic imagination of Kṛṣṇa's love game with the gopīs

---

[1] Hein in his 'Foreword' to Schweig's *Dance of Divine Love*, xv.

and the devotional intimacy. Vallabha's classicall commentary (with interpolation by his son Viṭṭhala) affirms that Kṛṣṇa is the source and medium of sexual love as well as the embodiment of all the moods. It is he who incites the mood of love on his devotees (gopīs) by his sound and sight. He gives the refined aesthetic taste to humans in different measures.

> For the love-making that occurred after that (i.e., after the Gopīs had gone to Kṛṣṇa in the forest) was no more or less than His gift of the Joy of His own Form after the manner of the mood of love, for His own Form has the moods as its very Essence, as holy scripture tells us in the words: 'Mood indeed is He.[1]

Joy which was once in every heart and then lost, was reawakened through the experience of the gopīs. At the same time 'Kṛṣṇa had an absolute unique experience of the mood of love with the Gopīs. It was different even from the mood He experiences with his wife Ramā (Lakṣmi), because the Gopīs are not married to him.'[2] Hence, there is a mutual fulfillment of the desire though Kṛṣṇa is eternal joy. The ambience and atmosphere of Vṛndāvana was most suitable for this mood. In Vallabha's words, 'what is fitting is what is according to the desire of the devotees.'[3] This is the case always and every where and whatever form a devotee sees or even hallucinates Kṛṣṇa. The gopīs were eligible for that night's experience because of their total love for Kṛṣṇa and his special grace bestowed on them. Their joy was complete. Vallabha's creative imagination has composed a concise and comprehensive verse placing the gopīs as the speakers:

> That is precisely why we address You as 'Lord of Love.' For wherever there is love, in the form of sexual union, in this world, You are its Lord. And without Your command

[1] J.D. Redington, *Vallabhācārya on the Love Games of Kṛṣṇa*, Delhi: Motilal Banarsidass, 1990, 7f; cf. Taitt. Up. II.7.1).

[2] Ibid., 8f.

[3] Ibid., 13.

> sexual love does not go forth into this world. Therefore we have been given to you, by Brahmā or Kāma (the gods of creation) as 'hired slave girls,' in order for You to introduce sexual love into the world...If sexual love should remain constrained and locked up in the Blessed Lord alone, then the mood of love would not exist in the world. We have come here so that You may make this love spread from Yourself over the entire world through us. But bringing that to pass must be the farthest thing from Your mind, because instead of that You are killing us! If this is so, then all the treatises on passionate love (Skt. *kāma-śāstra*) would be worthless, and the third of the four objects of human endeavour (i.e., *kāma*) does not even exist! Therefore You must by all means do what You have invited us here to do.[1]

Vallabha does not overtly spiritualize the sexual activity of Kṛṣṇa with the gopīs. He describes both preparation and the actual sexual intercourse in a far more realistic way.[2] In sum, it is not always easy to distinguish between allegorical sex and actual sex. What is clear, however, is that as the source of mood, joy and sexual love Kṛṣṇa shows that eros is part of the divine which his bhaktas can enjoy devotionally.

Unique Insights into the Nature of Unity and Diversity

Of all the books of the New Testament John's Gospel gives the greatest clues to the development of the concept and vision of God as one in three and three in one – one God known as Father,

---

[1] Ibid., 16f; Later BhP. X.21.27 is cited (24f) in which the gopīs mention in order, seeing, embracing, worshipping, touching, kissing, enjoying him sexually and the thrilling of the hair.

[2] Ibid., 137f; also see 200f, 213; it is again stated that 'Lakṣmi is 'the very Joy of Brahman' and by having the erotic play with a group of ordinary women who were not yet Brahman Kṛṣṇa acted 'just as a little boy.' 282 It is described that seeing Kṛṣṇa, the embodiment of passion, the gopīs became wounded by passion, and the moon in its effort to enter Kṛṣṇa too became wounded by passion and the moon 'represents Kṛṣṇa's semen.' There was ejaculation. 285.

Son and the Holy Spirit. Jesus clearly spoke that he and his Father were one in terms of holding deep intimacy and sharing in his radical mission. Several times he spoke about the same oneness to be experienced by their disciples and those who believed their words. Though the language is not easy to understand, one may see the vision so profound. Jesus prayed to the Father, 'that all of them may be one. Father, just as you are in me and I am in you. May they be also in us so that the world may believe that you have sent me…they may be one as we are one. I in them and you in me. May they be brought to complete unity to let the world know that you sent me and have loved them even as you have loved me' (17: 20-23). It is an astonishing insight that the unity among all Jesus' disciples, past and present, is in no way less than the unity between the Father and Jesus. The Holy Spirit (*pneauma* as neautral and its corresponding *Sophia* feminine gender) is mentioned in different connections. At the time of his baptism the Spirit came down from heaven as a dove and in turn it was realized that Jesus would baptize with Holy Spirit (1: 32-34). There is no special event in the Gospel of this peculiar baptism unless one takes it as the Spirit's transformation of persons ('born again') and unpredictable nature of her leading (3: 8). In his absence for a while, Jesus said, the Spirit will come from the Father to protect them and counsel them, and teach the truth. At the end the risen Jesus breathed the Holy Spirit on his disciples at the time of commissioning them for mission. We will come back in the conclusion reviewing the traditional formulation and suggesting a lesson from the Kṛṣṇa-gopīs' dance.

Sheridon suggests:

> Perhaps a homologue for the nature of this distinction is the Christian doctrine of the Trinity wherein otherness does not imply separation. Rather the perfection of the Deity requires a triune difference within the identity of the Godhead. In a homologous manner the *Bhāgavata* proposes a vision of a God who by his own power creates distinctions within himself. These distinctions derive

> reality from the Godhead without diminishing God's reality. To separate devotion from non-dualism as has often been done is therefore to trivialize the *Bhāgavata*'s vision of the devotee's love for Kṛṣṇa. Devotion is primarily an ontological rather than a moral phenomenon.[1]

This suggestion is confined to the identity and pluralistic personality of Kṛṣṇa himself. But there can be a reflection of the dynamic view of unity and plurality as we will point out in the conclusion.

The concept and vision of Trinity has been interpreted with reference to diversity or plurality. As early as 1970 Raymundo Panikkar published a seminal booklet entitled *Trinity and World Religions* in which he suggested Trinity as an inclusive framework to cover plurality as God himself embraces plurality.[2] Since then comments have been made in the form of both approval and criticism. The main point of caution has been to establish compatibility in specific ideas such as karma and transformation, dharma based on caste discrimination and a communal framework based on justice, peace, love and equality. Graham Schweig's reflection on the rasa dance from the perspective of religious pluralism is worth noting: 'The cowherd maidens linking arms in the dance represent the linking of human hearts and the solidarity of the human community of devoted souls. All souls, collectively, are invited to dance together with God, while simultaneously each individual soul is able to dance with God personally and exclusively. The Rāsa dance symbolizes the humility and passion of the devoted soul – the humility of love expresses through linking with other human beings, and the passion of love through souls linking with the supreme. This linking is the meaning of yoga, of which, as we have seen, the Gopīs are masters.'[3] Such

[1] Sheridon, *The Advaitic Theism of the Bhāgavata Purāṇa*, Delhi: Motilal Banarsidas, 1981, 148.

[2] Raymond Panikkar, *The Trinity and World Religions,* Bangalore: CISRS and Madras: CLS, 1970.

[3] "Vaishnava Bhakti Theology and Interfaith Dialogue" in *Journal of Vaishnava Studies*, 20/2 2012, 64.

linking or even inter-locking needs to be reflected further in the context of collaborative participation in a common human mission to address needs and challenges.

Social Appeal

Some may feel that in a bhakti study questions about socio-economic-political regeneration of India may not be asked. But others may want a reflection. In any case, as we have noted in this study, socio-economic factors cannot be ignored. Obviously, St. John's Gospel has more direct appeal to social realities than the Rāsalīlā section. Jesus' ministry and teaching took place mainly in his village, Nazareth which was most backward and rated insignificant in his time. Today though it is far improved Christian theologians and activists have identified such Nazareths all over the world and worked for their improvement. When there is mad rush to urban areas for various reasons, there are voices to urge to go back to the villages like Nazareth. It is asserted that life and hope lie in villages and one can have a better vision there of Jesus, crucified and risen yet giving solidarity with the victims of all forms of injustice. But churches are far behind realizing this vision and engaging in local mission.

Kṛṣṇa's solidarity with the cowherd community in Vraja is obvious. Whether this is interpreted to emphasise his identification with the poor and marginalized, can be established only by empirical studies. The Rāsalīlā experience was fundamental for the movement of Caitanya Mahāprabhu (1486-1533), the founder of Gaudia Vaiṣṇavism and Svami Bhaktivedanta Prabhupada (1896 – 1977), the founder of the International Society for Kṛṣṇa Consciousness (ISCON). Due to Caintanya's influence, his disciples built temples in Vraja and established it as a centre of religious learning. Today it attracts millions of pilgrims. There is a belief and even experience that Kṛṣṇa and his beloved consort Rādha are implicitly present and it is remembered as once the idyllic sight of a romantic place and Kṛṣṇa's eternal celestial abode (Goloka) or Garden of Eden. But those who have considerable experience of having lived there describe both the bhakti provoking atmosphere with numerous temples and in-depth dialogues as well as perplexing sights of stray dogs, roaming cows, begging lepers etc.[1] More recently the situation may have changed. Further, it is not clear if social engagement is an aspect of the mission of ISKCON. In the United States of America, there have been 'countercultural protests' against wars and certain policies of the government on education, religion, sexuality and so on.[2] A study of ISKCON centres in India with special reference to developing Vṛndāban and social engagements will be both revealing and updating.

Summary

It is important to decide on what we compare when we embark on a comparative analysis. A firm resolution not to exaggerate nor to distort is vital. John's Gospel and the Rāsalīlā section of the Bhāgavata Purāṇa come from two religious traditions or two communities, and their literary genres are different, one with historical events combined with interpretations and the other with purāṇic narratives of encounters, intense experiences and sports. In John Jesus is divine in the sense that he is the enfleshment of the Logos, cosmic Word, assumes the Jewish titles Messiah or Son of God and Son of Man, and above all intimately one with the Father sharing with him the works of liberation. Kṛṣṇa, on the other hand, has a long process behind his assuming the position of the supreme God Viṣṇu's avatāra, and here the supreme God himself although the names Viṣṇu and Vāsudeva occur towards the end. The disciples of Jesus and the gopīs who played with Kṛṣṇa are taken as representatives of bhaktas and their social standing and expression of bhakti are different. Both the groups respond to a divine call to be with their masters, to learn, to enjoy a casual intimacy, to experience a moment of bitter separation and profound oneness. But the bhakti of Jesus' disciples is connected to

---

[1] For example, see K. Klostermaier, *Hindu & Christian in Vrindaban*, London: SCM, 1969.

[2] J.S. Judah, *Hare Krishna and the Counterculture*, New York: Wiley Interscience Publication, 1974, 112-158.

a commitment to God's mission mediated through Jesus whereas the gopīs intrinsically enjoy the refreshing presence of their Lord. For the disciples the climax was Jesus' crucifixion, resurrection and sending them on a mission, and for the maiden of the Vraja the exhilarating dance with their lover and Lord. Number of insights are striking in the two separate narratives of bhakti and most notable are bhakti in relation to sexuality, and understanding more adequately the relationship between unity and diversity. They raise questions for further dialogue between the devotees of these two religious traditions.

Conclusions

The Multi-Dimensional Character of Bhakti

We have done an engaging study of bhakti with special reference to St John's Gospel and the Rāsalīlā section of the Bhāgavata Purāṇa. We started with observing the ongoing discussion on definitions and explications of the word and meanings of bhakti. Can we contribute to this discussion from this study? Obviously there are overlaps. However, what we have described in the first chapter we will recall and connect with the aspects of bhakti, both common and distinctive, we have observed in the two texts of our study. The following are the most remarkable.

First, bhakti lies dormant in every human psyche and consciousness and emerges to the surface when a person comes into contact with the compelling and fascinating reality, which one may call supreme, transcendence or sacred. The transcendent reality is often the immanent reality too and, more significantly, takes a personal form to manifest its love, to provide help in crisis and to reassure his/her continued presence until the end of the life's journey. In most cases, perhaps with certain amount of exaggeration, the bhakta outpours his/her inability, insufficiency, ignorance and sinfulness. In the saving grace offered there is a movement from confusion to clarity, restlessness to peace, and from depression to bliss. In some traditions, particularly in the Christian and Vaiṣṇava traditions, commitment to service and supreme surrender in different degrees are the culminating points of the bhakta's journey, having fixed one's mind on the transcendent reality named God.

Second, if one does not have attachment to a supreme person called God, as Krishna Sharma points out (we noted in the first chapter), his/her transcendent feeling may be directed to a special person (e.g. guru, the 'guru bhakti') or country (i.e. 'desa bhakti'). It is already observed that those who passionately belong to ideological systems such as Marxism, Communism or Humanism, may be said to follow a quasi religion. More recently, implicit religion has been introduced with the definition of commitment, integrating foci or common concern. From sports to IT hype, a variety of expressions are being studied. Today there is a talk about secular spirituality which shares features of implicit religion, and explains new centres and multiple belonging in contexts such as the multi-religious and secular India. However, these categories of people may not be agreeing to be called religious or devotional, and only a dialogue with them will bring out positions and views.

Third, the underlying fact of the non-material part of a human person is conceived differently and has been subjected to theological interpretation. For example, the Hebrew Bible declares that God created humans in God's own image (Gen. 1:27), and the word 'image' is interpreted as the inherent capacity to love and communicate with God and to participate in God's continued creation and humanization of all people. Also, another creation account mentions, 'The Lord formed a human being from the dust of the ground and breathed into his nostrils the breath of life, so that he became a living creature' (Gen. 2:7). The Hebrew word (*nephesh*) used here originally meant 'life-force', affirming humans as unitary beings without suggesting any dichotomy between body and spirit, but in the course of translations, particularly in Greek the word 'soul' came to dominate the Christian vocabulary. When the New Testament uses the terms body, mind, soul, heart and spirit in different orders, unless the reader is careful it may be confusing. John's Gospel is special in using consistently the word 'life' with adjectives such as 'eternal' and qualifiers such as fullness. Jesus calls for the involvement of the total person in God's ongoing mission with passionate love. In the Vaiṣṇava tradition, since the belief in soul or *ātma* was introduced in the Upaniṣads, its predicament and liberation from *karma saṁsāra* became the central factor in bhakti literature. Those who interpret Kṛṣṇa's pastime with the young milkmaids as allegorical, point out that the maids are embodiments of the souls of devotees. They add, with a distinctive kind of knowing bhakti as liberating, fulfilling and leading to bliss.

Fourth, in the name of bhakti a variety of religious activities happen. The elementary act of prayer trying to move, persuade and win the favour of God is most popular in all theistic religions. Particularly, in the present context of globalization there is a renewed concern about safety, security and stability. Even if there is assurance of all the good gifts in right times and gracious divine acceptance although unacceptable, why do Christians engage in a relentless pursuit of such things? Despite tragedies in stampede, pilgrim numbers swelling more and more in India is an expression of the same pursuit. Jesus did ask his disciples to pray to the Father in his name and promised that the prayers will be granted. The purpose is not to accumulate material wealth and gain mental peace but to be able to do God's will, to be guided by the Spirit and to dare to fight the evil forces in order to offer life in its fullness for all. For the gopīs the most precious gift is Kṛṣṇa himself, before whom all other possessions and bonds stand secondary or nothing. They enjoy their intimacy with their lover and Lord in a most dynamic way and win his love. St Augustine's words, 'Lord, our hearts are restless until they find rest in you' suit their experience. Such expressions should challenge the elementary bhakti of millions who are mad after wealth, health, happiness in this life and their abundance in the next life.

Fifth, in the Judeo-Christian tradition God is both impersonal and personal. As impersonal, God is transcendent of human imaginations though he is presented in anthropomorphic forms. The prohibition of idol worship in the Hebrew scripture is not only because such worship among other communities was tainted with superstitious and murderous practices such as child sacrifice, but also because God wanted his people to think beyond human made idols, being open with imagination. And God was personal in a particular sense of being able to inspire humans, to speak through prophets and lead them by God's Spirit. Jesus in John's Gospel is the enfleshment of the cosmic divine Word, beloved Son of the heavenly Father and Son of Man in solidarity with the suffering victims of injustice just as he saw the Father to be. He was receiving peoples' love and after resurrection became worship-able, but he refused to be idolized and tried to lead his disciples to experience the depth of divine love shared between the Father, Son and the Holy Spirit. However, in popular Christianity Jesus is taken the personal or favoured deity who is greater than other deities. Those who are aware of the history of traditions and theological formulations continue to maintain the vision of Trinity which is both personal and impersonal.

In the Vedāntic tradition there continued a discussion, even debate, on the question whether God the ultimate is personal or impersonal. Where the supreme is imagined as impersonal without any characteristic, the approach includes reading, listening and meditating until the mystical leap of union is achieved. What is the tool to verify the authenticity of that experience? And when it is ineffable, how can one express it? Earlier scientific investigations were applied and they included mescaline (R.C. Zaehner) but what was experienced was found to be inadequate. The Gītā relegates the impersonal Brahman to a stable state of mind and extols devotion to the personal Lord. This was elaborated by the Vaiṣṇava Vedāntins, Rāmānuja and Madhva, drawing on the experience of distinguished bhaktas such as the Tamil Āḷvārs. Notably, there is no trace that Rāmānuja knew or used Bhāgavata Purāṇa, but the description of bhakti in this text does not contradict any of his basic affirmations. In the Rāsalīlā section, Kṛṣṇa is both supremely impersonal and intimately personal. Thus, bhakti presupposes God being personal but its meaning needs to be carefully distinguished from the ordinary human perception of 'personal.' At the same time God cannot be possessed by particular individuals, not bound by idols, and this must create in the bhaktas a sense of awesome wonder and openness to see further unfolding of the reality.

Sixth, both mystic meditation and devotional outpouring may be possible as either alternatives or complimentary to each other. Claiming one as superior may be necessary to substantiate one particular metaphysical vision. But a bhakta may find meaning in both depending on his/her mood at a particular moment. Jesus and his disciples had their private moments of prayer, perhaps meditative prayer. At times they had open prayer with moments of rejoicing. Relating to the Father, Son and Holy Spirit was possible separately while relating to the mysterious reality of the Triune God also was possible. As we have already noted, Kṛṣṇa in the Gītā almost succeeded incorporating the experience of Brahman and of nirvāṇa into the supreme framework of bhakti. As the *viśvarūpa darśana* demonstrated, his cosmic body included all entities of life and experiences. Water, flower, controlled breathing etc can be accepted as offerings of loving devotion. In the Rāsalīlā narrative there is mention of those gopīs who could not rush to meet Kṛṣṇa, but who were engaged in meditating upon him and gained the same benefits as of those who participated in the romantic sport of love. Therefore, a clear-cut division between meditation and devotion seems unnecessary and artificial.

Seventh, imageries and imaginations are important corollaries of bhakti. Abstract ideas are dry and they may have appeal only to the intellect. King, father, Lord with compassionate glance, gracious smile and lotus feet, mother, kinsman, friend, lover, bride-groom and so on, are not only poetic embellishments but also having the power to kindle emotions and help imagination. Even the pain of separation is compensated with imminent joy of expectant deliverance. Their joy might find expressions such as singing and dancing. Also, there can be images of moving to the grading nearness to and union with God such as the deity's abode, body, and inseparable union.

Eighth, even if the vision of the Supreme is inclusive, a certain sense of being exclusive is characteristic of bhakti. The 'I am sayings' of Jesus and his claims such as 'I and my Father are one' and 'I am the way, truth and life, and no one can comes to the Father except through me' dominate Christian bhakti expressions. If they are studied in the original context they may present important challenges to the bhaktas themselves, but they throw them on outsiders and develop a superficial pride, even arrogance. For the gopīs there was no one like Kṛṣṇa in all the worlds. Even Brahmā, Śiva and Śrī (the goddess of fortune) place the dust of the feet of Kṛṣṇa on their heads to remove their sins. All the gods and their consorts are enchanted by his dance with the milkmaids. There should be a place for saying to God as per our vision 'you are the best', but to transpose it to interfaith conversation creates trouble.

Ninth, particular religious traditions and particular contexts colour the bhakti experience and expression. St. John's Gospel is set in the background of the persecution experienced by a group of Jewish Christians in the Jewish Diaspora. There is already in the tradition a vision of the Son of Man coming from the heaven and providing solidarity with those suffering persecution. This vision is tied with the root story of the Hebrew/Jewish community according to which God in the name of Yahweh liberated their ancestors when they were slaves in Egypt, made a covenant with them, gave them commandments and called them his people in the sense they were expected to be faithful to the covenant and establish a community based on the values of justice, peace and love. When they went astray the prophets reprimanded them and directed the proper way to go. For the prophets and the people bhakti was not an isolated event in an enclosure or enchanting natural spot. They sang, prayed and lamented with acute awareness of the challenges of their socio-political-economic context. Standing in the same tradition, Jesus and his disciples scantily expressed their bhakti in an open way. But all their activities for transforming persons and the society were governed by their constant relationship with God and acute awareness of living in the presence of God in the context of which the disciples needed correction and encouragement from their Master.

Tenth, continuity and discontinuity with the tradition and initiatives for a new movement seem to be characteristic of bhakti. Division, rejection and relativising are not avoidable. Jesus had to challenge the conservative and fundamentalist trends of his own religious tradition. He referred to other shepherds and pseudo-saviours when he claimed to be the good shepherd. He had a special intimacy with God that found tangible expression in liberation activities. As a new way, truth and life he presented before his disciples and people a new vision, tradition and action plan. At least the emergence of a new sect or movement in his name became unavoidable. In the case of Kṛṣṇa and his devotees the stated context had the quest of a dying king for fulfilling the dharma during the remaining few days. He was under a curse and such acts are plenty in the purāṇas. Whatever may be the purpose of such stories, quest for at least one concern of dharma seems to be important in the Bhāgavada Purāṇa. The Vedic or Ārya dharma was already in the fluid stage affected by challenges from the śramaṇas and from its amalgamation with the bhāgavata tradition and the inclusion of the divine hero Kṛṣṇa. If we analyse relevant sections of the Bhāgavada Purāṇa we can easily find the tensions created by the above challenges. But we have space to point out only a few clues found in the Rāsalīlā section. It is interesting that while Kṛṣṇa is the supreme Lord throughout the play, Viṣṇu takes over at the end. A separate study is needed to find out if this reflects the continued problem of having a hero from a shepherd community into the Ārya fold but having Viṣṇu's consort Śrī as his own, or betrays a sectarian modification of the text. In any case, reflecting the purāṇic pattern, the other two gods of the Triad (*Tirumūrti*), Śiva and Brahmā, are relegated to an inferior position. In response to Kṛṣṇa's doubts, the gopīs tell him that women straying away is proper to the Āryas. There is a mention of the rāsalīlā taking place in duration of Brahmā's night (4390 million years). Vedic gods with their consorts witness to the vigorous dance with great excitement while the celestial singers join in. All these seem to suggest that in spite of the fluidity and uncertainty of positions, this was Kṛṣṇa's supreme opportunity to establish his supremacy and reunion with his community of Vraja thereby inviting all people everywhere to join in the play which portrays the fulfillment of life not only for the dying king but the whole of humanity. The world reverberates the song! Every bhakti tradition may have such unique punch line.

Eleventh, commitment and openness should be the two eyes of a bhakti experience. Throughout the Judeo-Christian tradition there is the emphasis of being open to the further unfolding of the Reality. From liberation in the name of Yahweh at the beginning and struggle against an imperial power with the symbol of 'a lamb slain from the foundation of the world' in the end one can notice this. Jesus spoke about 'being born again' and being open to be led by the Spirit who was to lead the disciples and devotees into all truth. One experience leads to another and there is no room for tarrying and being rigid. Step by step Jesus led his disciples towards a vision and experience of the Trinitarian God. Kṛṣṇa too led his beloved gopīs from an ordinary meeting to an extraordinary experience of a whirlpool dance. He was compassionate towards those maids who could not keep pace with the vigorous movement of the dance and attended to their need. However, finally what happened to the young women, we do not know. But we know their successors of devotion today. The independence and movement, characteristic of the dance, is supposed to continue in devotional practices. Are they kept intact or restrictions are put in the name of ancient practice of ritual? This question may help to understand the present nature of Vaiṣṇava temple worship in general and Kṛṣṇa worship in particular. This question applies to Christian worship forms as well.

Twelfth, bhakti need not lead to be ascetic, alienating and introverted. Even world-denial is not the natural flow of it. Passion and affection in common life need not be sacrificed. Jesus had some wonderful friends and some of them were women. He trained his disciples to be good friends. His definition of true friendship is that there is no secret between friends. And also he declared that there is no greater love than one giving his/her life for friends. The Rāsalīlā takes such close relationship to a deeper level. Before their friend and Lord Kṛṣṇa the gopīs for a moment found all other attachments to be worthless. Romantic play or sexual game has a place if it is done with pure mind and mutual commitment. As the Lord of mood, joy and sexual love Kṛṣṇa was spontaneous and reveling himself and enabled his friends and devotees to have a share. In a world of sexual violence in many forms such interaction without the disease of lust enobles intimacy. At the same time where sexual description is allegorical and where actual, and in what form bhakti-bound sex should take, needs clarification.

It is hoped that these twelve observations on bhakti will contribute to the ongoing discussion on the nature and dimensions of bhakti.

Mutual Fecundation

In the introduction we mentioned that gaining a clarification about its meaning in practice as one of the aims of this study. This is often mentioned in interfaith studies and dialogue, but how it happens is not spelt out. Of course, there are unconscious influences between religious communities resulting in adopting certain beliefs and practices of a culture. For example, Christians often use the word karma in the sense of fate and predestination. Many of them are comfortable with dividing time as auspicious and inauspicious. But most of them refuse to use Indian music and architecture which are cherished by Hindus. At the same time, certain attempts of indigenization in areas of worship patterns and religious life style are not always appreciated by Hindus. Some revivalist Hindus even ridicule them as wolves coming in the guise of sheep. With a recognition of all such ambiguities, in the light of this study, we will point out four areas for mutual enrichment.

First, can we bring face to face the image of Jesus hanging on the cross with bleeding wounds and flute blowing Kṛṣṇa dancing with blossoming smile? As we have repeatedly pointed out, the God of the Bible suffers in solidarity with suffering people. God is kind and compassionate like a father and mother. Though God loves all people God has a special concern for victims of all forms of injustice and those who are vulnerable. This confession raises the question about the supreme power of God. One answer given is that the nature of God's power does match any form of power we know. God in love goes to the depth point of being crucified and died but with an inalienable right to survive and to give new life. Thus dying and rising seems to be the eternal rhythm of God's life and function and the power of survival and love works in mysterious ways.

The best expression of Christian bhakti, then, is sharing in God's pain and participating in the ongoing mission of transforming the world. There is joy in such bhakti which may be deep down hopeful for the future. Paul, who rejoiced in suffering and asked his church in Philippi to rejoice, writes: 'My one desire is to know Christ and the power of his resurrection, and sharing his sufferings in growing conformity with his death, in hope of somehow attaining the resurrection from the dead' (Phil. 3: 10-11). This may be difficult to understand fully but true in the life of many Christians. For example, Sadhu Sundar Singh (1889-1929), a Sikh convert, wandering monk and popular preacher, declared, 'the cross is heaven.'

The supreme Kṛṣṇa is always triumphant and smiling. His pastime with the milkmaids by singing and dancing with amorous behaviour invigorates the spirit of his bhaktas. The artistic presentations of Kṛṣṇa in temples including the icons of white marble are very attractive. As it happens in his temples, particularly in the temples of ISKCON, the devotees engage in dancing, singing and reciting his name repeatedly. The Ācāryas explain that the ultimate goal is to experience bliss, a transcendental vibration, which is not forced upon the mind but emerges in the course of dancing and chanting. Does God suffer according to the Vaiṣṇava visions? The Vedāntic traditions of Rāmānuja, Madhva and others identify Kṛṣṇa, Viṣṇu or Vāsudeva with the supreme Brahman of the Upaniṣads. Their exposition of God as both supreme and accessible is remarkable. But even in Rāmānuja's vision and interpretation of Viśiṣṭādvaita where God holds the whole world and all souls as his body, the question about the possibility of God the supreme soul of all beings to suffer has not been raised. Then it is natural for a Kṛṣṇa bhakta to see biblical vision of God, Christ, Spirit and the saints as gloomy and sad unless he/she is able to imagine with clues from the Bible that God is rejoicing too but always in relation to a faith community of ordinary people gaining new life and building up hope for a better future.

One may argue that fascination is different from simple attraction. Rudolf Otto's description of the mystery that is both terrifying and fascinating may be helpful here. This idea is not absent in Hindu bhakti texts. For example, Māṇkkavācakar, refers to the myth of Śiva being called by his father-in-law Dakṣa 'mad' etc as he wore necklace of human skulls and was roaming in cremation grounds. The poet-saint interprets it saying that the beauty of Śiva lies beyond conventional fashions and fancies, and he is indeed mad, but made in love! Perhaps more than any other symbol in the world history, the cross of Jesus may have fascinated more people. As Jesus said, when as the Son of Man he was lifted up from the earth (on the cross) he would draw everyone to himself (Jn. 12:32). It is true that his torture and cry of dereliction has caused many then and now to stumble, but when he breathed out last with a loud cry, a centurion who had watched him for a long time spontaneously declared, 'this man must have been the son of God' (Mk.15:39). Further, the early Christians realized that Jesus, even after his resurrection, continued to suffer which inspired them to suffer in faith or bhakti with others. Perhaps the balance between celebration of life including the risen life of Jesus and suffering in solidarity with the victims and the vulnerable, has not been creatively maintained in the Churches.

We live in a world where hard work is praised indiscriminately and hard work often leads to workaholism which in turn pushes people to mental health problems. Kṛṣṇa's regular pastime with his dear ones may call for a balance. In the Hebrew Bible, it is noted that, following six days of creation, God rested on the seventh day and made it sacred (Gen. 1: 27). Unfortunately, there is no detail about God's taking of rest, but, remarkably 'rest' is applied to labourers, land, animals and so on as the primary mark of a liberated life throughout Bible. Also, there are occasions on which devoted people could collect their sacred tithes and enjoy eating and drinking (wine) in the presence of God while remembering the landless, aliens, orphans and widows (Deut. 14: 22-29). There is a prophetic vision that in the new creation God and devoted people will delight and rejoice over each other (Is. 65: 18-19). While working to realize this vision Jesus celebrated life, eating and drinking with his disciples and the marginalized in the society. In the 'spiritualized' Christianity all these are forgotten. Christians need to recover the sense of joy which could be expressed meaningfully in worship services. Often the charismatic outpouring of emotion with shouting and jumping in churches and prayer meetings look artificial and irritating for outsiders. In some churches in Africa dancing in worship happens naturally. On the whole in majority of churches worship services are led with monochromic control, serious postures and ritual fast reading of the liturgies. Particularly the Eucharist, Thanksgiving, is conducted almost like a funeral service with sober music and participants with long faces. The most important acclamation in the liturgy is 'Christ has died, Christ is risen and Christ will come again.' If we don't demonstrate the meaning of it in gestures, with lively music and even simple steps of dance we convey to a Kṛṣṇite that the Christian gospel carries a kill-joy ethos. In turn, to balance, the Kṛṣṇites may take in the idea of suffering in solidarity with others in their devotional activities.

Second, the moral character or ethical content of bhakti needs to be recognized. As we pointed out in the first chapter, A.J. Appasamy, a distinguished theologian on bhakti, located it beyond emotional fervor and flights of speculation. For him bhakti implies 'the difficult yet joyous discipline of walking along His path of suffering. The attainment of salvation by suffering is not a specially Christian idea; the moral quality of suffering is.' The quality here needs unpacking. Just like other Indian Christian theologians of early phase, Appasamy also failed to recognize the quality defined in the Hebrew/Jewish tradition which produced Jesus. We have repeatedly maintained the Hebrew idea of God's suffering in solidarity with the victims and vulnerable and this continued in the life and teachings of Jesus and beyond. Jesus came to seek the lost sheep for which he was prepared to give his life. He chose a weak band of disciples and sent them on mission as representatives of the victim community with full right either to forgive or not to forgive those who victimize.

The Hebrew injunctions including the Ten Commandments were meant for establishing a model community which would have been attractive for others. Though some later interpretations of some of the commandments made things complex and worked in disfavor of women and aliens, the spirit of the commandments was never given up. The commandments revealed God's grace and obedience to them was the expression of loving devotion. The affirmations such as 'for the law was given, but grace and truth came through Jesus Christ' may be taken as representing exaggerations as part of anti-Jewish polemic. Jesus appealed to the conservative wing of Jews by reminding them what their ancestors did and how they had not deviated from a spirituality of being open to God's new doing. 'What I see my Father do, I do' was his motto. It was liberation and fullness of life he acted on. After recognizing the commandments of the tradition he added his new commandment of loving one another. In fact, this was based on the primary twin commandment of loving God with one's whole being and loving the neighbor as oneself. However, driven by a misunderstanding of the Hebrew/Jewish roots of the Christian gospel, there developed among the early Christians the antithetical view of law and grace. Martin Luther made it worse through his anti-Jewish polemic and presentation of a truncated gospel rejecting even the balance between faith and action as advocated by James.

Jesus was not passive in his devotional attachment to his heavenly Father. He was active in his mission until his end. He confronted those of his own religious tradition with their deviation and rigidity. When some of them claimed that they were the children of Abraham he declared they were the devil's (Jn. 8: 31-45). He pleaded with them for recognizing who he was and appreciating what he was doing. It is often pointed out in theology that Jesus was the greatest critique of religion. Uncritical acceptance of religious practices, even bhakti, would lead to blind faith and superstitious beliefs and practices. This critical approach too came from the prophets of his tradition. For Jesus, the test for true bhakti is to bear loving fruits in life, to participate in God's ongoing mission, and to be open to the unfolding of divine truth.

Kṛṣṇa's love and compassion found a profound expression in his concern about his people. He enquired about the welfare of his community in Vraja. The gopīs pointed out that he belonged to their community. After many ordeals he attained supremacy and now he is the supreme God. Yet he did not forget his shepherd community which was perhaps on the fringes of the Ārya society. Though he is not here simply an avatāra of Viṣṇu as used to be, he is able to take any number of forms he wants. He came from his highest place to the lowest and identified with his original community. The story does not say anything about his particular action for the benefit of the community. Perhaps it is not proper to ask for tangible benefit as an outcome of the self-engagement of the Lord either in apparent mischief or game. It is reasonable, however, to take the gopīs as the representatives of the community. Further, it is affirmed that his incarnation is 'for the good of the universe, and dispels the darkness of the people of Vraj.' Echoing the message of the Gītā it is affirmed that Kṛṣṇa descended into the world 'for the establishment of dharma and the suppression of non-dharma.' He removes ailment from the heart of his devotees and out of compassion and favour he spends his pastime with his devotees. Again we do not have details of the implications for his engagement outside his close circle of gopīs.

'Serving' is a key word associated with bhakti. Jesus washed the feet of his disciples thus setting an example to overcome the temptation of power and authority and to serve one another. Kṛṣṇa, after his reappearance, tells the gopīs that he was serving them without explaining. Then he comes with a chorus of praises for their acts of devotion. He admires them that they broke the enduring shackles of household, even transcending the Vedic dharma and came to serve him. More poignantly, he says that he cannot reciprocate 'even in the lifetime of a god' and declares, 'let your reward be your own excellence.' Such an open appreciation for dedicated service may be built into Christian bhakti expressions.

During the vigorous dance Kṛṣṇa multiplied his form in order to insert himself in between two pairs of the girls. There was no need for them to fight for the right side and the left side of their Lord as did two disciples of Jesus, who created a furor! And just as Jesus was concerned about the wellbeing of his disciples Kṛṣṇa too was concerned about his devotees. Most stunningly, he stopped when one or two dancers exhausted and attended to them and encouraged them with touches and embraces. Nevertheless, everything came to an end with pleasure. We have no account of Kṛṣṇa's further acts of compassion, nor of the gopīs.

We have already noted Kṛṣṇa's confrontation with devas and asuras, but there is no fight for justice, peace and love unless such mythological fights are taken as symbolical of actual and ongoing fights for justice and liberation. Certainly there was some tension between Ārya dharma and Bhāgavata dharma, but the author(s) of the purāṇa does not provide details. If the theory is right, the śramaṇa challenge to the extravagant ritual with belief in its intrinsic power generation of the Āryas and the discriminative varṇa system, was contained with the bhakti emphasis of the Bhāgavata tradition. And though one may imagine the transcendence of bhakti over extravagant ritual and caste discrimination, we have yet to know its operation among the Kṛṣṇites in any considerable manner. Here one can learn from Jesus, the greatest critique of ritualistic religion and champion of social and personal transformation.

Third, the Christian vision that God is one in three and three in one has confused not only outsiders but also Christians. After all efforts to offer some explanation with images and illustrations fail, it is declared to be a mystery! To start with, the perception of Trinity is not in the earlier parts of the scriptures although interpretations on certain passages are given and paintings done, which look artificial. It is more convincing to say that from receiving the revelation of God as liberator in the enigmatic name of Yahweh there were moments of new unfolding of God's 'person' and nature. The coming of Jesus as the Son of God and enfleshment of the cosmic Word opened a new window into the reality of God. Among the Gospels, St. John's comes closest to an evolving formulation of the vision of Trinity as it talks about Jesus in this way and the Holy Spirit as both empowering and replacing Jesus for some time. The baptismal and greeting formula of Father-Son-Holy Spirit found in Matthew and certain epistles, most probably, reflect practices in the early church. It was in the church councils that the matter was debated and finalized, although its explanation has continued. In the first place, as we noted in the last chapter, debates on the nature of the oneness between the Father and the Son was settled with the Greek word 'of one substance' (*homoousios*). In the explanation of Trinity also the word 'substance' was used. It appeared to be too abstract and therefore the word 'three persons' (*hypostases*) with shared existence of spiritual, divine and corporal natures was introduced but what kind of 'person' was a question. Further, to believe that the Son was begotten or generated of the Father was found to be easier than timing and locating the procession of the Holy Spirit. The controversy continued until the eleventh century when the Western Church settled with the formula that the Spirit 'proceeded from the Father and the Son', but the Eastern (Orthodox) Churches were firm with 'from the Father only'. This clause, called *filioque* ('from the Father and the Son') drove to the great schism, perhaps one of the silliest moments in the history of Christianity! Even after all such developments Christianity could not live with one or other of the above formula. The Unitarian Church and Oneness Pentecostals are examples of influential forms of Christianity in which belief in Trinity is dispensable.

Dynamic Trinity is something we suggest taking into account the essential features of the traditional concept of Trinity with insights from the extraordinary whirlpool dance of Kṛṣṇa with gopīs. What is known as the economic Trinity 'refers to the acts of the triune God with respect to the creation, history, salvation, the formation of the Church, the daily lives of believers, etc. and describes how the Trinity operates within history in terms of the roles or functions performed by each Person of the Trinity—God's relationship with creation.' The immanent Trinity, on the other hand, 'speaks of the interior life of the Trinity, the reciprocal relationships of Father, Son, and Spirit to each other without reference to God's relationship with creation.' They are complimentary. And it stands to reason that the creative and dynamic reality of Trinity has the centrifugal and centripetal movement, appearing in great speed, one and three. When Kṛṣṇa and gopīs danced in circle with the accompaniment of nature and celestial choir, the Lord in different forms inserted in between the pairs of the young women, with fast moments and splashing in the water, they appeared to be simultaneously one and many. This might be applied to the essential inner life of the three persons and their liberative actions in the world and enjoying fellowship with the devotees. In this moving circle we may perceive the presence of the one or three of them together. Not the abstract language of substance, but the dynamic communitarian movement gives a lively image of a living reality. There is a warning too: if any one 'person' in the Trinity is held in devotion permanently s/he becomes an idol and for this reason any form of a Jesus cult or Spirit filling becomes questionable.

The Kṛṣṇites may put forward the typical Hindu position of 'one and many.' Traditional shifts from polytheism to henotheism, to monotheism, to monism and panentheism, are now replaced by the open assertion that 'Gods are many.' The polycentrism of the ancient banyan is another suggestion. Some add spirits of all kinds. This is to confront all the subjugating powers of invaders and empires in the name of one God and one scripture. However, we have yet to hear a convincing explanation about the conflicts between gods and their winning which seem to mirror the political power conflicts on earth. Kṛṣṇa is said to have overcome the powerful Vedic god Indra. In the Rāsalīlā section he is presented as superior to Śiva, Brahmā and the Goddess. At the end it is said that it is Viṣṇu who enjoyed pastime with the gopīs and he is supreme deserving faithful devotion. As we have suggested, it either exposes the continued tension between the Vedic god Viṣṇu and the Bhāgavata divine-hero Kṛṣṇa who passed through many stages including an avatāra and became the Supreme Lord replacing Viṣṇu, or it betrays a sectarian modification. Today no one would deny the fact that some sort of a unified vision of the Divine would greatly facilitate concerted effort to transform communities and nations.

Fourth, bhakti and sexuality may be a relevant topic. Apart from the Song of Songs the Bible does not have a romantic poetry. The Yahweh God is very hot and jealous demanding chastity and faithful relationship between a man and woman. He cannot be perceived to have a wife though allegorically he is portrayed as the lover, bride groom and husband of his people. Jesus had friends among women but there is no indication of his amorous behaviour or spending pastime in the style of Kṛṣṇa. In the Christian tradition celibacy is extolled and the recent revelations of sex scandals of some celibates have raised new questions about sexuality and Christian morality. While there are clues of sexual mooring in certain songs and prayers among Christians it is a pastoral challenge to deal with young persons who either openly or secretly struggle with sexual instincts in a conservative surrounding. The distinction maintained between *eros* and *agape* which has further reinforced the idea that 'eros' is beyond the purview of the Divine should be challenged.

Kṛṣṇa-Gopīs sport in a romantic and even erotic posture, is revealing. The narrative is of course obscene (to non-devotees?) when we read of Kṛṣṇa caressing with his soothing hands the faces, breasts and thighs of the women thus arousing lustful desire (kāma) in them. At the same time Kṛṣṇa calls them 'chaste women.' In the text (BhP. 33: 26ff) itself there are shocking questions about Kṛṣṇa's behaviour. There is an explanation that just like fire can consume everything but nothing can affect it, Kṛṣṇa was self-content and of pure love without lust. More significantly, this story is spiritualized as the symbolic representation of the relationship between God and his devotees. He carefully differentiated their love for him from adultery of a woman without exception of good birth which does not lead to heaven. 'It is scandalous, fear-laden, worthless, fraught with difficulty and abhorrent.' The last verse, probably an interpolation, mentions the true identity of God and the true meaning of lust in relation to devotion: 'Achieving supreme devotion to the Lord, one quickly frees oneself from lust, the disease of the heart.'

In the Hindu religious traditions there is more positive view of sexuality than any other religious traditions. Texts like *Kāmasūtra*, stories of wedding between Gods and Goddesses, sleeping rooms in temples, phallic-yoni symbol and iconic-artistic representation of postures of sexual intercourse in certain temples are examples. There are some modern gurus who connect sexual act with young women with enlightenment. Though the extreme and excessive sexual activity as represented in certain Tantric cults is not appreciated by many within the tradition, one may find Hindus more open speaking about sex in connection with spirituality than others. It is interpreted that divine figures in human forms go through all the experiences of humans including mischief and romantic or erotic play. A logical conclusion may be to imagine that they engage in actual sexual intercourse as well. There is still room to interpret that the divinity shows meaning of such intercourse as true expression of pure love, and it has a great appeal to humans who often indulge in obscene acts and cruel acts of rape and intercourse whether it is within wedlock or without. 'Domestic rape', rampant in Indian society, has been recently highlighted. The Kristu bhaktas and Kṛṣṇa bhaktas need to dialogue with open mind. The following questions may help: In what way can the sex symbolism enhance bhakti? Are there boundaries between sex life and devotional life? Can there be sexual arousal without some element of lust? Can we jointly prepare guidelines on sexuality as an expression of pure love?

Hybridization

Hybridity or hybridization is seen as part of the 'dubious' view of post-modernism. To acknowledge, the dynamic process is identified as one of the dimensions of religion and the interrelatedness of both the Semitic religions and the Indian religions is studied rather thoroughly. In the process, a form of the loose term syncretism has taken place which is not always healthy for those who want to stict to the originality of their tradition. The Hebrew/Jewish prophets including Jesus attacked some forms of syncretism as signaling deviation from the original call and vision. Is the botanical-zoological analogy of hybridization suggesting something different? Let us refer to an instance of using this analogy. For Paul and his colleagues there was a crucial hermeneutical challenge as they propagated the new faith in the Hellenistic and Roman world. Salvation by undeserved divine grace, or accepting the unconditional acceptance of God already found in Christ, was the message he made central. Yet, this posture could lead to the extreme of forgetting and undermining the Jewish roots, even though the church was defined in Hebrew terms, i.e. 'kingdom of royal priesthood' (Ex. 19. 6; cf. 1 Pet. 2. 9). When excitement about the new faith went to the extent of undermining that Jewish heritage, the Jewish Paul had to tell the Roman church that even though some branches fell off, the root of the olive (Jewish) was holy and Christians were like wild olive shoots 'have been grafted in among the others and now share in the nourishing sap from the olive root, do not boast over those branches' (Rom. 11. 16-18). And when the idea of undeserved grace and new freedom was misunderstood, James brought out a balance, by reminding the church about the Hebrew tradition's emphasis on justice and harmony. St. John's Gospel, though it has taken the cosmic Word (not necessarily from non-Jewish stock), takes the Jewish roots seriously while challenging the deviation by unhealthy alliances and conservative rigidity. It is also significant to note that the book of Revelation, despite flashing and frightening images, somewhat like political cartoons, succeeded in working out a rapprochement between the Jewish and Christian traditions. Similarly, Kṛṣṇa embodies in himself the amalgamation of the Vedic Viṣṇu and the Bhāgavata divine hero and even after centuries of his independent identity the tension between the two traditions continue. Then in what way can we construct a hybridization between Kristu bhakti and Kṛṣṇa bhakti?

At this juncture, we should recognize popular slogans and imaginations in religious vocabulary and media projections. Most popular are 'only one way' on the one extreme and 'many ways to the one summit' on the other. Confusions are propagated to upset those who are zealous to maintain the distinctiveness of their faith who, in turn, may become agitated and even fundamentalist. For example, the name of the popular Hindu goddess Māri is said to be a synonym of Mary, the mother of Jesus. More glaringly, an imaginative vision is presented in a Tamil film named *Pudhu Vasantham* (New Spring, 1990). A group of five, including a stranded woman, live together and they are of different religious traditions. After a series of ordeal, in one of their dreams, the girl's wedding takes place with a dual ceremony: in a Hindu temple with Christian priests officiating and in a Christian church with Hindu priests solemnizing. Does this scene fall into the category of hybridization?

Love is a common human gift endowed with every human being and it has to be celebrated and shared. But in the name of love manipulation, excess and even violence can happen. In the case of divine human love, as Graham Schweig in his article "The Crucifixion and the Rāsa Maṇḍala: A Comparative Sketch of Two Great Symbols of Divine Love" (*Journal of Vaishnava Studies*, 20/2, 2012, 182) has pointed out God and devotees make their own sacrifices for the sake of love. In the Christian vision God makes the sacrifice and in Kṛṣṇite one the devotees make it. There is mutual change. The question is how such change can be effected in the lives of selfish and conservative devotees today and how can it be extended to all areas of life. Real meaning of hybridization will emerge not before but after attempts of bhaktas of different traditions to work together for restoring the eternal and divine worth of every human and to realize the 'divine community' (i.e., Trinity), a creative, dynamic and loving conglomeration or hybridity, in the common life of all.

Finally, there are possibilities of appreciation, accommodation and association for action. But what fundamentally matters for a true Jew or Christian is that God is in solidarity with the victims of all forms of injustice and those vulnerable because of many reasons. The vision of flute flowing, amorously behaving and dancing Kṛṣṇa can certainly give relaxation, pleasure and dynamic unity. But does such experience, whether in Christian heritage or Vaiṣṇava tradition, lead to the above mentioned solidarity? It is the biggest question for a functional and liberating oneness with the divine. Mystical depth, ecstatic height and intellectual breadth become credible only when they are connected with a commitment to cooperate with God for changing the world, individuals, communities and nations. And the immediate space for Kristu bhaktas and Kṛṣṇa bhaktas to come together in India may be the popular 'Clean India' project making it comprehensive. Such involvement will bring an interreligious group face to face to those secular minded people who may have been disillusioned about religion.

Does this restrict imaginative vision of hybridization applied at bhakti/worship level? Without prescribing details, one may visualize a possibility. In a mutually agreed enclosure, on a rolling base, there may be mounted up 'images' of Jesus hanging on the cross or rising from the dead with bleeding wounds on his body, and flute-playing and dancing Kṛṣṇa, who will be going around fast evoking both penitence and joy etc inside and among the bhaktas of both divinities. If dancing is too daunting for the novitiate, the Christian-Krishnite congregational act could be silent meditation. Again, what should be the outcome of such joint experience of two divine figures and their devotees with differing visions and emphases? Even if it proves to be a wishful thinking, it may still give an idea about moving towards more authentic forms of hybridization in future. But this need not tarry deliberate formation or revitalization of communities of bhaktas of both the traditions in different areas where the need of 'cleaning' is most urgent.

Select Bibliography

Appasamy, A.J., *The Theology of Hindu Bhakti*, Madras: CLS for the Senate of Serampore College, 1970.

______, *Christianity as Bhakti Marga*, Chennai: CLS, 1991.

______, *What is Mōkṣa? Study in the Johannine Doctrine of Life*, Madras: CLS, 1931.

Archer, W.G., *The Loves of Krishna: In Indian Painting and Poetry*, London: George Allen & Unwin Ltd., 1957.

Ashton, John., *Understanding the Fourth Gospel*, Oxford: Clarendon Press, 1993.

Bhaktivedanta, A.C., *Perfect Questions Perfect Answers*, Mumbai: The Bhaktivedanta Book Trust, 1983.

______, *Chant and Be Happy*, Mumbai: The Bhaktivedanta Book Trust, 1987.

Bhandarkar, R.G., *Vaishṇavism, Śaivism and the Minor Religious Systems*, Strassburg: J. Trubner & Co., 1913. (New Delhi: Asian Educational Services, 1983).

Bhuteshananda, Swami, *Nārada Bhaktisūtras*, Kolkata: Advaita Ashrama, 2009.

Blumfield, Vivienne, *Stories of Krishna*, Norwich: Religious and Moral Education Press, 2000.

Bowker, J., *The Oxford Dictionary of World Religions*, Oxford University Press, 2004.

Bryant, Edwin F. (ed.), *Krishna (A Source Book)*, Oxford University Press, 2007.

——, *Krishna: The Beautiful Legend of God, Śrīmad Bhāgavata Purāṇa*, Book X – With Chapters 1, 6 and 29-31 from Book XI, London: Penguin Books, 2003.

Carman, John B., "Bhakti" in *Encyclopedia of Religion*, New York: Macmillan Publishing Company, 1987, Vol. 2, 130-134.

Carr, Dhyanchand, "Development of Interpretative Perspective and Academic Ministry," *THE SATHRI JOURNAL*, 1/1 January 1991, 16-51.

——, "Some Exegetical and Hermeneutical Options in Reading the Gospel According to John to Promote an Inclusive Understanding of God" in *Discipleship and Dialogue: New Frontiers in Interfaith Engagement*, ed. by E. Lott, M.T. Thangaraj and A.Wingate, Delhi: ISPCK, 2013, 48-55.

Chakkarai, V., *Jesus the Avatār*, Madras: CLS, 1926.

Cracknell, K., *Towards a New Relationship: Christians and People of Other Faiths*, London: Epworth, 1986.

Dandekar, R.N., "Hinduism" in *History of Religions*: Vol. II: Religions of the Present, Leiden: E.J. Brill, 1971.

Doniger, Wendy, *The Hindus: An Alternative History*, London: Penguin, 2010.

Dunn, James D.G., *Christology in the Making: An Inquiry into the Origins of the Doctrine of Incarnation* (second edition), London: SCM, 1996.

Duraisingh, C. and C. Hargreaves (ed.), *India's Search for Reality and the Relevance of the Gospel of John*, Delhi: ISPCK, 1975.

Flood, Gavin, *An Introduction to Hinduism*, Cambridge: Cambridge University Press, 2008.

Francis, Dayanandan (ed.), *The Christian Bhakti of A.J. Appasamy*, Chennai, CLS, 1992.

Frith, Nigel, *The Legend of Krishna*, London: Sheldon Press, 1975.

Hawley, John Stratton, "Kṛṣṇa" in *Encyclopedia of Religion*, New York: Macmillan Publishing Company, 1987, Vol. 8, 382-387.

Hopkins, Thomas J., "The Social Teaching of the Bhāgavata Purāṇa" in *Krishna: Myths, Rites and Attitudes,* ed. by Milton Singer, Chicago: University of Chicago Press, 1968.

Hurtado, Larry W., *How on Earth did Jesus Become a God? Historical Questions about Earliest Devotion to Jesus*?, Cambridge: William B. Eerdmans Publishing Company, 2005.

Joseph, Martin P., *Srimad Bhagavatam for Greater Unity*, Thiruvananthapuram: Jeyamatha Training Institute Press, 1991.

Judah, J. Stillson, *Hare Krishna and the Counterculture*, New York: Wily-Interscience Publication, 1974.

Kinsley, David R., *The Divine Player: A Study of Krishna-Lila,* Delhi: Motilal Banarsidas, 1979.

______, *Hindu Goddesses: Visions of the Divine Feminine in the Hindu Religious Tradition*, Delhi: Motilal Banarsidas, 1987.

______, *The Sword and the Flute*, Delhi: Motilal Banarsidas, 1995.

Klostermaier, Klaus, *Hindu & Christian in Vrindaban*, London: SCM, 1969.

Lipner, Julius, *Hindus: Their Religious Beliefs and Practices*, London: Routledge, 2010.

______, "Avatāra and Incarnation" in *Revisioning India's Religious Traditions*, ed. D.C. Scott & I. Selvanayagam, Bangalore: UTC-ISPCK, 1996, 123-143.

______, "The God of Love and the Love of God in Christian and Hindu Traditions" in *Love, Sex and Gender in the World Religions*, ed. J. Runzo and N.M. Martin, Oxford: One World, 2000, 51-88.

Long, J. Bruce, "BHAKTI" in *Encyclopedia of Religion*, New York: Macmillan Publishing Company, 1987, Vol. 9, 31-40.

Losty, Jeremiah P., *Krishna: A Hindu Vision of God,* London: British Library, 1980.

Marchett, Freda, *Kṛsṇa: Lord or Avatāra?*, Surrey: Curzon, 2001.

Menon, Ramesh, *Bhagavata Purana*, New Delhi: Rupa, 2011, 2 Volumes.

Nicholas, Antonio T de., AVATĀRA: The Humanization of Philosophy through the Bhagavad Gīta, New York: Nicolas Hays, 1976.

Prentiss, Karen Pechilis, *The Embodiment of Bhakti*, New York: Oxford University Press, 1999.

Redington, James D., *Vallabhācārya on the Love Games of Kṛṣṇa*, Delhi: Motilal Banarsidass, 1990.

Renou, L., *The Destiny of the Veda in India*, Delhi: Motilal Banarsidas, 1965.

Robertson, S., *Bhakti Tradition of Vaiṣṇava Āḻvars and Theology of Religions*, Kolkata: Punthi Pustak, 2006.

Robinson, John A.T., *The Priority of John*, London: SCM, 1985.

Rosen, Steven J. (ed.), *Journal of Vaishnava Studies*, 20/2 Spring, 2012.

Schweig, Graham, *Dance of Divine Love*, Princeton University Press, 2005.

———, "The Crucifixion and the Rāsa Maṇdala: A Comparative Sketch of Two Great Symbols of Divine Love" *Journal of Vaishnava Studies*, 20/2, 2012, 171-186.

Scott, David, "The *parama-prema* bhakti of Narada *Bhakti-sūtra*, in *Discipleship and Dialogue: New Frontiers in Interfaith Engagement*, ed. by E. Lott, M.T. Thangaraj and A. Wingate, Delhi: ISPCK, 2013, 161-178.

———, "Radha in the Erotic Play of the Universe," *Asia Journal of Theology*, 12/2 October, 1998.

Selvanayagam, I., *The Dynamics of Hindu Religious Traditions*, Bangalore: Asian Trading Corporation, 1996.

———, *Vedic Sacrifice: Challenge and Response*, Delhi: Manohar, 1996.

———, "Components of a Tamil Saiva Bhakti experience as evident in Manikkavacakar's Tiruvacakam" in *Spiritual Traditions-Essential Visions for Living,* edited by David Emmanuel Singh, Bangalore: UTC (ISPCK, Delhi), 1998, 418-439.

_____, "Theological Education and Regeneration of the Church in India," in *Communion on the Move: Towards a Relevant Theological Education* (Essays in Honour of Bishop John Sadananda), ed. by Wati Longchar & P. Mohan Larbeer, Bangalore: BTESSC, 2015, 37-49.

Sharma, Krishna, *Bhakti and the Bhakti Movement: A New Perspective, A Study in the History of Ideas,* New Delhi: Munshiram Manoharlal, 1987.

Sheridon, Daniel P., "The Bhāgavata-purāṇa: Sāṃkhya at the Service of Non-dualism." *Purāṇa*, XXV (July 1983), 225-34.

_____, "Devotion in the Bhāgavata Purāṇa and Christian Love: Bhakti, Agape, Eros." *Horizons* (Duquesne University), 8/2,1981, 260-78.

_____, *The Advaitic Theism of the Bhāgavata Purāṇa*, Delhi: Motilal Banarsidas, 1981.

_____, "Manifestations of the Divine in the *Bhagavata Purana.*" *Purana*, XXVI (July 12, 1984), 2, 97-112.

Sheth, Noel, *The Divinity of Krishna*, Delhi: Munshiram Manoharlal, 1984.

Singh, D. Emmanuel (ed.), *Spiritual Traditions: Essential Visions for Living* (Essays in Honour of David Scott), Bangalore: UTC-ISPCK, 1998.

Sinha, P.N. *A Study of the Bhagavata Purana or Esoteric Hinduism*, Adyar, Madras: Adyar Library, 1950.

Smith, W.C., *Towards a World Theology*, London: Macmillan, 1981.

Vempeny, Ishanand, *Kṛṣṇa and Christ*, Anand: Gujarat Sahitya Prakash, 1988.

Vyas, R.N., *Melody of Bhakti and Enlightenment*, New Delhi: Cosmo Publications, 1983.

Index

A

Abraham 51, 58-59, 96, 171
Ācarya/s xxvii-xxviii, 21, 168
Acyuta 111, 115, 118-119, 121
Ādityas 41
Advaita 105
Āgama 68
Akkammādevi 131
Akṣara 11
Alastair McGlashan 9
Āḻvārs 10, 130, 162
Aṁsa 40
Aṁśa 11
Ananta 69
Āṇḍāḻ 130
Anders Nygren 149
Andhakas 40
Aniruddha 41, 68
Anurāga 12, 18
Appasamy, A.J. ix, xv-xvi, 4-5, 7, 13, 20, 22-23, 25-26, 53, 59, 61, 81, 105, 170
Aprakṛta 13
Archana 17
Arjuna xvii, 17, 37, 41, 67, 74, 80, 109, 135
Aruni 17
Āryans 114, 134
Ashtadhyayi 8, 67
Ashton 35, 56, 62-63, 135, 144
Aśokan 38
Ātman 15, 52, 59
Ātmanivedana 17
Avatāra/s xviii, xxiii, xxv-xxvi, 2, 7, 28, 37-38, 45, 47, 50, 54, 67, 69-80, 157, 172, 176
Ayodhya 10
Āyūrveda 37

B

Bādarāyaṇa 15
Bāla Kṛṣṇa xxiv, 74
Balarāma 72-73, 122, 149
Bali 17, 65, 72
Baron Fredrich von Hūgel 5
Barrett, C.K. 58
Bede Griffiths 59
Bhagavad Gītā/Gītā xvii-xviii, 2, 67, 71, 80, 151
Bhagavān xii, 11-12, 19, 22-23, 37, 45, 74, 110, 115-116, 119-121
Bhāgavata Purāṇa xv, xvii-xviii, xxvi, xxviii, 15, 22-23, 45, 70, 72-73, 78, 80, 83, 109-110, 115, 127 130, 135, 151, 157, 159, 162
Bhakti/bhakta ix-x, xv-xix, xx-xxviii, 1-26, 40, 46, 49, 53, 67, 70, 76, 81-110, 117, 124, 126-127, 129-170, 172-173, 176-177, 179
Bhandarkar, R.G. 18, 20

Bhāva 8, 12, 18
Bhima 40
Bowker, J. 2
Brahma 66, 69, 76, 115, 117-118, 123, 125, 153, 164-165, 175
Brahman xvii, xxvi, 11, 18, 40, 59, 66-67, 74, 78-79, 111, 162-163, 168
Brāhmaṇism 38-39, 67
Brahma-vaivarta-purāṇa 76
Brooke Foss Westcott xv
Bultmann 60-61

C

Caitanya 12, 44, 147, 156
Campakalata 139
Catherine Cornille xii
Chakkarai 9-10, 52, 71, 182
Chāndogya Upaniṣad 37
Chandragupta 41
Christ ix, xxii, 6, 13-14, 28, 30-31, 37, 46, 52, 55, 57-58, 61, 79, 84, 89-91, 94, 104, 131-132, 135, 141, 148, 168-171, 178, 185
Citra-devi 139

D

Daniel P Sheridon 11
Dāsya 17, 23
David Scott xxvii, 185
Dayanandan Francis 130
Devaki 38-39, 121
Dharma/dharma xxiv, xxviii, 23, 46, 68, 70, 73, 112-113, 120, 122-124, 134-136, 150, 155, 165, 172-173
Dodd, C.H. 81
Dunn, J. xii, 55-56, 61
Dvāpara 45
Dwāraka 37

E

Edwin F. Bryant xxviii
Ego eimi 58
Emerton, J.A. 63
Ensarkosis 71
Eric Lott xxvii

F

Farquhar, J.N. 5
Flood, G. 65, 182
Francis Clooney xxviii, 130
Francis J. Moloney 81
Freda Machett 38

G

Galilee 28-30, 82, 84, 132-133
Garga 17
Garuḍa 69, 78
Gautama Buddha 60
George Ụ Pope xx
Ghora Angiras 38
Gnosticism 56
Goloka 77, 133, 156
Gopāla 37-38
Gopīs/gopīs xvii-xviii, xxi, xxiii-xxiv, 11, 13, 24-25, 41-46, 70, 74-76, 78, 80, 109-117, 119-127, 134, 136, 139-141, 143, 145-147, 150-153, 155, 157-158, 161, 163-167, 172-175
Govinda 110, 115, 121
Grierson, G.A. 7
Guṇa xvii, 79, 111

H

Hanuman 17
Hare Hare xxviii
Harivaṃsa 41, 71, 73, 78-79
Heiler, F. 129
Hein 151
Hent de Vries 130
Homoousios 105, 174
Huizinga, J. 77
Hybridization x, xiii, xvi, xviii, xxii, xxvi, 130, 177-180

I

Indra 39-40, 65-66, 70, 117, 175

Indulekha 139
Indus Valley 38
Ishanand Vempeny 52
ISKCON xxvii-xxviii, 28, 127, 140, 157, 168

J

James Fredricks 130
Janmam 71
Jeremiah P. Losty 73
Jīva Gosvāmi 13
Jīvātmas 45
Jñāna 17, 40
John Dunne xii
John Sadananda 137, 185
John Thattamanil 130
Jose Maniparampil 82
Joseph 28, 88, 100, 183
Judah, J.S. 157, 183
Julius Lipner xxvii

K

Kabir 21
Kailāṣ 133
Kālindī 116
Kāliya 117
Kalki 73
Kāma 11, 110, 114, 116-120, 125, 127, 153, 176
Kāma-śāstra 153
Kaṃsa 37, 41, 70, 72
Kāraikkāl Ammaiyār 130
Karen Pechilis Prentiss 7
Karma 8, 17, 110, 123, 126, 136, 142-143, 155, 161, 167
Karma-Samsāra 8, 72, 161
Kārṣaṇaveda 37
Katha Upanishad 53
Kaustubha 69
Keith Ward 130
Kenneth Cracknell xxvii
Kingsbury ix
Kinsley, D.R. 43-44, 75-78, 183
Kirtan 17
Klostermaier, K. 157, 183
Kosambi, D.D. 21
Krishna/Kṛṣṇa x, xv-xviii, xxi-xxviii, 4, 8, 10-13, 17-18, 21, 24-25, 27-47, 49-80, 109-117, 119, 121-127, 129-158, 161-169, 172-185
Krishna Pillai ix
Krishna Sharma 7-8, 18, 160
Kristu x, xvi, xxvi, xxviii, 4, 7, 81-108, 129-158, 177, 179-180
Kṛṣṇaatreya 37
Kṣatriya 20, 37-38, 40, 72
Kūrma 72

L

Lakshmi 69
Lalita-devi 139
Lazarus 33, 91-93, 137, 139-140
Līlā 11, 13, 77, 122
Logos 50, 52, 54-57, 60, 157
Lord xxvi, 6, 15-17, 20, 24-25, 28-29, 32-33, 37, 39-40, 45-47, 49-53, 58, 62, 66, 70, 74, 76, 80, 85, 90, 105-106, 109, 111, 113-118, 120-127, 139-140, 145-146, 149-153, 158, 160-163, 165, 167, 172-173, 175-177

M

Madhva 11, 162, 168
Mahābhārata 37, 39-41, 67, 71-73, 80, 109
Mahānārāyaṇa Upaniṣad 67
Mahāprabhu 156
Mahāpurāṇas 41, 109
Maitrī Upaniṣad 66
Manasā 18
Maṇḍala 133, 147, 179
Martha 30, 32, 91, 97, 139-140, 143, 148
Martin Buber 60
Mary 28, 32-33, 82, 88, 100, 105, 139-140, 143, 145, 148, 179

Mary Magdalene 139, 145, 148
Mathura 38, 41, 45
Matsya 72
Megasthenes 41
Meister Eckhart 59
Michael Amaladoss xxviii
Michelle 130
Mīrābai 28, 131
Mohan Larbeer 137, 185
Moksha/Mokṣa xv, 4, 123
Monier-Williams 18, 21
Morna Hooker 64
Muṇḍaka Upaniṣad 66
Muslim xi, 50, 62
Mysticism xv, 4-5, 20, 24, 125, 130, 132

N

Nachiketa 53
Naimiṣha 109
Nāma 18
Nanda 41, 115
Nārada xvii, 16-17
Narasiṃha 72
Nārāyaṇa 40-41, 67, 79
Narayan Vaman Tilak x
Nārāyaṇīya 38, 41, 67-68, 71
Naṭarāja 42
Nathanael 28, 31, 143
Nāyanārs/Nāyanmārs 9-10, 131
Nazareth 28-29, 34, 49, 93, 132, 156
Noel Sheth 78

O

O'Flaherty, W.D. 42
OM 66
Orientalists 7, 18, 20-21

P

Pādasevana 17
Padmapurāṇa 9
Pañcarātra 68
Pāṇḍavas 37, 80
Panini 8, 67
Paramatman 53, 74
Paraśurāma 72
Parīkṣit 44, 111, 122, 135, 149
Patañjali 2, 40
Peshitta 63
phallic-yoni 149, 177
Phillips ix
Pneauma 154
Pradurbhāva 71
Pradyumna 68
Prakṛta 13
Prakṛti 79, 111
Prema/n 12, 18
Premā-netra 141-142
Primus inter pares 63
Prophet xxv, 3, 5-6, 28-29, 46, 49, 59, 79, 91, 93, 134-135, 144, 162, 164, 172, 178
Proskyneo 33

Q

Qumran 63

R

Rabbi 29, 49, 85
Rādha xxvi, 44, 70, 74, 115, 139, 147, 156
Radhakrishnan, S. 39-40
Rāga 18
Rāgānuga Bhakti 12
Raimon/doPanikkar xii, xxii, 155
Rajas 111
Ramā 10, 43, 52, 72, 115, 152
Ram Mohan Roy ix
Rāmānuja 10-11, 20, 79, 162, 168
Ramesh Menon 43
Rangadevi 139
Rasa 12-13, 15, 24, 45, 121, 131, 133, 147, 151, 155, 179, 184
Rāsalīlā xviii-xix, xxi, xxv-xxvi, xxviii, 11, 15, 41-42, 44, 46-47, 53, 70, 73, 83, 109-127, 130-131, 133, 135-136, 139, 146, 151, 156-157, 159, 162-163, 165-166, 175

Ravi Gupta xxviii
Redington, J.D. 152, 184
Renou, L. 71, 184
Ṛgveda 37
Robert Neville 130
Robertson, S. 10, 184
Robin Boyd 105
Robinson, J.A.T. 54-62, 82, 184
Rudolf Otto 5, 169
Rudolf Schnackenburg 64
Rūpa 18

S

Sādhana 12
Sadhu Sundar Singh 168
Sahajiyā cult 23
Śaiva xi, xviii, 9, 17, 21, 28, 45, 69, 71-72, 131, 184
Sākhya 17, 23
Śakti 45, 119
Śaktimat 45
Sālokya 19
Samādhi 15
Sambhava 71
Samhīta 68
Sāmipya 19
Saṁkarṣaṇ 41
Sāṁkhya-yoga 38
Śāndilya xvii, 15
Śaṇkara 20
Sanskrit xxviii, 1, 10, 13, 50, 65, 124
Śānta 23
Sārṣṭi 19
Sārūya 19
Sattva 22, 79
Sātvatas 37-41, 67, 117
Saviour 28, 33-34, 58
Schweig, G. 131, 141-142, 147, 155, 179, 184
Sedgwick, L.J. 4
Selvanayagam, I. ix-x, xiii, xix, 3, 17, 39, 98, 137, 183-184
Sesa 69
Sevā 18, 142
Sharon 131
Shesha 17
Shuka 17
Siddheśvara Bhaṭṭācārya 78
Śiśupāla 39, 67, 70
Śiva xxvii, 2, 9, 37, 42, 66, 69, 71, 77, 115, 123, 131, 164-165, 169, 175
Skanda 37
Smaraṇa 17
Soma 2
Song of Solomon 131-132
Son of God 28-31, 46, 50, 55-56, 58, 62-63, 79, 84, 91, 94, 134-136, 157, 169, 174
Son of Man xxv, 6, 28, 30-33, 46, 50, 56, 63-65, 80, 88, 90, 94-95, 97, 100, 103, 134, 136, 139, 157, 162, 164, 169
Sophia 54, 154
Śramaṇas 2, 38, 165
Śravaṇa 17
Sri/Śrī xxvi, 69-70, 74, 115, 117-118, 121, 146-147, 164-165
Srivatsa 69
Sṛjana 71
Sṛṅgāra 12
Stanley Samartha xx
Streeter, B.H. 5
Sudevi 139
Śūdra xvii, 21
Śuka 44, 111, 123, 150
Sunni xi
Sūta 109
Sutra 8, 15, 17
Svami Bhaktivedanta Prabhupada 156
Svarūpaśakti 13
Śvetāsvatara Upaniṣad 4
Swami Bhuteshananda 16
Swami Cidbhavananda xxviii

T

Tamas 111
Tamil ix, xviii, 9, 17, 21, 130-131, 162, 179
Tanujā 18
Targums 63
Thomas 33, 50, 62, 80, 86, 98, 105, 137
Thomas Thangaraj 130
Tirupperuntokai 131
Tiruvācakam xviii, 17, 147
Trinity xxii, 27, 53, 56, 105, 154-155, 162, 173-175, 179
Tulasī 113, 147
Tungavidya 139
Tyāganetra 142
Tylor, E.B. 129

U

Uddhava 17
Ugrasena 41, 70
Upaniṣads 4, 8-9, 37, 39, 78, 161, 168

V

Vaidhī 12
Vaikhanāsa 68
Vaikunta 133
Vaikuṇṭha 19
Vaiṣṇava xv, xviii-xix, xxi, xxvi-xxviii, 10, 22-23, 28, 38, 43-46, 68-69, 71-72, 76, 79, 130, 140, 159, 161-162, 166, 168, 180
Vaiṣṇavism 12, 18, 39, 44, 71, 127, 156
Vaiśya xvii, 21, 40
Vallabhā/chārya 11, 18, 21, 152-153
Vāmana 72
Vandana 17
Varāha 72, 127
Vardhanī 18
Vāsalya 23
Vāsudeva xxi, xxvi, 37-38, 40-41, 67-68, 70, 80, 123, 126, 157, 168
Vedāntic xxii, xxvi, 17, 162, 168
Vedāntins 18, 162
Vedas 7-8, 16, 37, 39, 46, 72, 119-120, 134
Venkaṭeśvara xxviii
Viraha Bhakti 6, 13
Vīra Śaiva 131
Viṣaka-devi 139
Viśiṣṭādvaita 168
Viṣṇu xviii, xxi, xxiv-xxvi, 2, 10, 17-18, 28, 37-38, 40-42, 44, 47, 65-74, 77-80, 114, 119, 123, 126, 135, 150, 157, 165, 168, 172, 175-176
Viśvarūpadarṣana xvii, 41, 68, 74
Vittayā 18
Vraj xxiv, xxvi, 110-111, 113-114, 117-118, 121, 123-127, 150
Vraja 37, 41-42, 70, 77, 133, 140-141, 147, 156, 158, 166, 172
Vṛndāvana 13, 44-45, 75-77, 80, 115, 125, 133, 152
Vṛṣṇis 38, 40, 45
Vyabhicāri 11
Vyas, R.N. 15, 17, 19-20, 24, 185
Vyāsa 17, 123
Vyukas 68

W

Wati Longchar 137, 185
Weber 18
Whitehead 54
Wilfred Cantwell Smith xx, 92
Winslow, J.C. x

Y

Yādava 37-38, 40, 67, 80
Yahweh 3, 32, 58, 164, 166, 174, 176
Yajña xviii, 2, 40
Yasoda 41
Yoga xxviii, 2, 12, 16-17, 22, 111, 120, 123, 125-127, 155
Yogis 2, 45, 76, 121, 125
Yuga 118